THE ECONOMICS OF TIME

THE ECONOMICS OF TIME

Clifford Sharp

A HALSTED PRESS BOOK
John Wiley & Sons · New York

Published in the United States of America
by Halsted Press, a Division of
John Wiley & Sons, Inc., New York

ISBN 0-470-27263-5

Printed in Great Britain

Contents

Acknowledgments

I should like to thank Jeanne Cretney, Joan Cook, Mavis Johnson, Dorothy Logsdon and Jaqui Coleman, all overburdened secretaries in the Economics Department at Leicester University, for managing to interpret my manuscript and type out this book for the publishers. I am very grateful to my colleagues at Leicester who gave me their comments and suggestions, and particularly to Alan Baker, Derek Deadman and Leo Katzen who read parts of the final draft and helped me to improve them. The mistakes that remain are, of course, my own responsibility.

List of Tables and Figures

TABLES

FIGURES

CHAPTER 1

Introduction

There is no absolute relation in time between two events but there is an absolute relation in space and time. [A. Einstein]

Time is a mystery. It cannot be tied down by a definition or confined inside a formula. Like gravity, it is a phenomenon that we can experience but cannot understand. We are aware of the ageing of our bodies, of the effects of the movements of our planet, and of the ticking of the clock. We learn a little about what we call the past and we know that change is built into our lives. But neither philosophers nor scientists have been able to analyse and explain all of the meaning of time. Not only have they failed to provide easy explanations, but their efforts sometimes seem to have made mystery more mysterious and to have shown us that our lack of understanding was even greater than we supposed.

Some philosophers have argued that the passage of time is an important metaphysical fact, but one that can only be grasped by non-rational intuition. Others tell us that the flow of time is an illusion and that the future can no more be changed than can the past. Some believe that future events come into existence as the present, the actual 'moment-in-being' (Shackle, 1958, pp. 13–14), reaches them; others suggest that they are already in existence. According to Einstein's special theory of relativity, separate co-ordinate systems in relative motion each have a different time system so that event *A* can occur before event *B* according to the clocks of one co-ordinate system, but *B* can happen before *A* on the clocks of another system (Bondi, 1970). If we were able to travel faster than light, time would move backwards and, if we encountered one of the recently hypothesised black holes, it might slow down or stop. A forty-year journey away from earth and then back to this planet during which we were accelerating at the same speed as the pull of earth's gravity would return us to an earth 48,000 years older than the one that we left forty years before.

Economics is not mysterious even if the writings of some of its high priests do sometimes appear to pass all human understanding. If its subject matter is now being shown to be not quite so factual and clearly demarcated as has sometimes been supposed, nevertheless some kind of definition can be devised and the economics that matters will in the end be that which has some relevance to the lives of people in what we believe to be a real and existing world. It may therefore seem an impossible task to try to link the still unsolved mystery of time to the practical issues of economics. But fortunately there are different kinds of time. There is the 'psychic phenonemon' that we have been discussing. There is time measured from the movements of planets and time measured by the rate of radioactive decay. And for our purposes there is the much more limited and comprehensible concept that we may call human or economic time. This is the time that human beings have at their disposal and that must be allocated between alternative activities.

One well-known definition of economics said that it was about the decisions that must be made in allocating scarce resources that have alternative uses (Robbins, 1945, p. 16). Time is a scarce resource, although in a rather special way. The amount of iron-ore in the world is fixed. When it has all been converted to iron and steel then we will have to make do with recycling or start mining on the moon. Time, in a sense, is inexhaustible. We do not know when it began and we cannot understand how it may end. But economics is concerned with men and men are subject to three time-linked constraints. At least in their present form, human beings are not built to last. Psalm 90 tells us rather optimistically that 'Seventy years is the span of our life, eighty if our strength holds'; but the actual life expectancies of people in many countries in the twentieth century are somewhat less. There may be, some of us believe that there is, another kind of life beyond this one where new aspects of time may be revealed. But economics is concerned with this life on this planet so that everyone has a stock of years that will eventually run out. No one knows the size of his remaining pile of time and it cannot be hoarded. As Shackle has written: 'The moment-in-being rolls, as it were, along the calendar-axis, and thus ever transports us willy-nilly to fresh temporal viewpoints' (1958, p. 15). Since the scarce resource of time must be spent, a basic problem of human existence is to spend it well, to use it to bring in the greatest return of happiness that can be achieved. Even though we shall sometimes narrow it down to such specific issues as the case for buying a dishwasher or the value of reducing the time taken travelling to work, this problem of the optimum allocation of time will be the underlying theme of this study.

The third constraint, which makes choice necessary, is that people cannot use the same lump of time to carry out more than one or perhaps two activities. My children have sometimes attempted to learn French vocabulary and watch a TV programme during the same time period (though not perhaps quite simultaneously), but most activities demand an exclusive consumption of time. No one can use the same two hours of his life for playing tennis and for planting vegetables. The time during which we exist must be allocated between all the alternative and generally mutually exclusive activities that are available to us.

This book is therefore a study of the main problems involved in using the scarce and unhoardable resource of the timespan of our lives. Some of these problems are familiar in economic literature and in these cases all that is attempted in this relatively short study is to bring together a discussion of these scattered bits of economic theory. In other areas some gaps are shown to exist in the treatment of the economics of time and some possible new lines of thought are suggested with the main emphasis being given to actual choices that may have to be made by individuals or by society. Even with established theory however, it is hoped that looking at issues from the view of obtaining the optimum expenditure of time may sometimes provide new insights.

A major result of trying to concentrate on the choices that must be made in 'spending' time can be mentioned in a preliminary discussion even at this early stage in this study. In the past, fairly strict boundaries have been placed around the subject matter of economics. It has been restricted to those things to which the 'measuring rod of money' can be applied or to the welfare of human beings in so far as this is affected by their possession of goods and enjoyment of services. More recently, the boundaries have become somewhat extended as the practitioners of cost–benefit analysis have struggled to deal with 'intangible' external benefits and dis-benefits, which are very difficult to measure in the common currency of money. 'Multi-criteria analysis' has also become fashionable. But still the old 'material welfare' concept has some influence on the treatment of time in economics. When the allocation of time is considered it does not make much sense to distinguish between economic and 'non-economic' activities. Time spent in meditation or reading yields utility in the same way as time allocated to paid work or to growing vegetables. Robbins' definition of economics as 'the science which studies human behaviour as a relationship between ends and scarce means which have alternative uses' rather than as dealing exclusively with the causes of material welfare clearly suggests that time is part of the proper subject matter of economics (1945, p. 16). He argues that 'The time at our disposal is limited. There are only twenty-four hours in the day. We have to choose between the different uses to which they may be put' (1945, p. 15). This viewpoint is generally accepted today, but nevertheless some uses of time seem to be regarded as being different from others so that separate models have been developed for dealing with time in which paid work is done and with leisure time. A utility-maximising exercise would involve allocating time in such a way that the marginal utility of the last unit spent in each activity was the same, and it would be necessary to include all types of activity.

The receipt of income as a reward for undertaking some activities and the need to make payments in order to be allowed to enjoy others is a complicating factor that will be discussed more fully in chapter 2. It makes it necessary to define what is meant by the utility received from an activity very carefully but it does not imply that the economist should regard time spent on unpaid activities as essentially different from time spent at work. In this study an attempt is made to develop an integrated analysis of the problems of allocating time without having separate models for leisure and for working time.

Another familiar problem, which also relates to the word 'utility', is how far it can be regarded as being synonymous with 'welfare' or 'happiness'. Utility is usually defined as anticipated satisfaction, or the happiness that a consumer expects to receive when he decides to buy a good or service. The actual happiness obtained may be greater or less than he expected but it is the happiness that he hoped to receive that is relevant to the decision on whether or not he buys the commodity (or to his decision about the quantity that he will purchase). The same principles apply in allocating time, and 'utility' will be used in this study to describe the expected net increase in happiness to be received from spending units of time in a particular activity. 'Welfare' and 'happiness' are regarded as being synonymous. This leaves unresolved the difficult philosophical problem of determining what constitutes happiness. Are people the best judges of their own state of happiness or may they sometimes be deluded, spending their store of time on second-best activities that yield less welfare than could be obtained from some alternative occupation? Should we accept a man's free choice to spend thirty minutes watching 'Top of the Pops' when we believe that he could obtain greater happiness from using the time to listen to a broadcast of one of Bach's Brandenburg concertos? In this study the normal assumption made by economists that each individual is the best judge of his own interests is accepted as a working principle, though this does not imply that it necessarily has a sound philosophical basis. It is a working principle that has exceptions; again, the existing situation in which society, while still leaving individuals a wide area of choice, may decide to encourage some activities and to discourage, or even prohibit, others is accepted. The objective of maximising happiness is therefore only likely to be fulfilled in so far as individuals, partly circumscribed by state action, are the best judges of their own interests.

The more specific topics discussed in this study include the possible extension of the total 'stock' of time by extending life expectancy, and the possible trade-off between the length and quality of life; the problems created by technological change, including the choice between reducing the size of the labour force or reducing hours worked; the extent to which measurements of productivity changes need to be modified to allow for the size of the input of time into the process of production; the value of the time savings produced by using 'labour-saving' domestic appliances; the choice between professional and 'do-it-yourself' labour; the special problem of the value of transport time savings in relation to transport investment decisions; the relationship between earnings and the length of the working day; the nature of leisure and leisure-time budgets; the choice between present and future satisfactions and the implication of current discounting techniques.

One major factor that receives very limited attention in this study is that of uncertainty. As will be shown in chapter 2, some economists have regarded the creation of uncertainty as the principal activity of time. The existence of 'our future all unknown' has led to the development of many strategies for minimizing the effects of uncertainty. In this study, although some references will be made to uncertainty, particularly in chapter 3, it is generally assumed that the results of decisions are reasonably certain, or that people act according to the *a priori* probabilities that they attach to alternative outcomes that may result from their decisions. The justification for this is that some abstraction from reality is necessary in order to concentrate on the problem of choice in allocating time and that very many of the decisions discussed relate to the near future when uncertainty is minimised. The different treatments of time in economics and the arguments for concentrating mainly on the allocation problem in this study are considered more fully in chapter 2.

Throughout the study 'he' and 'his' (except where they refer to a specific male person) should be taken to mean 'he' or 'she' and 'his' or 'hers' respectively, while 'man' means 'man or woman'. Female readers will, I hope, regard this contraction as a matter of economy of space rather than as representing any kind of masculine prejudice.

The final point in this introduction is to consider whether the study is intended to be descriptive and analytical or also partly prescriptive. In a relatively underdeveloped field of study, there is, it is suggested, considerable interest in trying to examine the process by which time is allocated and it might be over-ambitious to attempt to base any policy conclusions on such a short and mainly theoretical study. Nevertheless, some fundamental questions are raised in this book, even if they cannot be answered. The choices made by people in spending their stock of time are restricted and strongly influenced by state action, by the pressures of society and by the economic organisation of the nation. It is therefore of very considerable interest to consider how far the activities of the state and of society and the operations of a market economy appear to help or hinder people in their attempt to allocate time in a way that will yield them the maximum amount of welfare.

CHAPTER 2

Time in Economic Theory

But at my back I always hear
Time's wingèd chariot hurrying near,
And yonder all before us lie
Deserts of vast eternity.

[Andrew Marvell]

1. GENERAL SURVEY

In this chapter some of the main economic studies dealing with time are reviewed and discussed, and an attempt is made to build up a theoretical framework that may be used in the rest of the study. In the examination of the literature, most of the attention is focused on the more general theories. Detailed references to specific issues, such as the valuation of transport time savings or the determination of social time discount rates, are contained in the chapters dealing with these issues.

There is very little specific discussion of the economic problems of time in books on the general principles of economic analysis. A typical textbook may contain a reference to time as a scarce resource but the concept is not usually developed. There are, of course, a number of important issues that have been discussed widely in economic literature where some aspect of the passing of time does come into the analysis. The processes by which the length of the working day is determined have received considerable attention since the discussion was started by Ricardo and Marx. Much more recently, writers like Owen (1970) and Vickerman (1975) have dealt with the other part of our daily ration of time by studying the choice between work and leisure and the problems involved in the allocation of leisure time. Time has been brought into the analysis of interest, particularly by those who regard interest

7

payments as a reward for waiting. Closely allied to this concept has been the discussion of the choice between present and future satisfactions, which has included technical arguments about methods of discounting and the more interesting debate on how society should determine the rate at which the value of future benefits should be discounted. Time has been regarded as a form of input required in production using capital equipment by those who have followed Böhm-Bawerk in regarding the use of machinery as a roundabout method of production. The only direct mention of time in Samuelson's standard textbook on economics is a reference to time being consumed in indirect methods of production, followed by the argument that 'Economic activity is future-oriented . . . current productive efforts . . . produce for the future in order to repay the past for present consumption' (Samuelson, 1948, pp. 46–7). Another more recent development has been the attempt to put a money value on the time savings that arise from transport improvements.

Many of the references to time in economics are not concerned with its allocation but use time as a proxy for change. It is also a convenient unit for 'spacing out' measurements of economic indicators such as those relating to output, prices and wages. Interest calculations and payments are related to time periods that are determined by the calendar. There is no particular economic reason why interest should be paid or dividends declared every time the earth completes one circuit around the sun. Since a day on Venus is longer than a year, Venusian businessmen and economists (once they had overcome the problem of the temperature and the excessive supply of carbon monoxide) would have to decide whether to relate interest payments and economic data to this local day (243 earth days) or to the time taken by their planet in its orbit round the sun (225 earth days). Here on earth an astronomically determined calendar will no doubt continue to be used as the natural unit for economic measurement, although, except perhaps in activities based on agricultural output, there is no particular reason why the affairs of a company should be judged, or interest paid, at intervals of 365 earth days. But the earth calendar has been built into economic calculations. In forecasting exercises, time (usually measured in years) is the standard independent variable. Economic models attempting to measure growth in the economy or to explain important economic factors such as investment, savings and employment have generally started out dealing with one point in time but then changes in time have inevitably been introduced. The inadequacy of purely static models for dealing with some such essentially change-dependent concept as growth is obvious and so the difficult task of turning them into dynamic models has been attempted. But, as Carlstein and Thrift have argued, '. . . the procedure was one of "dynamising" the conventional equilibrium formulations . . . time was only incorporated as a kind of appendix to the existing body of theory' (1978, p. 242).

As was stated in chapter 1, the main concern of this study will be with the allocation of the scarce resource of time. This means that the study of time-saving values — which measure the benefits of being able to transfer time from one use to another, the choice between present and future consumption; the choice between work and leisure; and the uses of leisure time — falls within the scope of the book. On the other hand, time as a proxy for change or as the independent variable in equations used for forecasting the future level of some economic activity does not form part of the allocation problem and is thus excluded from any detailed consideration. As already explained, the problem of uncertainty is also largely (although not wholly) excluded, but this is in order to simplify the discussion and to keep the study within its prescribed length, rather than for reasons of logical classification.

The argument so far has shown that there is no single clearly defined concept that comes into the mind of economists when the word 'time' is mentioned in relation to their subject. This is clearly illustrated by examining the distinguished writings of Professor Shackle who, although he includes the word 'time' in the titles of two of his books (1958, 1969), deals largely with the area of discussion that has been excluded from this study. In discussing the factors that are left out of a static equilibrium model of the Walras–Pareto type, Shackle writes of 'Time and everything that belongs to time: expectation and uncertainty; change and growth; ambition, hope and fear; discovery, invention and innovation; novelty and news' (1958, p. 93). The economic problems of time for Shackle are uncertainty and change. In *Time in Economics* he deals with the philosophical concept of time as 'a moment in being, which is the locus of every actual sense experience, every thought, feeling, decision and action' (1958, p. 13). Shackle thinks of decisions as a kind of instantaneous 'cut' between the past and present that introduces a new strand into history. He contrasts space, in which people can change their position, with time, in which they cannot. (As we have seen in chapter 1, people can theoretically change their relative place in time, but Shackle's conclusion is effectively true for the world in which economic choices must be made.)

Apart from his extensive treatment of decision making when there is uncertainty, Shackle deals with a few more specific economic issues. These include the investment cycle and some aspects of the determination of interest rates. In criticising the view that interest is a reward for waiting, he points out that some waiting periods may increase the pleasure received from an expected future event because of the pleasures of anticipation. In discussing economic models, Shackle makes clear the distinction between a stationary state and a static system for an economy. In the theoretical stationary state, an economy has worked itself into a position of equilibrium so that there is no further tendency to change. In a static system, time, or change, is assumed not to exist or, in Shackle's phrase, 'we abolish it altogether' (1958, p. 94). Shackle is concerned with the argument that the static state is a useful theoretical concept whereas the stationary state is useless and unrealistic, since it involves seeking to 'put time in fetters or rob it of its essence' (p. 94). It is apparent that, for Shackle, time is synonymous with change. He is not concerned with the problem of allocating the scarce resource of time except in so far as uncertainty is involved. In a sense, Shackle's work on time may be said to deal with an important complication – the existence of uncertainty in relation to the future – rather than with the basic issue of how choices are made when the outcome is known or assumed to be highly probable. Since we cannot make decisions about the past, all economic choices relate to the future and uncertainty exists. But the degree of uncertainty about using time is not necessarily greater than that associated with the consumption of any other good or service. If a man wishes to have central heating installed in his house he must make decisions despite uncertainty about the severity of future winters, the price of alternative fuels, the relative aesthetic appeal of radiators and open fires and the possibility that he may move. The uncertainties are no greater in deciding what length of journey to work is acceptable or in choosing between an hour of overtime work and an hour of leisure activity. Time in economics, for Shackle, would be abolished if there was no economic change. But time is a scarce resource and individuals will be forced to make choices about its use in this world so long as man is neither omnipresent nor immortal.

The body of economic literature is so extensive that it is dangerous to designate any particular author as being the first to discuss any given issue. According to Carlstein and Thrift, the American economist George Soule was one of the first writers to deal extensively with the time-allocation issue. Soule argued that economists had not developed a comprehensive theory for dealing with time as a scarce resource and that 'economic theorists have not absorbed the concept of time into their basic thinking' (Soule, 1955, p. 89). He also raised the fundamental question of whether the market system could be relied on to allocate time to the uses best fitted to satisfy human needs. The best-known basic study of time allocation is probably contained in Becker's article 'A Theory of the Allocation of Time', which was published in 1965. This paper resulted from the work of several economists at Columbia University, which involved 'introducing the cost of time systematically into decision about non-work activities' (Becker, 1965, p. 494). Becker's own work related to the use of time in education and training activities. Despite its title, his paper deals only with the use of time in non-work activities.

In his analysis Becker makes use of an idea, developed by Cairncross (1958), of the household as a small factory or purchasing unit that manufactures what Becker calls 'basic commodities', which it then consumes itself. The production process of the household involves combining time with market goods. The time input is the time required to consume Becker's 'basic commodities'. These commodities are not defined except by giving the two examples of seeing a play and sleeping. The inputs for seeing a play would be actors, script, theatre and the playgoer's time. Becker does not distinguish between time spent watching the play and any travelling time involved. Becker represents his basic commodities by Z_i so that

$$Z_i = f_i(x_i, T_i)$$

where x_i and T_i are vectors of market goods and time inputs. For durable capital goods, x refers to the services that they produce. Following Becker's formulation of his model, households maximise utility and their behaviour can be represented by the equation and identities

$$U = U(Z_i \ldots Z_m) \equiv U(f_1, \ldots f_m) \equiv U(x_1, \ldots x_{mi} T_1, \ldots T_m)$$

which is subject to a budget constraint

$$g(Z_i, \ldots Z_m) = Z$$

where g is an expenditure function of Z_i and Z represents the resources

constraint. The goods and resources constraints can be written
separately. The goods constraint is given by

$$\sum p_i x_i = I = V + T_w \overline{w}$$

where p_i represents the money prices of the goods x_i, I is total
income, V is 'other' (presumably unearned) income, T_w is the
hours at work and $\overline{w}$ is average earnings per hour. The time constraint is

$$\sum T_i = T_c = T - T_w$$

where T_c is described by Becker as the total consumption time and
T is total time available. This suggests that all non-work time is
spent in consumption. Becker rewrites the household production
functions as

$$T_i \equiv t_i Z_i$$

$$x_i \equiv b_i Z_i$$

where t_i gives the input of time per unit of Z_i and b_i gives the input
of market goods. He then points out that one of the two constraints
can be removed because 'time can be converted into goods by
using less time at consumption and more at work' (1965, pp. 496–7).
The single constraint becomes

$$\sum_i p_i x_i + \sum_i T_i \overline{w} = V + T \overline{w}$$

which can be rewritten as

$$\sum_i (p_i b_i + t_i \overline{w}) \, Z_i = V + T \overline{w}.$$

Thus Becker's basic commodities (Z_i) have what he calls a full price
representing both the money price of the goods consumed and the
time required for consumption. Becker develops a similar concept
of 'full income', which would be the total amount of money that
could be earned if all possible time was devoted to paid work 'with
no regard to consumption'. This does not mean working twenty-
four hours a day, however, as Becker recognises the obvious fact
that some time must be spent eating and resting if money income
is to be maximised. This full income must be 'spent' either directly
on goods or on time given to consumption when it is not actually
earned but is forgone. Time and goods, Becker argued, must be
allocated between work-orientated and consumption-orientated
activities and costs could be divided into those resulting from allocating goods and those caused by allocating time.

The basic ideas contained in Becker's *Economic Journal* article were expanded in a book written with Ghez (1975) to cover longer-period time-allocation decisions and to include the activity of education, or the creation of 'human capital', as well as the activities of work and leisure.

Becker's work is of considerable importance as a pioneering attempt to deal with the problem of time allocations and it has given us some valuable insight into the issues involved. Inevitably, as Carlstein and Thrift have pointed out, the attempt to express the problem in econometric equations has led to some abstractions from reality, and Carlstein and Thrift make a number of other criticisms of Becker's work. They complain that the threefold classification of activities is simplified and crude and that there is no 'spatial dimension' in his analysis. (Although it does not appear in the model, Becker does have a section on travel time in his *Economic Journal* article.) They summarise their criticisms by arguing that Becker's model '. . . is thus hardly a genuine theory of time allocation, but a basically untested model, which relates certain crude and aggregate measures of time use to certain aggregate measures of pecuniary flows affecting an aggregate of households' (Carlstein and Thrift, 1978, p. 247). These criticisms are perhaps rather severe. It is not clear what 'spatial dimension' means in this context and Becker's model does have some explanatory power. But some criticism may be justified.

The distinction between Becker's 'basic commodities' and 'goods' is not always clear. Basic commodities are goods combined with time that directly enter the utility functions of households. But some activities, such as eating a piece of chocolate, do not require any exclusive allocation of time since they can be carried out during time that is already allocated to another activity (such as going for a walk). Chocolate is therefore perhaps a good but is also a basic commodity. Conversely some activities, such as meditation, do not require any goods input. Becker passes over the distinction between durable goods and those that cease to exist when they are 'consumed' rather lightly. There is an important difference between goods that are literally consumed when they 'enter a utility function' and that must consequently be replaced and those whose 'consumption' involves zero marginal money cost. Once it has been purchased, the enjoyment of a painting involves only time costs. Marginal money costs are zero and the average money cost will therefore fall continuously as the period of enjoyment is extended.

A possibly more important criticism is that many activities do not fall very clearly into any of Becker's two or three categories. Housework, do-it-yourself home repairs and gardening may not produce any immediate satisfaction at all and can hardly be regarded as combining 'goods' with time to produce utility. A housewife may enjoy making jam but quite probably she will not do so and the utility-producing activity will occur later when the inputs of jam, bread, butter and time are combined in the activity of enjoying afternoon tea. Becker does deal with some aspects of this problem in his discussion of the application of his model to the relationship between earnings and hours worked. He points out that the forgone earnings for some leisure activities are greater than those for others. Since there may be no opportunity to earn money during weekends, the forgone earnings, or opportunity cost of leisure, will be less than they would be during a weekday. Becker also argued that the cost of time is less for 'productive consumption' activities such as sleeping and eating because these contribute indirectly to earnings. It is not clear, however, whether housework and do-it-yourself activities are supposed to contribute to earnings. There is a difference between sleeping and eating, which provide workers with the necessary health and strength to work for money earnings, and decorating a room in one's own home. The latter activity means that money income that might be allocated to pay professional decorators can be spent on some other good or service but it does not increase earning capacity. Becker argues, quite correctly, that not only is it difficult to distinguish leisure from other non-work but also non-work from work. But his argument that the idea of productive consumption was introduced to cover 'commodities' that contribute to paid-work activity as well as to consumption clearly suggests that he is not thinking of such activities as gardening, do-it-yourself work and housework. These are forms of unpaid work that contribute to consumption and do not seem to fit into any of his categories.

Carlstein and Thrift appear to have been slightly confused by Becker's treatment of the different categories of non-work time. They suggest that full income is the money income people earn if they worked 24 hours per day for 365 days per year. But Becker is more realistic than this, allowing for necessary inputs of eating, sleeping and even some leisure activities, which do not involve forgoing earnings but rather make them possible. However, as we have seen, Becker is a little unclear about the extent of these necessary inputs, and he does not deal at all with unpaid productive activities. Indeed he largely avoids using the word activity and writes instead of commodities in what is sometimes a rather confusing context. He argues for example that 'pure consumption could be a limiting commodity in the opposite direction in which the contribution to work was nil' (1965, p. 504). This seems to apply the word 'commodity' to some such activity as watching the Eurovision Song Contest or going for a walk.

Becker replaces a world of work and non-work time by one divided between work and consumption. 'Pure work' is a limiting commodity of joint commodities that contribute both to work and to consumption in which the contribution to consumption is nil and vice versa. But the consumption/work dichotomy is, perhaps, a not very much more satisfactory classification of human behaviour than the work/leisure division it replaces. We have already seen that some activities do not contribute indirectly to work in the way that Becker describes for productive consumption; that is they do not help to make the performance of paid work possible. But these activities, such as home decorating, are hardly cases of pure consumption. If 'consumption' means deriving some direct satisfaction from carrying out an activity then it is clear that work may also be a form of consumption and the work/consumption division may be no more easy to maintain than is the work/leisure classification. All activities consume the scarce resource of time. Time may be used to create goods or services and the worker may be rewarded by being paid a money wage or by selling the product for money. Alternatively, the worker may keep the goods or benefit from the service himself. He may eat the vegetables grown in his garden or enjoy the improved reflection in the mirror after he has shaved. Some time may be spent in Becker's activity of combining time with goods and enjoying the product although it is only in some of these activities that the goods input is literally consumed. If a man eats a chocolate then no semantic difficulties are created by saying that the chocolate has been consumed and there is no difficulty in picturing the chocolate and the time taken to eat it as a market good being changed into one of Becker's 'basic commodities'. (But even this simple illustration contains a difficulty. As already argued, it is possible to eat a chocolate and to listen to the radio or operate a capstan lathe simultaneously so that this particular activity does not demand an exclusive time input.) If a man reads a book then the book is consumed in the sense that the pleasure that it can give to the reader is likely to be diminished, although the book continues to exist. Other goods such as paintings and musical instruments may yield pleasure when they are combined with time without in any sense being consumed. Finally, time may be spent in ways that give satisfaction but that do not require any input of market goods at all. A man may enjoy watching a sunset or simply sitting and thinking.

The points of departure from the Becker model and areas where an attempt has been made to build further developments on his original ideas may perhaps be usefully summarised at this stage. Three main points have been put forward in the discussion of Becker's work. Firstly it is suggested that Becker's concept of basic commodities produced by the household is too restrictive as it seems to apply only in cases where there is an input of market goods. In 1966 Winston wrote that 'Time can be spent either on the earning of income (work) or on a host of alternative non-economic activities (leisure)' (p. 28). Becker goes a long way towards dispelling the idea that leisure activities are not the concern of the economist, but perhaps it is necessary to go a little further and establish that all uses of time, even when there is no input other than time, are part of the legitimate area of study of economics. The word 'activity', even if this is also used by geographers and sociologists, seems to be more appropriate to describe different ways of using time than Becker's production of 'commodities'.

A linked point is to accept Becker's arguments that it is difficult to find a logical basis for a distinction between work and non-work time but to suggest that his own classification into pure work, pure consumption and intermediate commodities is also unsatisfactory. Some activities are excluded and there is an implication that work is carried out exclusively in order to earn money income. The important possibility exists that work may itself 'enter directly' into people's utility functions.

The third point follows from the other two. Although his work reveals the artificiality of the work/leisure dichotomy, Becker still appears to support separate treatment for work and non-work time, even in his later study (Ghez and Becker, 1975), which incorporates education and training. Although it may not be possible to test it in the real world, there is a case for developing a single model that can be related to all uses of the scarce resource of time.

Another important examination of some more general issues relating to time in economics is contained in DeSerpa's article 'A Theory of the Economics of Time' (1971). DeSerpa's main aim is to modify neoclassical consumer theory to allow for the use of the scarce resource of time. It is interesting that DeSerpa considers that Becker's *Economic Journal* paper is not a general discussion of the problems of time in economics, but that it relates only to the specific issue of the effect of forgone earnings upon consumer choice. DeSerpa's model is supported by three basic arguments: that the utility received from consumption is a function not only of the commodities consumed but also of the time allocated to consumption; that in making consumption choices individuals face both time and money constraints; and that some minimum amount of time may be required for some acts of consumption but the individual may spend more than the minimum time in consumption if he wishes. DeSerpa concentrates on the simplified case where goods are consumed one at a time and all free time is spent 'in the consumption of some commodity'. His model is based on the choice of the individual rather than the household and DeSerpa assumes that each person has a fixed amount of time available, which is equal to the length of the decision period, and also a fixed money income. This means that the possibility of exchanging time for money by working for a longer period, which is discussed by Becker, is excluded by DeSerpa from his basic model. An important feature of DeSerpa's theory is that there are no fixed time prices for consumption. This represents a step towards reality as many utility-yielding activities can be extended according to the wishes of the consumer. There is no fixed time price for playing tennis or for fishing although, as DeSerpa also points out, there may often be a minimum time input required. Travel time may represent an absolutely unavoidable minimum time input for many activities. This would apply to our examples of playing tennis and fishing, except for people with a tennis court or a river in their own grounds. These activities also require minimum inputs of time to be allocated to them directly. Even if a man was eccentric enough to want to play tennis for a one-minute period he would be unlikely to be able to find an opponent who would be willing to fit in with his plan. Fishing is clearly an activity requiring a minimum time allocation of considerable size.

DeSerpa's model thus has two time constraints. He calls the total time available for all consumption activities the time-resource constraint, while the minimum time allocation required for particular activities is described as a time-consumption constraint. DeSerpa expresses the problem of obtaining the maximum utility for an individual from the most efficient use of his time and money resources as a Lagrangean function. The shadow variables λ, μ and K_i are generated. These represent the marginal utilities of money, of time and of saving time in a particular activity respectively.

DeSerpa stresses the distinction between time as a resource and time as a commodity. In his notation, K_i/λ is the value of saving time. DeSerpa puts forward the argument, which has also been developed by Evans (1972) (and which is perhaps self-evident), that little meaning can be attached to an absolute value of time (or value of time as a resource) since we cannot acquire an increased total stock of time. (Possible exceptions to this conclusion are discussed in chapter 3.) Practical economic interest must centre on the value of time savings that make it possible to transfer time from one use to another. Thus a road improvement might reduce the travel time input required for some activities and enable some of DeSerpa's time-consumption constraints to be relaxed.

The main new feature of DeSerpa's model is the attempt to deal with the problem created by the need to allocate indivisible 'lumps' of time to some activities. Utility-maximising positions could be calculated only with the use of a new linear programming model. DeSerpa claims that his model 'is neither a theory of working time, nor a theory of leisure time, nor a theory of travel time, but a theory of time' (1971, p. 843). While it is true that the level of abstraction of DeSerpa's arguments makes his analysis of general applicability, it may perhaps be going too far to suggest that he has developed an all-embracing theory of the economics of time. His model is similar to Becker's in that it deals with the significance of the time input in the consumption of market goods. It does not seek to analyse the wider issue of how maximum utility can be gained from the allocation of time over all possible activities. DeSerpa has little to say about the determination of the length of the working day or of the time allocated to non-working activities that do not involve the consumption of market goods. A further reference to DeSerpa's analysis of the theory of the value of travel time savings is contained in chapter 5, and his definition of leisure time is mentioned in chapter 6.

2. THEORY OF TIME ALLOCATION

The basic assumptions of this analysis are that time is in some senses the ultimate scarce resource and that the most fundamental economic decisions made by an individual are about how he will allocate the future time that he expects will be available for his use. Most of the difficulties and complications arise because of the existence of various limitations on the freedom of choice. The main restrictions that may affect the free allocation of time may be described as being legal; institutional or organisational; climatic; the effect of prior decisions; the required cooperation of other people; and the need to possess market goods or to be able to command market services. Legal restrictions may forbid some uses of time or enforce others. People in Britain are not allowed to use their time to take some harmful drugs or to practise firing revolvers in their gardens. The most important positive state interference with the freedom to allocate time is the institution of compulsory education. Children in Britain are compelled to allocate about eight hours a day (allowing for travelling and homework but assuming that lunchtime is free) to school and school work for five days a week and for thirty-nine weeks a year over a minimum period of eleven years. Assuming that average children of school age would have twelve hours of free time per day if it was not for the obligation to attend school, this means that during school years the state forcibly allocates about 36 per cent of the total annual free time of children. Another example of compulsory time allocation is committal to prison. It is interesting that one of the two main forms of punishment for law-breaking in most countries is the forcible allocation of a period of an individual's time to the 'activity' of being in prison. Those who are 'doing time' still have some choices left in allocating their time in prison between different activities or 'sub-activities' but they suffer from a large number of extra constraints.

The institutional and organisational restrictions on the use of time may have an economic basis or be mainly the result of custom. Their effect is to lead to fixed hours, which are not determined by the consumer, during which consumption, or the pursuit of an activity, is possible. A play, once it is started, must be acted through to its conclusion so that, even if it was repeated continuously throughout the day, it would only be possible to begin to see it at fixed intervals. But economic and human considerations usually confine the performance to one or at most two occasions. Actors cannot usually repeat their efforts more than once or twice a day and, presumably, the marginal cost of an extra performance would normally exceed the marginal revenue. Films, however, can be shown again at relatively low extra cost so that film shows can be continuous and it is possible to enter a cinema over a long time period, providing that one is not too concerned about seeing the end of a film before its beginning. But with falling cinema attendances the continuous performance has become less common and in smaller towns cinemas may now have fixed programmes so that a complete programme can only be seen by entering the theatre at some specific time. Perhaps the most important organisational restriction on time use in Britain is the limitation on shopping imposed by having shops open only at fixed hours. This issue is too complex to be dealt with in this introductory discussion and it is examined more fully in chapter 6. This area of restriction on the allocation of time has not received very much attention from economists (except in some studies of the use of leisure), from politicians or from the information media. On the other hand, elections are fought on the extent to which the state should interfere with the ways in which an individual spends his money budget. The question of how far organisational or legal restrictions on the allocation of time are beneficial to society requires much more attention and it will be considered again in this study.

Climatic limitations on time allocation are fairly obvious, and in so far as they cannot be altered are no special concern of the economist. However, if the climate cannot be changed its effects can sometimes be overcome, so that the provision of indoor tennis courts and the protection of football pitches against snow and frost are examples of methods of increasing people's freedom to watch or take part in these sports at times of their choosing.

The freedom to allocate time to specific activities is limited as the result of many previous allocation decisions. It is not possible to decide to spend thirty minutes playing Beethoven's Moonlight Sonata, even if the inputs of a piano and the music are available, unless a previous decision has been made to allocate, say 1000 hours in earlier time periods to the task of learning to become a pianist. These prior decisions also have a spatial dimension. We cannot, in the morning, decide to spend the afternoon of the same day surfing at Bondi if previously made choices have resulted in our being located in Stoke on Trent rather than in Sydney. The use that can be made of future time periods may also be limited because of previous decisions committing those periods to some specific activity. It may be physically possible to play a third set of tennis but if we have previously promised to meet a friend during the required time period then we may feel unable to change the earlier decisions.

Another restriction on the freedom to allocate time to some activities arises because the agreement and cooperation of other people may be required. I might decide that the maximum utility that I could obtain from time allocated to paid work would be received if I was the Chairman of ICI. But the people who control the appointment to that post might base their decision on some criterion other than the maximisation of my utility. Some activities can only be pursued by one person in any given time period. The appointment of a Prime Minister normally precludes any other person from following the same activity in the same country.

The constraint on a free choice of activities with which economists have been mainly, perhaps almost exclusively, concerned is the need for inputs of goods and services. Many activities involve consuming goods and/or services so that they can only be chosen by those to whom these market goods are available. Sailing requires the availability of a yacht and reading demands at least temporary possession of a book. There is a sense in which every activity requires some direct or indirect market input. Suppose that we live in a house with direct access to a beach from which nude bathing is customary and free. Then we can engage in the activity of swimming without requiring any direct market inputs. We will not need to pay for transport to the beach nor need we buy bathing trunks. We could even dispense with a towel if it was a warm day and we were prepared to allocate time to getting dry. But swimming requires us to be reasonably healthy and well fed, so that indirectly it demands inputs of food, clothing, shelter and fuel. This distinction between the direct and indirect market inputs that may be required for a given activity to be undertaken is analogous to, but not identical with, the division between average and marginal costs. The direct inputs are those goods or services that would not be consumed if time was not allocated to a particular activity. In our example of swimming it would normally include the inputs of swimming trunks, a towel, transport costs and, in the case of a swimming pool or private bathing place, admission costs. Since the costs of using these inputs would not be incurred if the activity was not undertaken they are clearly very similar to marginal costs. But the comparison is a little confused because some inputs are not consumed on each occasion that time is allocated to an activity. The marginal cost of wearing trunks for a particular swim is virtually zero. The indirect inputs may be regarded as those basic market goods and services that are required to enable an individual to take part in any activities at all. They include shelter, food, clothing and heating. The costs of these inputs are similar to fixed costs, but again the comparison is not exact since the quantities of 'indirect inputs' consumed may sometimes be increased when an activity is undertaken. Swimming and other forms of athletic exercise may increase our need for food. Rough walking may result in a marginal increase in our expenditure on shoes while staying indoors to read could add to our annual fuel bill. Some items such as clothes could be classified as either direct or indirect inputs. Specialised clothes such as swimming trunks or riding breeches may be regarded as direct inputs while the ordinary clothes that we need to wear to go shopping or visit the cinema are indirect inputs. But it is apparent that the classification is not completely rigorous. English people in Switzerland tend to walk on the mountains in 'ordinary' clothes whereas Germans and Swiss wear special breeches, boots and socks even for the most gentle walk along the mountain paths. It is apparent that the 'direct' and 'indirect' input distinction, though generally valid, is not entirely satisfactory.

Much of the attention in the economic analysis of people's behaviour in allocating their time has centred around the need to undertake paid work in order to earn money, which can be exchanged for the market goods that are required as direct or indirect inputs for other non-work activities. As we have seen, Becker's model is based on the assumption that time can be changed into market goods through the medium of paid work. But exclusive concentration on the work and non-work choice has tended to obscure the fact that though this may involve a particularly important decision it is not essentially different from other choices in time allocation.

The six constraints affecting people's choice in allocating time are not necessarily mutually exclusive. If a man wishes to spend three years as President of the USA he will face legal constraints relating to his age and country of birth, he will probably require a considerable input of market goods and he will need the co-operation of many other people. Sometimes market good inputs can be used to relax other constraints. A rich man might be able to buy a special performance of a play at a time of his own choosing or he might find that some shops were prepared to open out-of-hours for his benefit. In chapter 5 the possibility of relaxing travel time constraints by using faster, but more expensive, means of transport will be discussed.

3. A TIME-ALLOCATION MODEL

The basic problem in the use of time, it has been argued, is not the choice between work or leisure; nor is it the allocation of leisure time or of 'free' time. The fundamental issue is to consider how time can be allocated between all available activities so that maximum utility can be obtained. The simplest situation is where the allocation decisions relate to a specific short time period, where there is no uncertainty and where the market goods input constraint is eliminated. Let us take the case of a multi-millionaire who is planning the allocation of the next day's twenty-four hours. If he is sufficiently wealthy the market goods input constraint will not be operative. He will be able to buy any inputs that he requires and need not allocate any time to paid work. This does not mean that paid work will necessarily be excluded from his list of possible activities, as he might obtain sufficient utility from the work itself to make this a chosen activity. There will therefore be a number of alternative activities on which the millionaire could spend his time. The list will be limited by the legal, institutional, climatic, 'prior decision' and 'cooperation of others' constraints that are still applicable even when the market goods constraint is removed. These constraints cannot be built into a manageable economic model but they can be represented by considering only activities that are available. Out of all possible activities, a set a_i are available to be chosen by the decision-making millionaire. Suppose that the decision-maker chooses to take part in a sub-set, a_n, drawn from the total available activities a_i during the twenty-four-hour period for which plans are being made. If the situation is simplified further by ignoring the 'DeSerpa' problem of the necessity of allocating minimum time inputs to some activities, and if it is assumed that very small units of time can be transferred from one activity to another, then the essential basic issue remains. This is the problem of allocating time between different activities on the 'chosen list' so that utility is maximised.

Suppose that the a_n chosen activities are represented by a series $a_1 \ldots a_n$ and that the time allocated to activity a_1 is represented by t_1, and similarly the time for activity a_2 is t_2 and for the last activity, a_n, is t_n. Then, if U is total utility, the simple expression

$$U = U(t_1, t_2 \ldots t_n)$$

must be maximised. The only constraint is the twenty-four-hour time budget, so that (if time is measured in minutes)

$$1440 - \sum_{i=1}^{n} t_i = 0.$$

This maximum utility position would be found (in these simplified conditions) where

$$\frac{\partial U}{\partial t_1} = \frac{\partial U}{\partial t_2} \cdots = \frac{\partial U}{\partial t_n}$$

or where the marginal utility of the last small unit of time that can be allocated is the same for all activities. It must also be the case that the marginal utility from the last unit of time allocated to one of the chosen activities must be greater than that which could be obtained from any excluded activity. This could be written

$$\frac{\partial U}{\partial t_n} > \frac{\partial U}{\partial t_{n+1}}.$$

It is interesting to compare the situation with the maximisation of utility in normal consumer theory where the well-known equilibrium condition can be represented, where p is price and there are two commodities x and y, by

$$\frac{U_x}{P_x} = \lambda = \frac{U_y}{P_y}$$

where the ratios of marginal utility to price are equal to each other (and to the common ratio λ). In the time-allocation problem, given the simplifying assumptions of the absence of a market goods input constraint and of indivisibilities, all the activities can be said to have the same time price. If different commodities have a different money price per unit, then the equilibrium position will be reached when the ratio of the last increment of utility from the last unit purchased is the same as the ratio of the prices. Thus if rice costs 20p per pound while cheese is 80p per pound, then the utility-maximising consumer would (assuming that he could buy these commodities in very small units) allocate his money so that the last unit of cheese purchased was expected to yield four times as much utility as the last unit of rice that he bought. But the costs of one minute spent in reading, or of one minute walking in the garden, or of one minute engaged in any other activity would all be the same (when market inputs are costless, or are not required) and equal to one minute. There is an extra factor involved in turning money into goods that does not apply when expenditure is measured in the currency of time. When money is exchanged for market goods the consumer must consider both the utility he will gain from the goods, and also the quantity of the goods that can be obtained for a unit of money. When time is 'spent' it is only the amounts of utility that are expected to be gained from different activities that need to be compared.

The analysis so far may seem to be highly simplified but it is not wholly unrealistic, and there are, indeed, some real world situations in which it may be at least partly applicable. It is not only extremely rich people who can ignore the problem of the market goods inputs required for time-consuming activities. As has been shown, some activities do not require any 'direct' market good inputs. We need to be fit and possess clothes and shoes in order go for a walk, but these are 'joint goods' that we also require in order to carry out many other activities. Even when specific market good inputs are required, the marginal cost of using them may be zero. Once we own a garden fork the marginal cost of using it for an extra hour's digging would be effectively nil. Where there is a positive marginal cost associated with some activities, ordinary non-millionaires may be temporarily, partially or wholly freed from the market goods input constraint. A family on their annual holiday may have saved enough money to pay for all the required goods inputs for their list of possible activities. If their holiday savings are already dedicated to that use, and if the amount available is adequate for any possible combination of market inputs, then the problem of maximising the utility from their holiday will be basically the same as that illustrated in our simple model. The family must allocate time in order to yield the maximum satisfaction but they are not concerned, for the duration of the holiday, with making any decisions about earning money income.

People who have retired from work and those who live on unearned, but limited incomes do have to deal with money budget constraints. But if (whether by their own choice or not) there is no possibility of these non-workers turning time into money by undertaking paid work, then their position is also not altogether dissimilar from that represented in the 'millionaire model'. The budget constraints will not lead to the complications, shown in the Becker and other models, and discussed later in this chapter, that arise when a choice must be made between activities for which money is received and those that involve net market inputs. The budget constraints for people living on pensions or unearned income will reduce the list of available activities by making it necessary to exclude all those uses of time that demand market good inputs for which money is not available. But given the reduced activity list the basic problem thus becomes one of allocating time between alternative uses in a way that will maximise utility. The main difference from the 'millionaire model', apart from the reduction in the size of the list of available activities, is that where the money cost of an activity increases with the length of time that is allocated to it, the monetary as well as time opportunity costs must be considered and money prices as well as time prices will be significant.

Since the analysis of this section of the study is partly unfamiliar, some recapitulation with a slightly more rigorous statement of the arguments is perhaps desirable before proceeding to further issues. Economists are accustomed to thinking of individuals as consumers of goods and services who can maximise their satisfaction by an efficient allocation of their money resources. Time is an additional constraint that has been examined by a few specialist writers, but its importance is usually largely ignored in the analysis of the behaviour of consumers. In this chapter an attempt is made to treat people as consumers of time, and to regard the allocation of time between different activities as the fundamental choice that they must make. The availability of money, or the power to obtain a supply of market goods and services, then becomes the additional factor that must sometimes, but not always, be considered. When money resources are more than adequate for any required input of market goods, consumers only need to allocate their budget of time between alternative activities, all of which have the same time price, in a way that will maximise utility. Suppose that a time consumer's preferences led him to produce a 'short list' of only six activities that he expected to use up his budget of free time, and that, ranked in order of preference, these were:

> Sleeping
> Eating
> Sailing
> Swimming
> Cycling
> Theatre attendance.

He would then, if market good input constraints were inapplicable, maximise his utility by allocating his time between the activities so that the marginal utility of the last unit of time allocated was the same in all activities and no gains could be made by any reallocation of time. It must be assumed that marginal utility diminishes for all activities as the amount of time allocated to them increases, otherwise all the available time would be devoted to the activity with the highest initial utility ranking.

The next degree of complication is found when money income cannot be increased and is insufficient to buy all the inputs that would be required if time was allocated to all the preferred list of activities, but where the inputs for each activity have a fixed money cost that does not vary with the amount of time that is allocated to them. People living on pensions or on unearned income may be in the position where they cannot easily turn time into money but it is unlikely that they will only take part in activities for which the money cost is fixed in relation to time. Given the assumptions, the money costs of activities are equivalent to a set of weights that affect the exchange rate between activities. While it is still true that the time costs of each activity are identical (the time opportunity cost of one minute spent swimming is one less minute devoted to reading), the differing money costs mean that a 'lump' of time given to one activity may have to be exchanged for a larger or smaller lump of time if it is reallocated to another activity. The total money income available forms a second budget constraint. If the previous notation of $t_1 \ldots t_n$ is used to represent the amounts of time allocated to the n preferred activities, then each activity will have a price, p_i, which represents the money price of required market inputs. The consumers must therefore maximise the utility received from t_n activities subject to the two constraints

$$\sum t_i = Y$$

and

$$\sum p_i = B$$

where Y and B represent the time and money budgets respectively. If both time and money could be allocated continuously in very small units, then the utility-maximising position would be similar to that found for the consumption of market goods and would exist where the rates of the marginal utility of each activity to its price was the same. If Ut_1 is the total utility received from activity number 1, while activity n yields Ut_n, the utility-maximising equilibrium position can be represented by

$$\frac{\partial Ut_1}{p_1} = \frac{\partial Ut_2}{p_2} \cdots = \frac{\partial Ut_n}{p_n}$$

Suppose that, for the six preferred activities already listed, the time periods allocated by the 'millionaire' consumer and the fixed money costs were as shown in Table 2.1. It is assumed that the allocation decisions relate to a time budget of eighteen hours. Now suppose that another consumer, with identical tastes to the millionaire, had a fixed income of £5 that he could spend during the eighteen-hour time period. He could not reach the utility-maximising position that he would choose if he was not restricted by his budget constraint. If the consumer insisted on eight hours

TABLE 2.1
*Time allocated to chosen activities by 'millionaire'
consumer, and fixed money costs*

	Time (hrs)	Money price (£)
Sleep	8	0
Eat	2	2.0
Sail	3	3.0
Swim	1	0.5
Cycle	1	0.5
Theatre	3	2.0
	18	8.0

sleep and two hours spent eating, then he would have £3 of his money budget still to allocate, and could choose either sailing, or the three activities swimming, cycling and visiting the theatre. Suppose that he chose to give up sailing. The consumer would then have three hours available from his time budget that he could re-allocate between the three activities swimming, cycling and theatre attendance. In practice, of course, theatre attendance cannot be extended by a small extra unit of time (except when the time allowance includes travelling time) and an extra 'lump' of time spent in seeing a play would involve additional money expenditure. If the consumer had to eliminate sailing he might revise his 'short list'. He might not allocate all the time made available between the three remaining 'short-list' activities of swimming, cycling and theatre attendance, since he might find that the marginal utility gained from allocating some time to a seventh zero-price activity, such as walking, would exceed the marginal utility obtained from extra time periods spent on swimming or cycling.

The next complication that arises is that the money cost of an activity may vary directly with the quantity of time that is allocated to its pursuit. For some activities market goods inputs may be hired for a price that increases with the period of use. The use of a hired car is an obvious example. In the list of activities chosen for our imaginary consumer, swimming and sailing costs may increase with time (though not continuously) and even the extension of a period of eating may require some extra input of food! If it is assumed, for simplicity, that all the selected activities, except sleep, have a money price that increases with time, and that the hourly rates are based on the total costs already shown, then the

TABLE 2.2
Assumed hourly costs of chosen activities

	Hourly rate (£)
Sleep	0
Eat	1.0
Sail	1.0
Swim	0.5
Cycle	0.5
Theatre	0.67

hourly money prices would be as shown in Table 2.2. This means that if a consumer had a time budget of eighteen hours and a money budget of £5.00 and if it is assumed that the time allocated to eating could not be reduced, then the whole time budget could not be used up on activities having money costs. Even if only the cheapest activities, in money terms, of swimming and cycling were selected, the maximum time that could be allocated to them would be six hours. With eight hours sleeping and two hours eating time this would add up to only sixteen hours, so that two hours must be allocated to a 'money–costless' or zero-price activity.

In the real world some activities will have a fixed cost for a discrete lump of time (such as admission to the theatre), some will have a money cost that varies with time, and many others will have zero or near-zero marginal money costs (such as taking a walk or reading a library book). The money cost of inputs may also be less rigid than our example suggests. The cost of the food 'input' to eating can usually be varied. A consumer with a limited money budget might therefore have to choose between pairs of activities such as eating with superior food plus costless activity, or eating with inferior food plus an activity with a money cost. Typical time budgets (which will be discussed in chapter 6) contain several activities with zero or very low marginal money cost and most people's money budgets are probably used up before their time budget is exhausted. Linder (1970) has argued that, with increases in the productivity of working time, more 'consumer goods' will be used per unit of leisure time. The truth of this conclusion is discussed in chapter 6, but it is apparent that increases in wealth (whether obtained from work or in the form of 'unearned' income) will relax money budget constraints and allow consumers to undertake more activities requiring the consumption of market good inputs.

4. THE NATURE OF TIME-ALLOCATION UTILITY

Before considering the problems that arise when our major simplifying assumption that consumers receive a fixed 'unearned' money income is removed, some further examination must be made of the nature of the utility that is expected to be received when time is spent. In the discussion so far, the utility from undertaking an activity has been equated with the expected benefit that will be derived from taking part in the activity itself. The utility from allocating a lump of time to playing tennis has been regarded as being the utility received from the activity of playing tennis itself. But in order to take part in many activities time must also be spent making the activity possible. It may be necessary to engage in what may be called ancillary activities. The most obvious ancillary activity is travel. In deciding whether to swim, or fish or go to the theatre a consumer must also take into account the time that must be spent in travelling to the swimming pool, river or theatre. The problem of evaluating travel time is the main topic of chapter 5. Other ancillary activities may also be required. In order to play tennis it may also be necessary to prepare the court, to change clothes before the game and to change clothes and take a shower after playing. The total utility received from playing tennis might therefore be made up of a mixture of different levels of utility obtained from the tennis itself but also from several other activities. Suppose that a person is considering spending two hours playing tennis (U_1) and that this involves the following ancillary activities and time consumption:

U_2 Travelling   40 minutes
U_3 Changing clothes   6 minutes
U_4 Preparing court   4 minutes
U_5 Taking shower & drying   10 minutes

If the activities playing tennis, travelling, etc., are numbered 1 to 5, and if the expected utilities per minute that will be received from the activities are represented by U_1 to U_5 respectively, then the total utility expected from the decision to play tennis (assuming that utility is constant per minute over the time periods involved) would be

$$U_t = 120\, U_1 + 40\, U_2 + 6\, U_3 + 4\, U_4 + 10\, U_5.$$

The decision maker must consider the total utility that he expects to receive from a package of different activities that he must choose.

Thus our prospective tennis player might choose between tennis and an alternative gardening package. If the same amount of time was available (three hours) and the gardening activities and time consumptions were:

U_6 Changing clothes 6 minutes
U_7 Preparing tools 10 minutes
U_8 Digging 70 minutes
U_9 Weeding 60 minutes
U_{10} Planting 22 minutes
U_{11} Taking bath 12 minutes

then the total utility would be (if the numbering system is continued):

$$U_t = 6\,U_6 + 10\,U_7 + 70\,U_8 + 60\,U_9 + 22\,U_{10} + 12\,U_{11}.$$

Even if, for the decision maker, the utilities of the individual gardening activities were lower than that of player tennis ($U_8 < U_1$, $U_9 < U_1$, $U_{10} < U_1$) the gardening package might be chosen if, for example, the utility of the gardening activities was much higher than the utility of travelling to play tennis ($U_8 > U_2$).

It is apparent that it is necessary to distinguish between different types of utility that may result from the allocation of time. The utility that is obtained from the time spent directly on some chosen activity might be called specific utility, while the utility that results from choosing a package of interlinked activities could be described as composite utility. But this classification does not make allowance for all the complexities that may be found when consumers try to allocate their stock of time in a way that will yield maximum satisfaction. People who make decisions about spending their time must also consider what might be called the indirect costs and benefits, or gains and losses in utility, that may be associated with some activities. The 'costs' of activities have already been considered in the discussion about market good inputs. The most important benefit, which has been excluded from the analysis so far, is the receipt of money earnings or profits as a reward for carrying out some activities. As has been shown, it has been customary in the economic literature dealing with the allocation of time to base the analysis on the existence of the two separate constraints of time and money. This approach has been used for some of the earlier discussion in this chapter and it can be used to explain consumers' behaviour and to work out the effects of changes in prices or in income levels. But it does have disadvantages. It can lead to a preoccupation with the problems of consumers' behaviour with which economists are most familiar, those of maximising the utility received from goods and services, rather than from activities. Time becomes the awkward extra factor that may be mentioned but that usually disappears from analysis concentrating on the utility received from the goods and services for which money can be exchanged. The money budget approach also fails to deal with the many non-monetary 'indirect' benefits that may be gained by taking part in some activities. Some utility may be gained from the activity of being at the hairdressers, but most of the benefit will result from having one's hair cut, permed or otherwise improved. Similarly, the activities of planting vegetables or redecorating a room may yield some satisfaction, but a major part of the utility, for most people, will be found in the form of eating the vegetables or enjoying the refurbished room. These 'indirect' benefits of activities are examined in chapter 4.

Unfortunately, the two classifications of utility cannot be combined to produce sub-groups of activities. The specific/composite classification relates to the act of decision making. In some cases the decision to undertake a particular activity involves engaging in a package of activities, each having its own specific utility. All activities will have a direct utility but some will also yield an indirect utility or will have a negative utility in the sense that they involve the consumption of market goods. Where activities have a money cost it would be possible to develop a concept of gross and net utility measurements. Gross utility would be the amount of satisfaction yielded by the activity itself, while net utility would make allowance for the forgone utility that could have been obtained from using the money cost to buy market goods purchasing some alternative form of satisfaction. A millionaire, who has no effective money budget constraint, and who is considering spending a fortnight's holiday in Acapulco, need only be concerned with the utility that he expects to receive from the package of activities involved in the holiday. If that utility seems likely to be greater than the benefit he will receive from any alternative use of the two weeks, then he will choose to take the holiday. Anyone whose unearned income is insufficient to pay for any possible combination of market goods that might be consumed must make the same comparison but must also carry out more complicated calculations involving, for example, the utility that could be obtained from using the money cost of the holiday to buy new furniture for his home. Whenever time is spent on one activity rather than another there is an opportunity cost representing the alternative uses to which the time could be allocated. But when the decision maker has a fixed and limited money income then this is an additional opportunity cost for all activities that require an input of market goods.

5. UNDESIRED ACTIVITIES

So far in the discussion it has been assumed that all activities yield positive utility. But are there any circumstances in which activities might be said to produce negative utility or disutility? There are clearly some ways of spending time that people may wish they could avoid. We may not enjoy cleaning blocked drains, visiting the dentist or sitting examinations. But if an activity is freely chosen can it be said to produce disutility? The distinction between direct and indirect utility is useful in examining this issue. Cleaning a drain may be a very unpleasant task and the activity may well be regarded as yielding negative utility or as being a disutility. But the total utility produced when allowance is made for the indirect benefits of having non-smelling unblocked drains may be positive. It is, perhaps, not very obvious when the direct utility provided by an activity is very low or is negative. The fact that we would regard a reduction in the time that must be allocated to a particular activity as a benefit does not necessarily mean that the direct utility yielded by that activity is negative. The benefit may arise from being able to transfer time from a less attractive to a preferred activity when both activities produce positive direct utility. Thus we may prefer spending ten minutes listening to the radio at home rather than sitting in a train, so that we would welcome a reduction in train journey times. But we may obtain some pleasure from travelling by train and even if its marginal utility falls rapidly with the length of the journey it may remain positive. Direct utility might be said to be negative when a consumer would, if it were possible, choose to have the time period allocated to an activity annihilated. In some cases this choice is available through the use of anaesthetics that cause total insensibility. A person may choose to be made unconscious rather than experience the activity of having a tooth removed. The state of doing 'absolutely nothing', which has been used by Evans (1972) in discussing the money valuation of time savings, is clearly different from unconsciousness. In a dreamless sleep or state of anaesthesia, it can be said that the individual is not experiencing any activity, and that, in one sense, the time period has been abolished. Doing 'absolutely nothing' when we are conscious could be extremely boring and might be regarded as yielding disutility.

The concept of direct and indirect utility helps us to give an economic explanation of why people undertake activities that they dislike. The total combined utility will normally be positive because the gains in indirect utility outweigh the losses in utility obtained from the activity itself. The unpleasantness of visiting the dentist is more than offset by the freedom from toothache that is expected to be the result of the session in the dentist's chair. A consumer allocating lumps of time will decide that the total utility resulting from spending thirty minutes with the dentist will be greater than (or equal to) the utility that he could obtain from any alternative use of the thirty-minute time period. This argument leads us to the consideration of whether the total utility resulting from undertaking an activity can ever be negative. It is not difficult to construct theoretical situations in which the total of direct and indirect utility received by a consumer (whether from a specific activity or from a composite package of activities) would be negative. This could be the case even if the consumer chose the disutility-producing activity. There is an important difference between consuming time and consuming commodities. If the consumption of a commodity would yield a disutility then we will choose not to consume it. It is difficult to imagine a situation in which a consumer would use some of his stock of money to buy a commodity that he expects will yield disutility. There is no compulsion to spend money. But time must be spent and it is quite possible to envisage circumstances in which it must be used on an activity that would yield a net disutility.

Two simple theoretical situations may be used to illustrate this point. Suppose that there are n activities available for a consumer (for simplicity it is assumed that there is no composite 'package' problem), that the utilities yielded are constant per unit of time, that these are represented by

$$U_1 + U_2 \ldots U_n$$

and that the activities are numbered in order of declining utility so that

$$U_1 > U_2 \ldots > U_n.$$

Now some of these possible activities might yield disutility and it is assumed that this applies to the fifth and all subsequent activities so that

$$U_5 < 0.$$

If the consumer was free to allocate all the available time Y to activities 1–4 then he would of course be able to avoid the negative utility of activities 5–n. But suppose that activities 1–4 all had money prices $p_1 \ldots p_4$ per unit of time allocated while activities 5–n were free and that the consumer's money budget B was exhausted by the allocation of time (represented by $t_1 \ldots t_n$) so that

$$t_1 p_1 + t_2 p_2 = B.$$

If the total time budget that must be spent was Y and if

$$Y = t_1 + t_2 + t_3,$$

then it would be necessary to allocate t_3 minutes to the activity yielding the disutility U_5, the least objectionable of the activities with zero-price. In the real world these activities that do not produce any positive direct or indirect utility will be mainly those that involve little action and are considered to be boring. Unemployed or underemployed people and schoolchildren at the end of long holidays may find time 'hanging on their hands' and might wish that part of their daily ration of twenty-four hours of time could be removed. Prisoners who are forced to spend many hours in their cells in activities that they find boring are sometimes able to extend the periods during which they are asleep so that, in effect, part of the surplus of time is eliminated. For many people, boring activities yielding negative utility could be replaced by activities producing positive utility if the market goods input constraint was removed. Those who are unemployed for long periods and people in poor 'developing' countries may be in this position. The situation when life appears to offer only negative utility is discussed further in chapter 3.

6. WORK ACTIVITY

For the final discussion of this chapter the problem of paid-work activity must be taken into consideration. The analysis so far has been simplified by assuming that all consumers enjoyed only unearned income (or income that was obtained independently of any work effort). The two basic situations have been examined where unearned income is sufficient to pay for any required input of market activities and the much more common state of affairs where the scarcity of money income means that some preferred activities are not available or can only be enjoyed for limited time periods. As soon as allowance is made for the possibility of undertaking paid work the position becomes much more complicated because time can be turned into money income, which can be used for the purchase of the market good inputs that are required for some preferred activities.

There is a very considerable body of economic literature dealing with the determination of wages and with the relationship between wages and hours worked or the supply of labour (e.g. Hicks, 1963; Gilbert and Pfouts, 1958). The main issues have been set out in a number of standard books on microeconomic theory (e.g. Henderson and Quandt, 1980; Laidler, 1974; Layard and Walters, 1978) and no attempt is made to work over the ground again here. It is possible to explain the effect of changes in wages on the supply of labour without developing a theory of the use of time. Much of the debate has dealt with the relative strength of the income and substitution effects of a rise in real hourly wages. Empirical evidence suggests that in Western countries the income effect has been stronger than the substitution effect for adult males in the last 100 years and rising real wages have been associated with falling average weekly hours worked. For women, however, rising wages may have increased the supply of labour though not necessarily the hours worked per woman, as women have been persuaded to substitute paid work for housework.

The formal analysis of the wage rate and supply of labour relationship is customarily based on the apparent assumption that work is undertaken entirely in order to earn wages and yields no utility or disutility in itself. As Layard and Walters have remarked, 'the theory . . . seems to imply that people have no feelings whatever about work as such' (1978, p. 308). But paid work is an activity in which time is used and may yield utility quite apart from that which is represented by the money payments received. The idea that wages must be paid in order to compensate people for surrendering leisure time represents a considerable oversimplification. There are several factors that may motivate people to undertake paid work apart from the basic need to 'earn a living'. The work itself may be enjoyable and some identical activity might be undertaken even if it were unpaid (although the receipt of wages may persuade people to spend longer at this activity than they would do otherwise). Fishing, gardening, wood or metal working and other craft work and the provision of professional services are all examples of paid work that may be enjoyable for its own sake. Work provides the greatest opportunity to exercise power and to have some control over the lives of others available to most people and there are many managers in industry, commerce and government who would be extremely distressed and consider themselves to have suffered a large loss in utility if they were compelled to retire early from their work, even if their full wage payments were continued indefinitely. Probably much more common is the situation in which the actual work activity yields little direct utility but where the fellowship with other workers is highly valued.

The utility provided by paid-work activity is not simply a psychological phenomenon; it may also have significance for economic analysis. There may be no easily discernible relationship between the utility provided by work activity and the level of earnings in different occupations because often factors such as training requirements determine the supply of workers and because the value of the marginal product is not related to work utility. But this does not mean that the pleasantness or unpleasantness of a job has no influence on wage rates. The effect of tax changes or wage increases on the work effort purchased by managers and entrepreneurs may be considerably reduced if work activity is regarded as an end in itself that provides utility. The long-term decline in hours worked by adult male workers has been partly explained by the suggestion that the real costs of the market goods inputs for leisure activities have fallen. Another partial explanation would be provided if it was shown that the utility of work for typical workers has been falling at a time when real wages have been rising. Surplus earnings, above those required for the 'necessities' of life, could be used to buy market goods inputs that would make leisure activities more attractive when the utility received from work activity was falling. This would help to explain the greater force of the income effect compared with the substitution effect when real wages increase for some workers. The fall in work utility would be most likely to occur where skilled craft work was replaced by repetitive relatively unskilled assembly work, and where the growth in the size of industrial organisations made the workplace less attractive. The special position of the 'harried leisure class' is considered in chapter 6.

In their analysis of the relationship between wages and the supply of labour for work, Layard and Walters extend their model to take some account of the theory of time allocation. In order to reach the highest attainable levels of utility, consumers must maximise

$$u = u(v, T, H)$$

where y is money income, T is leisure time and H is hours worked. The equilibrium conditions, where w represents the wage rate, include

$$w = \frac{u_T}{u_y} - \frac{u_H}{u_y},$$

which tells us that wages must compensate workers for the marginal utility of leisure time surrendered, minus any positive utility gained from work. As has already been argued in this chapter, it is possible to envisage circumstances in which the utility received per unit of working time could be higher than that received from any alternative leisure use of the same time period. Layard and Walters also introduce the concept of activities into their analysis. If there are two leisure activities, Z_1 and Z_2, then the full price of each of these activities includes both the money cost of required market inputs (represented by $p_1 A_1$ for activity Z_1) and the wages forgone by devoting time to leisure activities rather than to work (wt_1 where w is the wage rate and t_1 is the time allocated to activity Z_1). Expressed with the budget constraint of full income that would be obtained from working twenty-four hours a day plus unearned income (y^0) on the right-hand side, Layard and Walters' equation for the two-activity case becomes

$$(p_1 A_1 + wt_1)\, Z_1 + (p_2 A_2 + wt_2)\, Z_2 = 24w + y^0.$$

It is customary for economists to turn time into money, as in this model, and for many purposes this may be the most useful approach. However, there is no reason why the reverse procedure should not be followed and money income expressed in terms of the time required for it to be earned. The concept of the 'hours of work' required to purchase specific goods is already used in making international comparisons of living standards. Suppose that a consumer engages in only three activities (or groups of activities) A_1, A_2 and A_3, and that A_1 represents basic living requirements (eating, sleeping, housework), whereas A_2 is a recreational leisure activity and A_3 is the activity of paid work. Activities A_1 and A_2 have fixed money input requirements (for each decision period) of p_1 and p_2, while activity A_3 produces a constant wage rate of w pence per minute. Suppose that in an original equilibrium position m_1 minutes are devoted to activity A_1, m_2 minutes to A_2, and that the decision period, or total time budget available, is Y. Then

$$m_1 A_1 + \frac{P_1}{w} A_3 + m_2 A_2 + \frac{P_2}{w} A_3 + x A_3 = Y.$$

The surplus time at the paid-work activity above that necessary to pay for the inputs required for the chosen activities A_1 and A_2 is represented by x. Our assumption that only three activities are chosen, and that the time spent at activities A_1 and A_2 is already determined, implies that any surplus time must be used for paid work. Arranged according to activities, the equation becomes

$$m_1 A_1 + m_2 A_2 + \left(\frac{P_1 + P_2}{w} + x \right) A_3 = Y.$$

This implies that when choosing whether to allocate time to an activity that requires a market goods input a consumer must consider both the utility he expects the activity will yield and the utility that will be provided by the extra increment of paid work he must undertake. The situation is not very different from that already discussed in which secondary activities such as travel must be undertaken in order to enjoy a chosen activity. The need to earn money to pay for the market inputs, which is imposed on all those who do not possess sufficient unearned incomes for this purpose, serves to make the package of activities, between which effective choice is possible, a little more complex.

Neither the time-allocation model developed here nor the more traditional model in which time is changed into potential money earnings appears at first sight to be very realistic psychologically. People do not regularly calculate how much extra work they will need to do in order to be able to visit the theatre, nor are they likely to cost a game of tennis in terms of the earnings that are forgone. Money has sometimes been described as acting as a veil that hides or obscures economic realities. Money can be saved, borrowed or obtained as unearned income so that people may make decisions as though they had to face two independent budget constraints, those of time and money. But in so far as consumers are free to vary the length of time that they spend on paid work then they may have to make a choice between longer periods of leisure activity requiring little or no market input and shorter periods of an activity needing more costly inputs plus an extra length of time undertaking paid work. The choice between two different packages of activities, one of which includes some paid working time, is most apparent when consumers choose to work overtime or take on an extra job in order to be able to enjoy some high-cost activity such as taking an expensive holiday or making pleasure trips in a new car.

In our simple time-allocation model no allowance has been made for the existence of any activity that would not require a specific market input (such as going for a walk), so that the introduction of a new activity with a higher money price would mean reducing the time spent on some existing activity that also had a money price. Suppose that activity A_2 in our model was fishing and that the consumer decided to take up golf instead and that golf demanded a higher-priced market good input. (The assumption that the cost of the input is fixed in relation to the decision period or time budget, and does not vary with the number of minutes allocated to the activity per decision period, is retained.) If the new activity of golf is represented by A_4, while the utility obtained from a package of activities is U, then this change would imply that

$$U\left(m_4 A_4 + \frac{P_4}{w} A_3\right) > U\left(m_2 A_2 + \frac{P_2}{w} A_3\right).$$

Since golf has been assumed to be more expensive than fishing, it follows that $p_4/w > p_2/w$ (so long as wage rates remain constant). If it is assumed that the surplus work time xA_3 cannot be reduced (this point is discussed below), then the golfing 'package' could contain a longer period of paid-work activity than the fishing package. If the marginal utility of time spent fishing was greater than that of paid work then, for a consumer choosing the fishing package, it must be the case that the utility gain from substituting a shorter period of golf for a longer period of fishing is greater than the utility loss resulting from transferring some time from fishing to paid work.

The 'surplus' working time or balancing item xA_3 would, of course, generate income of xw. This could be regarded as providing savings and there might be a minimum savings requirement S in which case there would be an extra constraint

$$x \geqslant \frac{S}{w}.$$

On the other hand, when a consumer has unearned income or is prepared to borrow money, x could be negative. The hours worked could in these circumstances produce less money income than that needed to buy the required input of market goods for the chosen activities.

Established theory has shown that the effect of a wage rate increase on hours worked is uncertain, since when income is traded against leisure (and if leisure is a normal good) the income and substitution effects work in opposite directions. In Figures 2.1 and 2.2 indifference curve analysis is used to illustrate situations in which

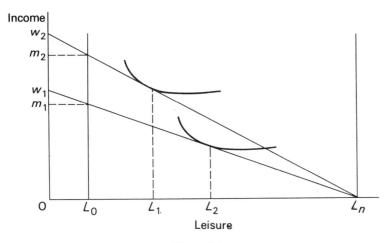

Figure 2.1

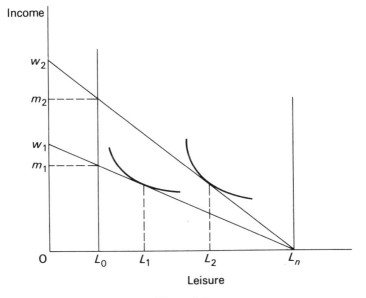

Figure 2.2

wage rate increases could lead to an increase or a decrease in the hours worked. It is assumed, for simplicity, that the individual consumers whose preferences are mapped have no unearned income. L_n represents the maximum amount of leisure available if no paid work was undertaken. This would be 24 hours or 1440 minutes in a one-day decision period. $L_n w_1$ represents the original wage rate (or rate of exchange possible between income and leisure) and $L_n w_2$ represents the possibilities with a higher wage rate. It is assumed that a minimum amount of leisure time L_0 must be reserved for eating, sleeping and other unpaid activities, so that the effective maximum money incomes available are Om_1 and Om_2. In Figure 2.1 the rise in wages causes work to be substituted for leisure, leisure time falling from OL_2 to OL_1 and work time increasing from $L_n L_2$ to $L_n L_1$. In Figure 2.2, the nature of the consumer's preferences means that when wages increase from $L_n w_1$ to $L_n w_2$ leisure time increases from OL_1 to OL_2 and work time falls from $L_n L_1$ to $L_n L_2$. A supply curve relating hours worked to wage rate for the consumer of Figure 2.2 would be backward bending.

As Laidler has argued (1974, pp. 57 et seq.), if income and leisure are regarded as substitutes, then a rise in wage rates will increase the demand for income and hours worked will rise. But if income and leisure are complements then an increase in the wage rates will lead to a fall in the number of hours worked. When analysed from the point of view of the allocation of time between different activities, income is seen primarily as a complement to leisure activities, making it possible to purchase the required market goods inputs.

Given the simple basic situation shown in our model

$$m_1 A_1 + m_2 A_2 + \frac{p_1 + p_2 + S}{w} A_3 = Y,$$

a rise in wage rates could have a number of different consequences. These could include (i) increasing the savings above the minimum S, with the length of the working day remaining constant; (ii) reducing the length of the working day and allocating the spare time to activity A_2 while keeping S constant; (iii) introducing a new activity that would use up extra earnings and some spare time, which could be obtained by shortening the working day, but by a lesser amount than in the second option; and (iv) introducing a high-cost activity that would wholly or partly replace A_2 and might conceivably involve working longer hours. If the second option was chosen and the working day was reduced by the maximum amount possible, subject to the constraints that savings must not be reduced and that the other activities must continue, and if all the surplus time was allocated to activity A_2, then the new equilibrium position would be

$$m_1 A_1 + m_2 A_2 + \frac{w^1 - w}{w^1 w}(p_1 + p_2 + S) A_2 + \frac{p_1 + p_2 + S}{w^1} A_3 = Y$$

where the increased wage rate is w^1.

Suppose that the following data applied to the model:

Time budget (Y) = 1440 minutes
Time originally allocated to A_1 (m_1) = 10 hours (600 mins)
Time originally allocated to A_2 (m_2) = 6 hours (360 mins)
Fixed price of market goods inputs –

$$A_1 \ (p_1) = 360p$$
$$A_2 \ (p_2) = 720p$$

Savings requirements (S) = 840p
Original wage rate (w) =   4p per minute
New wage rate (w^1) =   6p per minute

Then the new equilibrium allocation if the second option was chosen would involve reducing the time at work from 480 to 320 minutes and increasing the time devoted to activity A_2 from 360 to 520 minutes. If the consumer chose the third option and decided to use his pay increase to give him some extra time for a new activity, but also had to pay the market good input price, p_4, for this activity, then, if all other factors were to remain constant, the new equilibrium position would be

$$m_1 A_1 + m_2 A_2 + \left(\frac{p_1 + p_2 + p_4 + S}{w^1}\right) A_3$$
$$+ \left(\frac{p_1 + p_2 + S}{w} - \frac{p_1 + p_2 + p_4 + S}{w^1}\right) A_4 = Y.$$

If the figures used for the previous options applied and if the market input price of activity A_4 was 240p, then the hours worked would fall to 360 minutes and the spare 120 minutes would be used for the new activity, A_4.

There are a number of alternative 'scenarios' that could be produced by considering the effect of an increased work rate on the variables in the time-allocation model, and the situation becomes more complicated as some of the simplifications of the model (such as a fixed cost for market goods inputs to activities and a constant wage rate) are removed. Theory by itself is not very helpful in showing which of a number of possible outcomes is most likely to occur, but it is possible to make some intelligent guesses based on different assumptions about a consumer's motivation. There are some situations in which consumers might be expected to react to a wage rate rise by working longer hours. A man who had a strong desire to maximise his earnings, but for whom the marginal utility of paid work was very low or negative, might be persuaded to surrender a little more leisure if his wage rate was increased. This effect would, of course, be much stronger in all cases if it was the wage rate for extra work that was increased and if basic wages remained unchanged. People who give a high priority to increasing their savings are likely to be more ready to work longer hours than those who want to use earnings for immediate activities. Building up savings could be described as an activity that demands a money input but requires only a very small or negligible time input. Unless the saver is a miser the savings will presumably be required for some form of consumption and 'consumption' usually implies taking part in an activity that will consume both market goods and time. Individuals who give a high priority to saving will in any case be likely to be ready to work long hours, but may still be influenced by wage rates in making this choice between paid work and other activities. Savers who only require to save a fixed amount, as was assumed to be the case in the time-allocation model, would, on the other hand, be influenced by the income effect when average wage rates were increased, and might well reduce the length of their working day if they found that they could do this and still save the necessary sum and continue to meet their other financial needs.

In the example given above, introducing a new activity that required a market goods input when wage rates were raised still resulted in shorter hours being worked. But if the new activity was very costly a consumer might conceivably work longer in order to pay for it and might sacrifice some previous activity in order to be able to spend time in the new occupation. As has already been suggested, however, in developed countries the most important situation in which an increase in wages may lead to an increase in the hours of paid work is with housewives. A housewife who does no paid work herself is, in some respects, in a similar position to a person living on a limited unearned income. She will have a money budget provided by her husband and must adapt her activities according to the limitations of this budget, but she cannot herself turn time into money income. Her initial time allocation position might be represented by the equation:

$$m_1 A_1 + m_2 A_2 + m_4 A_4 = Y$$

where A_1 is 'basic' living time (eating, sleeping, personal hygiene), A_2 is houswork plus care of children, A_4 is social or pleasure activity and Y, as before, is the time budget. The money costs of the three activities (p_1, p_2 and p_4) do not have any time implications since the income is obtained from paid work carried out by her husband. The housewife will have a separate money budget constraint

$$p_1 + p_2 + p_4 \leqslant B$$

where B is the income provided by the family's wage earner. Now the direct utility of housework, at any rate at the margin, might well be lower than that of paid work so that (if u is the direct utility obtained from carrying out an activity)

$$\frac{\partial u}{\partial m_2} < \frac{\partial u}{\partial m_3}$$

where, as before, m_3 is the time allocated to paid work (activity A_3). But if total utility was measured the inequality might be reversed. The housewife might enjoy some forms of paid work more than housework, but this enjoyment plus the benefits received from a low wage could be more than offset by the disadvantages of having a dirty home and neglected children. But where wage rates rise two factors might persuade the housewife to undertake some paid work. The money income received from paid work might enable her to buy labour-saving household equipment that would enable her to reduce the time, m_2, allocated to housework without any corresponding reduction in the quality of service provided. This possibility is discussed more fully in chapter 4. Secondly, and more obviously, the utility yielded by paid work itself, plus that provided by a higher wage rate, might offset some drop in the quality of household services and child care.

For paid workers of either sex who are already working for a 'full' day (i.e. the average hours for full-time workers) it is easier to envisage circumstances in which a wage rate rise will lead to a fall in hours worked than it is to construct a situation in which the working day will be lengthened. People who 'live for their jobs' and obtain a very high utility from paid work will already work long hours if they have the opportunity and are unlikely to extend these because wage rates are increased. Many people in this category will in any case be paid an annual salary so that daily hours worked would not affect earnings and the only way in which more time allocated to paid work would increase earnings would be by postponing retirement.

For the worker paid on an hourly rate for whom the marginal utility of paid work time was declining, an increase in wage rates would give him a larger hourly income so that, as has been shown, the paid-work time necessary to buy the market goods inputs for 'basic living' and for recreational activities, and to maintain a required level of savings would fall. If any reduction in working hours was smaller, proportionately, than the rise in wage rates, the total income would rise and time would be likely to cause an increase in the utility obtained from leisure activity. It would become possible to substitute superior market input goods for use in existing activities or to follow new, preferred activities requiring more expensive inputs. Thus a consumer enjoying a wage rate increase might be able to watch his local football club from covered seats instead of open ones or he might find that he and his wife could now afford to entertain friends regularly instead of watching television. This use of more expensive market good inputs would be likely to increase the utility of leisure time. The direct utility of extra paid-work time would remain the same while the marginal utility of extra income would be likely to fall as total income would have been increased. In order to persuade a worker to work longer hours, the gain from earning $w + \Delta w \ (= w^1)$ instead of w for each extra minute worked would have to be great enough to offset the increased marginal utility of leisure and the reduced marginal utility of money. The pre wage-rise equilibrium position may be represented by

$$\frac{\partial u}{\partial m_2} = \frac{\partial u}{\partial m_3}$$

where the marginal utility of an increment of time spent on activity A_2 was equal to the marginal utility of an increment allocated to paid work (A_3). If the extra income from the higher wage rate was used to buy superior inputs and caused the marginal utility of time spent on A_2 to rise, then it would be the case that

$$\frac{\partial u}{\partial m_2} < \frac{\partial u}{\partial m_2^1}$$

where m_2^1 is time spent on A_2 with the superior market good input. The utility obtained from work is made up of the direct utility of work activity itself, $u(A_3)$, and of the indirect utility from the wage earned $u(w)$.

The analysis of the effect of a wage rate increase on hours worked made on the basis of the time-allocation model comes to essentially the same conclusion as conventional analysis, which is that the results are uncertain. The relative strengths of the income and substitution effects will depend on individual preferences. But the time-allocation analysis does suggest that the circumstances in which full-time workers would choose to work longer hours may be relatively unusual. (In a detailed study of the relationship between wages and the hours of work, Gilbert and Pfouts (1958) concluded that although Robbins (1930) was logically correct in arguing that the direction of the response of hours of work to wage rate changes was indeterminate, in practice hours were likely to fall following a wage rate increase.) If money income is considered to produce utility only when used in some time-consuming activity, and is not regarded as a good in itself, then it clearly becomes unlikely that a change that increases income will lead to the use of more time to produce even more income. The time-allocation approach also has the advantage of removing an over-rigid separation between paid work and other activities and makes full allowance for the utility that can be obtained from the paid-work activity itself. The analysis assumes the existence of a 'Western' standard of living in which recreational or pleasure activities play an important part in the typical individual's time budget. The situation in an economy moving from a subsistence farming to a wage-earning basis might be similar to the housewives' case. Rising wage rates might lead to a rapid increase in paid work as subsistence farming was wholly or partly abandoned. Empirical evidence on wage rates and hours worked is considered in chapter 6. In cases where hours worked have increased with rising wage rates it may not always be easy to distinguish between the effects of wage rates on people's willingness to undertake paid work and the possibility that opportunities for undertaking paid work have been increasing.

The time-allocation model could be used to support the fairly obvious conclusion that high overtime rates paid for extensions of the working day are much more likely to increase the supply of paid-work labour than are general wage rate increases. As people who do not work overtime will not have enjoyed any increase of income, the utility of their recreational activities will not have been increased nor will the marginal utility of income have been reduced. Changes in tax rates that increase average hourly income will have the same effect on hours worked as would a wage rate increase, while changes that only increased marginal overtime earnings would have the same effect as overtime rate increases. The discussion does not, of course, tell us anything about the effect of wage rates, overtime, or income tax changes on the intensity of effort of workers during the time that they are engaged in paid-work activity. The analysis has dealt only with wage rate increases. In theory, moving along a backward bending supply curve to lower wage levels would lead to an increased supply of labour, but in practice cuts in money wage rates are so unlikely that there would be little point in analysing this situation. A long-term fall in real money earnings is, of course, a possibility that some of the more gloomy economic forecasts envisage. This could lead to a willingness to work longer hours, but it is obviously doubtful whether a depressed economy would generate any demand for people to allocate more of their time to paid-work activities.

CHAPTER 3

The Supply of Time

Seventy years is the span of our life,
Eighty if our strength holds.
[Psalms 90 v. 10]

One crowded hour of glorious life
Is worth an age without a name.
[Thomas Mordaunt]

1. THE LENGTH OF HUMAN LIFE

In this short chapter all that can be attempted is to put forward a few untested ideas in an area that is largely unexplored by economists. While the rest of the study deals with the problems involved in making the best use of a given 'stock' of time, some consideration needs to be given to possible means of varying the amount of time that each individual is able to enjoy. In one sense the supply of time is not under human control. Time happens and its flow cannot be increased or reduced. But human experience of time on this earth can be varied. The average length of life of human beings can be extended, within limits, by the provision of adequate food supplies, by medical care and by the avoidance of activities that increase the risk of an early death. There are, at present, very considerable differences between the life expectancies, or average amounts of time available, of people in different parts of the world (see Table 3.1).

These large differences in life expectancy are influenced by even larger variations in infant mortality rates (death within the first year of life), which range from less than 20 per 1000 live births in developed countries to from 100 to over 200 per 1000 births in developing countries. Life expectancy is closely associated with

49

The Supply of Time

TABLE 3.1
*Average life expectancy in different parts
of the world*

Country or area	Life expectancy at birth (years)
All developed countries	72
All underdeveloped countries	57
Africa	49
Asia	51
Angola	Less than 45
Afghanistan	Less than 45
Somalia	Less than 45
Mali	Less than 45
Niger	Less than 45

Source: Mahler (1980).

living standards as measured by gross domestic product per head. The poorer countries suffer from a double disadvantage: low income levels may lead to many people having such a poor diet that their health deteriorates; and medical services are very inadequate. Developing countries not only have less income to spend but also spend a lower proportion of that income on medical services. Typical spending levels on health services in developing countries range from under 1 per cent to 2 per cent of GDP, while the equivalent figures in developed countries are in the range 6–12 per cent.

If there was an agreed world plan to seek to maximise the average length of life of all mankind, this would clearly involve a transfer of resources from rich to poor countries. The transferred resources would be spent on food and on the provision of the kind of medical services that would do most to prolong life. In theory, in an unselfish world, resources would be transferred until the marginal increase in life expectancy resulting from an increase in expenditure on food and all forms of health service and education was the same in all countries. However, even in a world that was much richer in loving-kindness than the one in which we live, a policy aimed at maximising life expectancy would still produce problems. In particular, an outstanding difficulty, which underlies most of the rest of the discussion in this chapter, is that it may be necessary to choose between length of life and quality of life.

The ultimate purpose of a world government would be to maximise the welfare of all people. In these circumstances it might be argued that the happiness of those transferring their wealth would fall, even if their life expectancy remained constant, and that this fall in welfare could be greater than the rise in happiness resulting from the increased life expectancy in poorer countries. If it is believed that obtaining happiness (or that part of happiness with which economists are concerned) from the use of time depends upon the possession of market goods, then extending the life of those who lack these goods at the expense of reducing the supply of goods available to people in developed countries would not necessarily increase the sum of happiness. This is an unconvincing argument in our real world, however, where rich countries spend significant proportions of their income on weapons of destruction and on very non-essential goods and where there may be no clear relationship between the supply of market goods and the happiness obtained from time. But it does focus attention on the importance of the quality of life. One of the main advantages of improved medical services and food supplies in poor countries would be not just to extend life but to free those who are alive from the burden of ill-health. Another important aspect of this problem relates to the optimum population size for a country or for the world.

If maximising the amount of time available for individuals (which can be called 'human time') is an acceptable objective, then it might follow that the more people there are around, the greater will be the sum of welfare. If each lifetime of seventy years is a source of potential happiness, then more lives will mean more happiness. Time only exists for men who exist: 200 million people will have twice as much time, and therefore twice as much welfare, as 100 million people. The flaw in these arguments is, of course, apparent. Too large a population may use up so many resources that life expectancy is reduced. But before this point is reached the quality of life may be reduced so that a smaller population could generate more welfare than a larger one and it is clear that the relationship between population size and happiness is not linear.

The idea of an optimum population leads to almost insoluble problems. These can be illustrated briefly by means of an analogy with the theory of road congestion. Beyond a certain traffic flow, roads become congested so that every additional car will slow down all other road users. If all road users were made to pay the marginal cost of road use (including the time costs of delays caused by congestion), then road use would be optimal because anyone who valued his use of the road below the marginal cost would not travel. (Even in the road case there are welfare problems when income is not distributed optimally.) But it is not possible to know how much people would pay in order to be born into a congested world. The value of life to someone who does not exist cannot be estimated by even the most powerful tools of economic analysis. In the road case it is assumed that a tax is imposed by an outside body that raises average cost to the level of marginal cost. But if the road was controlled by a body of regular users then this optimum position would probably occur at the point when congestion began. If 5000 existing users controlled a road that was uncongested and if one more car would cause congestion, then the current users would gain by excluding the additional car unless its driver was able to arrange to pay compensation to all those using the road in its uncongested state. Similarly a potentially congested world, or country, would gain from holding the population at the point where congestion, which would make all living people worse off, began.

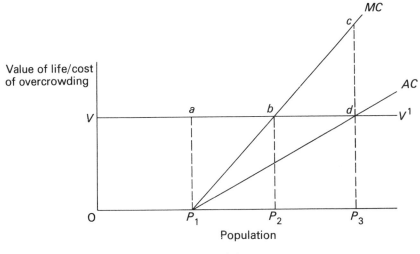

Figure 3.1

In Figure 3.1 the vertical axis measures the money value of being alive and the cost of overcrowding. The line VV^1 represents the value of life and can be regarded as the 'demand curve' for life where everyone puts the same value on being alive. OP_1MC and OP_1AC are the marginal and average costs of overcrowding. Below the population level OP_1 the costs of overcrowding are zero. A selfish world that could control population would maintain the level at this point, although the theoretical optimum would be OP_2. Moving from OP_1 to OP_2 would increase welfare by P_1abP_2 but the costs would only be P_1bP_2. As these costs would fall partly upon the existing population, OP_1, they would be worse off. (This argument assumes that the benefit of life accrues only to the individual who is alive.) Moving from OP_2 to OP_3 would reduce welfare since benefits would only increase by P_2bdP_3 while costs would rise by P_2bcP_3. The value of life to the extra population would be less than the reduction in the quality and possibly in the length of life caused by overcrowding.

In the real world, population levels are likely to rise beyond OP_2 and could even move above OP_3. Population cannot easily be controlled by governments but its level depends mainly on innumerable individual decisions. The selfish level OP_1 could not be maintained by any acceptable policies. In the road congestion example, car drivers make the decision about the use of a road and if the average cost that they would have to pay was higher than the benefits that they would obtain from using the road then they would not use it. Congestion would thus not increase beyond the position that is equivalent to OP_3. But people do not choose to be born themselves and do not know that they may be entering a world where the costs of living could exceed the benefits and life be literally 'not worth living'. How far prospective parents can be said to perceive the 'average cost of life', which must be interpreted as the unpleasantness of living in an overcrowded, disease-ridden and hungry world, is not clear. When life is generally unpleasant people may seek the pleasures of sex regardless of the consequences. It is a well-known phenomenon that birth rates have for many years been higher in poorer than in richer countries. At present, the average natural rate of increase for all developed countries is 0.6 per cent while that for developing countries is 2 per cent. The fertility rate, or births per woman, is 2.0 in developed countries and 4.4 in developing countries. But governments in many poor or semi-poor countries are attempting to reduce population growth. China (which contains about one-fifth of the population of the world) has succeeded in reducing its birth rate in the last ten years as a result of an intensive government campaign. According to the Director General of the World Health Organisation, 'in response to the very real negative impact of excessive fertility on individuals and individual countries . . . efforts to spread the message of family planning through the developing countries have proliferated in the past 25 years' (Mahler, 1980, pp. 71–2).

Political restrictions on the movements of people mean that the single relationship between population and quality of life for the whole world represented crudely in Figure 3.1 does not exist. Different countries are at different positions. Some, like Australia, may not even have reached the position OP_1, where increases in population start to reduce the quality of life. Other countries are in various positions between OP_1 and OP_3, or even a little beyond OP_3. Richer countries, where the existence of more resources means that the point OP_1 would come at a higher population density than in poorly endowed countries, tend to add to their advantage by restricting population growth more successfully. This restriction comes from individual choice rather than government action. The extent to which countries fail to develop their resources adequately because they are overpopulated is a complicating factor that cannot be explored here.

Local population optima may be applied to towns as well as to countries. Urban economists and geographers have argued that there may be a different optimum city size according to different criteria (e.g. Button, 1976; Richardson, 1973). The optimum sizes for a city as an efficient administrative unit, as an area purchasing goods and services and as a pleasant place for its inhabitants may all differ. But since it is possible to have more smaller towns or fewer larger ones, the size of the optimum urban area need not influence the size of total population and the number of people who can be brought into the world to make use of time by living out their lives.

2. THE VALUE OF PREVENTING ACCIDENTS

Before discussing the 'value of life' issues, the construction of a very simple model may help in working out the choices that are open to society. The total 'stock' of time available in a country (T) may be thought of as a function of the average length of life (L) and the average population (P) so that

$$T = fP, L.$$

Average length of life might depend on the amount of resources devoted to medical services (X) and to accident prevention (A) and, it is assumed, will decrease with population growth. (This would not, of course, apply in some countries, and in most others the coefficient for the effect of population growth would be very small.) These assumptions give

$$L = aX - bP + cA$$

and

$$T = P(aX - bP + cA).$$

But governments are concerned not only with the total stock of human time, or hours of life, but also with its quality. Their objective might therefore be defined as the maximising of T_q — the product of the stock of time and quality per unit. The quality of life, it is assumed, depends positively upon the expenditure on goods and services (G) and is negatively associated with population so that

$$q = jG - kP.$$

T_q is thus given by

$$T_q = (PaX - bP^2 + cAP)(jG - kP).$$

If B was the total amount of resources available, then the maximisation of T_q would be subject to the budget constraint

$$G + A + X = B.$$

This produces a number of different trade-offs between population size and the length and quality of life and in the allocation of resources between 'goods', accident prevention and medical services.

One area in which there has been some work carried out by economists is in investigations of the 'value of life' (e.g. Weisbrod, 1961; Schelling, 1968; Mishan, 1971). This discussion does not refer to the benefits of being, or not being, born, or to the value of an extra life, however, but to that of preventing the premature ending by accident of existing lives. This issue has aroused interest mainly because real world decisions must be made in which the value of saving a life is an important factor. About 20 per cent of the benefits from new road building in Britain come from accident prevention (not only fatal accidents in this case of course); the value of saving life is also important in such decisions as how much money to allocate to mountain rescue teams or coastguard services, the determination of speed limits and fixing of other safety regulations, and on the allocation of resources for the elimination of road accident black spots.

Some non-economists have objected to the process of giving a money value to human life, but there are many decisions made by society that imply that life does have a finite value. A study of the value of life by Jones-Lee (1976) contains a valuable summary of some of the attempts that have been made to value life or to consider how it ought to be valued. A basic issue is to decide whose judgement should be the basis of evaluation. The normal assumption of cost–benefit analysis is that individuals are the best judges of their own interests and it seems logical to suppose that the man whose life is threatened is the one who should judge its value. But there are difficulties with this approach in accident avoidance evaluation. If a man knew that he would be the victim of a fatal accident he would, if he was enjoying a reasonably happy life, value very highly an investment that would save his life. If he had to pay for the investment himself he might be prepared to raise money on future earnings, leaving himself only just enough income to keep alive. He would also appeal to his friends and his family for help, as people will do to find the money to pay for a life-saving operation or to meet a ransom demand. But a system that valued the life of a poor man at less than that of his rich neighbour might not be acceptable to society, and in public decisions about investment it may be the valuation of society that is relevant. The other difficulty is that in practice no one knows who will be killed in an accident. It may be possible to say that a given investment will save lives, but no one can know whose lives will be preserved. For this reason some economists have concentrated on attempting to evaluate changes in the risks of accidents (Needleman, 1975; Jones-Lee, 1976) rather than the direct value of a saved life.

One particularly important attempt to measure the value of accident reduction is the method developed by Reynolds (1956) and Dawson (1967, 1971), which has become the basis of the official values used in road investment appraisal. The basis of the method as developed by Dawson was to estimate the average discounted value of the lost output of people who are killed (or injured) in a road accident. In his first report (1967) Dawson deducted the estimated value of consumption, arriving at a net output figure. This had the unfortunate result that the average value of a female fatality (in 1965 prices) was −£1120. The low value placed on housework in Dawson's calculations meant that, on this narrow basis, society gained when a woman was killed in a road accident. But Dawson added a 'subjective' value for life, originally £5000, to allow for the possibility that the victim, and his friends and relatives, would suffer subjective loss if he was killed. In a later Transport and Road Research Laboratory Report (1971), Dawson revised his method by using a gross output measurement, without any deduction for goods and services that would be consumed by the potential accident victim if his life was spared. This technique, with updated figures, is still the basis of the valuations used in investment appraisal by the Departments of Transport and of the Environment. The average cost of a fatal road accident in 1976 prices was assumed to be £44,000. This average figure covered the total accident cost including injuries and damage to vehicles and, in a few cases, accidents involving more than one death.

The Reynolds–Dawson approach has the advantage of being based on costs that can be measured, but its philosophical foundation seems to be somewhat insecure. The discounted value of a man's earnings for the rest of his life is an approximation to the largest sum that he could raise to pay for the investment that would enable him to avoid a fatal accident, but if there is no allowance for the cost of his consumption then he would become dependent on state aid for the rest of his life if he actually had to pay for the investment himself. The addition in the official calculations of a subjective value of life to the gross product value seems to involve some double counting, since the gross product valuation already involves some contribution from society.

The choice for society, which is reflected in the model, is whether to make a potentially life-saving investment and lower the general quality of life by reducing the quantity of goods and services that are available or to maintain the quality of life but risk more fatal accidents. Apart from the road investment case it is probably true that it is the level of cost that determines whether an accident-reducing or life-saving investment will be made and there may be no very careful comparison with the value of benefits.

When someone is lost on a mountain or at sea the rescue forces do not normally stop their search as soon as a certain level of cost has been incurred, although the size of the rescue services available may imply some kind of decision about the value of life-saving. To some extent, the frequency of a particular kind of accident may determine the cost that will be incurred to prevent its occurrence. The government may be prepared to keep a fleet of helicopters available to rescue the relatively few people who are in danger climbing cliffs but it may not be prepared to spend the vast sums necessary to provide shelter for all those who would be at risk in a nuclear war. There is a psychological though not necessarily a rational economic difference between the rescue of a particular individual who is lost on a mountain and investment in a road improvement scheme that will save the life of an unknown person at some time in the future. It is not therefore surprising that, as some of the figures in Jones-Lee's survey show, the implied value of life saving varies considerably in different public decisions.

One interesting area, where there is a form of trade-off between the quantity and quality of time (or between T and q in the model), is in the fixing of safety regulations. These involve action by government to prevent people taking risks that they would otherwise choose to incur. Where the risks affect only the person undertaking the risky activity, this means that the assumption that people are the best judges of their own interests is discarded. This can sometimes be justified by assuming that individuals have insufficient knowledge to make a proper decision. The prohibition of bathing on dangerous beaches is an example. But there are cases where the state is in effect assuming that consumers are wrongly choosing activities that they believe will add to the quality of their lives but that will also reduce their stock of time by shortening their life expectation. Two examples are cigarette smoking and the choice of speeds by car drivers.

Governments, even if they are convinced that they know best, may find it difficult to overrule the wishes of large sections of the population. Smoking, which is an example of what Mishan (1971) has classified as a direct voluntary risk, is discouraged but not banned by most governments. If the tax on tobacco is high enough to cover all the social costs of smoking (such as the cost to the health and fire services and the unpleasantness caused to non-smokers) and if the 'government health warning' ensures that smokers are fully informed about the risks that they run, then the economist who adopts the 'consumer knows best' rule would argue that no further control of smoking is required. However, the assumption that consumers are the best judge of their own interests is itself a value judgement, so that the need to make a moral decision cannot be avoided by sheltering behind the protective fence of Paretian welfare economics. The arguments that apply to tobacco could also be applied to the use of harmful drugs, which are generally banned by society. The issue of how far people are allowed to shorten their own lives by taking actions that they believe will improve the quality of their living is a moral problem that will be decided by public opinion through the political process. Economists can try to measure the costs and benefits of alternative policies, but they cannot prescribe measures unless they are prepared to be involved in the messy business of making value judgements. Both economic analysis and common sense suggest that there may be some occasions when a shorter, 'high-quality' life will produce more happiness than a longer, low-quality period of existence.

Most governments have some form of speed limits on their roads though the West Germans still resist the imposition of compulsory limits on their motorways. Time is involved in both sides of the trade-off that is made when speed limits are fixed. Motorists wish to travel quickly mainly so that they can transfer the time saved to a preferred alternative use. But in so far as higher speeds involve more accidents, the total stock of time will be reduced. During the 'oil crisis' of 1973–74, Britain, the USA and many other countries reduced their speed limits in order to conserve fuel. In Britain, a speed limit of 50 mph was imposed on all roads not already subject to a lower limit from 8 December 1973 to 29 March 1974. There is clear statistical evidence that all the countries reducing their speed limits enjoyed a fall in accident rates. Compared with the previous year, reported accidents in Britain in the period November 1973 to October 1974 fell by 16 per cent on motorways, by 15 per cent on all-purpose roads with previous speed limits of 50–70 mph, but by only 6 per cent on all-purpose roads not affected by the new speed limits. In the USA fatal accidents fell by 27 per cent on controlled access roads on which the speed limit was reduced from 65 mph to 55 mph. The lives saved in the countries reducing speed limits were a kind of bonus resulting from actions intended only to save fuel. Speed limits have generally been put back to their former levels as supplies of fuel became more readily available. When the announcement that speed limits were to be raised to 70 mph on dual carriageways in the UK was made in 1977 it was welcomed by the Royal Automobile Club as a 'splendid Easter gift for motorists'. Some countries, like France and West Germany, have higher speed limits than Britain and also consistently higher accident rates.

These few facts about speed limits raise the issue of how accurately governments are able to express the wishes of their citizens in bringing about the right balance between 'quality' and 'quantity' of life. Do the current speed limits and accident rates (it is not, of course, suggested that accident rates are determined solely by speed limits) in Britain represent the true social choice of the population? It is possible that the machinery of government can react more readily to the need to conserve oil than it can to the problem of reducing accident rates. Similarly it seems uncertain whether different speed limits and road accident levels in different countries represent real differences in social choice or are the accidental product of the imperfect working of the machinery of government and the relative strength of conflicting 'pressure groups'.

3. PROBLEMS OF LOW-QUALITY TIME

A peculiarity of time, already noted at the beginning of this study, is that it must be used. While we are alive we are compelled to spend our store of hours. Other goods and services that may yield displeasure need not be acquired, or can be given away or remain unused. But time must be spent even if it produces boredom or unhappiness or pain. It is possible to use alcohol or drugs as a means of escape from reality, but these uses of time may bring more severe problems of their own. What policy can be adopted when time must be spent but its only possible use will bring unhappiness? The only alternative must be either to endure the unhappiness or to bring life to an end, to 'bear the whips and scorns of time' or 'end the heartache, and the thousand natural shocks That flesh is heir to . . . with a bare bodkin'.

The rights and wrongs of suicide and euthanasia are generally believed to be matters for the philosopher or the theologian rather than the economist. If a religious belief suggests a total and immutable ban on suicide, then for those who accept that teaching there is no more to be said. Those who are prepared to consider bringing their own lives to an end will, if they are the best judges of their own interests, be able to decide for themselves whether life continues to be worth living. No economist is equipped to make a balance between the expected pain and pleasure in another man's life. But despite these severe difficulties there is perhaps one slightly surprising conclusion that can be derived from economic reasoning. This is that if the case for suicide was to be decided on a utilitarian 'net balance of pain or pleasure' principle then usually the longer the potential suicide's expectation of life, the less likely it is that he would gain from ending it. Even if an immediate period of unhappiness is in prospect there must nearly always be uncertainty about a long time period, and in the more distant future time spent may yield a net surplus of pleasure. If a man has a painful, incurable and eventually fatal disease, then he knows that the rest of his life may produce little happiness. But a man who can expect to live for thirty or forty years, or even longer, cannot be certain that the rest of his time on earth will bring a net sum of unhappiness even if he knows that he has to live through one or two years of guaranteed misery. In the real world, of course, those who are likely to kill themselves are basically people who are unable to make a rational assessment of their future prospects, so that this estimation of probabilities may be irrelevant to individual decisions.

But the conclusion is not entirely without interest for decisions made by society.

The simple 'quality' or 'quantity' model in this chapter showed the state trading goods and services, which are intended to raise the quality of life, for expenditure on accident prevention or medical care and research that may prolong life. One issue that was ignored was the quality of the particular lives that might be saved. Since in accident prevention it is not known whose lives will be saved, it is obviously quite impossible to distinguish between happy and unhappy lives. (Dawson's first study did take account of the average age distribution, and thus also the average life expectancy, of people killed in road accidents.) But with medical care the situation is different. If resources are to be allocated between accident prevention, preventative medicine, medical research and the prolongation of the lives of those who are incurably and painfully ill, then account should be taken of the poor quality of life that the unlucky invalids must expect. It is not good economics, or sound common sense or even easily defensible morality to regard the extension of all human life as being of equal value to society or to the individual concerned. The use of the scarce resource of medical skill to keep alive those whose time has become a burden both to themselves and to their families and friends seems difficult to justify and the situation would not be very different even if the resources were in unlimited supply.

Another case where society has some kind of decision to make is that of long-term prisoners. Now that, in Britain, the state is no longer prepared to end a man's life because of a criminal offence, men may receive prison sentences of twenty or thirty years. People having to spend very long periods in prison are an exception to the previous argument that those with a long life expectancy cannot foretell whether their future lives will bring a net surplus of happiness or unhappiness. Long-term prisoners may know that most of the rest of their lives will be of very poor quality. A state policy for which a case could be argued would be to guard new long-term prisoners extremely carefully until they survived the first impact of prison life and then to allow those who so chose the means to end their lives.

4. THE 'FUTURE LIFE HYPOTHESIS'

A final area into which an examination of the size of the stock of time may lead is the *terra incognita* of life after death. If a man believes that he will continue to live outside time when his body dies, then it will affect the ways in which he uses his stock of time on earth. The 'future life hypothesis' is not entirely without relevance to the subject matter of economics, the allocation of resources. The argument that we do not know whether the hypothesis is true or false, and that it can therefore be ignored, is not tenable. Innumerable decisions must be made where there is great uncertainty. If a hypothesis that demands action is ignored, then this amounts to an assumption that it is untrue. A society in which the hypothesis was widely accepted might allocate resources to activities that were believed to be relevant to the anticipated future life, while a state in which it was rejected would plan for the concentration of resources or activities that yield benefits only in this world. The decline in the study of theology at universities in Britain and the greatly increased importance of such subjects as engineering presumably reflect changing attitudes towards the future life hypothesis. Some countries like West Germany and Sweden give state support to the churches (or to the main 'state' church), while in other countries like Britain and the USA this is denied. This probably reflects historical 'accidents' or different attitudes towards the role of the state in society rather than different assumptions about the relevance of religion to man's needs. But it is, of course, in private decision making that beliefs about the future life hypothesis are most relevant. Methods of attempting to maximise the happiness obtained from the seventy or eighty years of human life must be influenced by acceptance or rejection of the belief that life on earth is the prelude to another kind of existence.

CHAPTER 4

Time and Technology

Not in vain the distance beacons. Forward, forward
  let us range
Let the great world spin for ever down the ringing
grooves of change.   [A. Tennyson]

1. INTRODUCTION

It is not necessary to be an economist to realise that technological
changes may bring both gains and losses to society. While new
technological developments usually lead to an increase in the supply
of goods and services, they may produce unwanted side-effects in
the form of environmental pollution; bring economic or psychological losses to those who were involved with operating out-dated
technologies; provide problems for those workers who have to
learn the skills required by the new technology; and lead to a
possibly too-rapid depletion of stocks of irreplaceable raw materials.
An examination of technology in relation to time reveals problems
that are mostly already well known, but it may help to solve some
of these problems when they are approached by an unfamiliar route.
The main specific issues discussed in this chapter are those of technological unemployment; the nature of productivity with a reference
to the special problem of depletable resources; the problems associated with asking workers to undertake repetitive or unpleasant tasks;
the economic calculations that might be carried out when deciding
whether or not to buy labour-saving equipment for use in the home;
and the similar calculations that might be made when choosing
between do-it-yourself activities and professional services.

2. TIME AND PRODUCTION

It is very curious that, in the development of economic theory, the adoption of capital-intensive techniques has been considered as consuming more rather than less time in the production process. In his analysis of capital and interest (1959) Böhm-Bawerk put forward his well-known argument that the use of capital equipment means the adoption of a roundabout method of production. He argued that 'the disadvantage which attends the capitalist method of production consists in a sacrifice of time. Capitalist roundaboutness is productive but time consuming. It yields more or better consumption goods but not until a later time' (1959, p. 82). A labour-saving invention would result in the output of the same quantity of product for a smaller input of labour or a greater amount of the product from the same labour input.

The 'sacrifice of time' idea may help to explain the payment of interest but it is a somewhat artificial concept. Technological development can be said to save time, or allow time to be transferred to other uses, in the same way as it is supposed to 'save' labour or capital. One of Böhm-Bawerk's illustrations of roundabout, time-consuming production is that of a farmer drawing water from a well. Instead of making a daily journey to the well, he could adopt a 'roundabout' capitalist method of production by felling trees and making a wooden pipeline to bring the water to his house. It is true that the time spent making the pipeline could be used to produce more water immediately but whether or not there is a sacrifice of time in any other sense depends upon the time period over which production is measured. Suppose that the output of water was measured over a one-year period and that it took thirty minutes to fetch two gallons from the well before the pipeline was built. If the pipeline delivered one gallon per minute and took six weeks to construct, then the rate of delivery of water to the house would rise from 0.06 gallons per minute to 0.88 gallons per minute for the year during which it was constructed. On the other hand, if the farmer had worked on the pipeline for seventy hours per week, and assuming that he had also had to collect two gallons of water per day from the well during the construction period, the total labour input in the year of construction would be 441 hours while the input in a previous non-pipeline year would have been only 182.5 hours.

Labour-saving innovations could usually also be described as time saving. A machine that enables a worker to produce ten times as much per unit of time than he could do using a simpler hand-tool technology may be said to 'save' the work of nine men since the output that formerly required ten workers can now be produced by only one man. But the new technology could also be said to save time since ten workers could produce their former output in one-tenth of the previous time period and transfer the surplus time to an alternative use. The study of the combination of factors of production has usually been associated with an analysis of the ways in which the product (or the proceeds from selling the product) is divided between the different factors involved in its production. The most commonly used model is the production function, which relates the output of product per unit of time to a combination of factors of production. Thus if q is the output of some good per fixed time unit, a production function could be written

$$q = q(x_1, x_2, \ldots x_n)$$

where x_1 to x_n are the different factors of production. Empirical evidence suggests that the Cobb–Douglas form of the production function can be used as a model of real-world relationships. In its simplest form this function can be written

$$q = a \, L^\alpha \, C^\beta$$

where L and C represent labour and capital inputs and q is output per unit of time, and where $a > 0$, $0 < \alpha < 1$, $0 < \beta < 1$. The powers α and β can be regarded as the elasticities of production for the two inputs. When $\alpha + \beta = 1$ then the model represents a firm having constant returns to scale. In some versions of the Cobb–Douglas function, time is said to be included as an independent variable but this does not mean time treated as a direct input to the process of production. Time periods are included to represent changes in technology, and the time element is simply a proxy for technical change, which is assumed to take place as a continuous process in the whole of manufacturing industry. Ferguson has argued that 'aggregate technological change can be represented by a smooth time trend' (1969, p. 216) so that time can represent technical development in a macroeconomic production function.

It is possible to construct a simple production function in which time is explicitly included as an input. Suppose that only one type of machine is used, that each machine requires one worker and that one unit of man/machine input (M) and one unit of time input (H) (which can be assumed to be equal to one hour) produce one unit of output (X). Then, if R is the required input of raw material,

$$R + MH \rightarrow X.$$

(The arrow symbol is used since the production process is not reversible and the normal properties of an equation are not present.) If the daily output that could be sold was aX then this could be achieved by increasing the inputs to

$$aR + bMcH \rightarrow aX$$

where

$$bc = a$$

and b is a positive integer. If the hourly wage rate and machine running costs were constant then a profit-maximising firm would seek to use the smallest possible number of machines, thus avoiding the cost of buying extra capital equipment. Labour and machine running costs would remain the same whether a small number of machines and workers was used for a large number of hours or vice versa. The profit-maximising position would therefore be

$$aR + M(aH) \rightarrow aX$$

subject to the constraint that

$$aH \leqslant 24.$$

If 800 units of output per day could be sold, then the profit-maximising position would be

$$800R + 34M\,(23.537H) \rightarrow 800X.$$

But if a maximum working day of eight hours existed and if shift working was not practicable then the profit-maximising position would become

$$800R + 100M(8H) \rightarrow 800X.$$

If there was a major technological advance then this would have the effect of reducing the required man/machine hours of input and there is no reason why it should be automatically assumed that hours will remain constant while the man/machine input is reduced. (If capital equipment is measured by value, rather than by machine units as in our simplified example, then the higher cost of more sophisticated capital equipment may mean that it is only the labour input that is reduced.) It is possible that welfare could be increased by reducing the time input instead of the labour force, although arguments relating to economic efficiency normally suggest that it is labour rather than time that should be 'saved'. Suppose that after a major technical improvement the position for the firm in our example became

$$10R + M^1H \rightarrow 10X$$

(where M^1 is the new machine), then the previous output X could be produced by using ten workers and ten machines for eight hours per day. (In real-world situations the new technology might reduce costs so that prices could be lowered and the daily quantity sold increased to $X + \Delta X$. But in our example it is assumed that there is only a small cost reduction and that this is used to increase the profits of the firm, which is not operating in conditions of perfect competition.)

As has already been pointed out, the straight labour versus time saving choice is usually confused because technical changes that reduce costs may increase the sales of the product and a great deal of discussion of the significance of technical change has concentrated on its influence on the total demand for labour in these circumstances. The debate goes back at least to Ricardo and Marx, Marx taking a pessimistic view about the extent to which compensating new employment would replace job opportunities that were lost by the introduction of new machinery (Marx, 1961). The possibility of having smaller time inputs and more workers was not considered. The issue is also usually less clear than in our greatly simplified example, since there will normally be a number of different processes and machines involved in manufacture and complicated relationships may exist between the required labour and capital inputs for these processes. The well-known history of cotton weaving and spinning during the Industrial Revolution in Britain showed how the mechanisation of one process could increase the demand for labour in a complementary process that had not experienced any similar technological development.

The important question is how far the market solution, or indeed the apparently most efficient economic solution, to the problem of combining the inputs of workers, capital equipment and time also maximises welfare. There are situations in which an efficient solution in terms of the use of scarce resources may not produce the greatest degree of welfare for the community. In our example, if the eight-hour maximum working day constraint is removed, then the most efficient combination of the three factors of production, after the technical improvement, would be four men and four machines working for twenty hours. Why then is this efficient combination not achieved? The most usual reason is that the marginal cost of labour increases steeply beyond a certain daily maximum so that it becomes cheaper for the firm to employ more capital than is strictly necessary for the required output, rather than to use a smaller amount of capital equipment more intensively. Where capital equipment is particularly elaborate and expensive, as in a car assembly plant, or where industrial processes cannot easily be stopped and restarted, the problem can be overcome by the adoption of a shift-working system. But there are very many plants in which the use of a complete extra shift of workers would not be justified or practicable and where, in effect, surplus capital equipment is required because of the shortness of the working day. In some cases, government regulations or trade union agreements prevent the full utilisation of capital equipment. The maximum driving hours imposed on lorry and bus drivers by government and EEC regulations mean that lorries and buses cannot be utilised fully, and that more vehicles and drivers are required than the minimum number necessary to meet the demand for freight and passenger transport. In this case the shift system is usually prohibitively costly because a second driver cannot normally be provided at the point where the first driver 'runs out of time' unless he accompanies him for the entire trip.

The existence of surplus capital equipment as a result of limitations on the length of the working day is not usually noticed as employers may be more concerned with the reduced utilisation of capital equipment that is caused by fluctuations in the demand for their product. When the management of a firm complain that their plant is working to only '60 per cent of capacity' they often mean that it is producing 60 per cent of the output that could be turned out during a full working day rather than 60 per cent of the output that would be produced if machines were operated continuously. 'Short-time' working is related to a day of seven or eight hours rather than to a working period of twenty-four hours. The main reason for limitations on the length of the working day is that people do not like working long hours, or, in extreme cases, are physically incapable of doing so. The rapidly falling utility (or increasing disutility) of work is reflected in an increase in the price of overtime labour, and through the pressure of organised labour for reductions in the length of the working week.

In his discussion of the nature of a working day, Marx argued that it was twenty-four hours less the minimum time required for eating and sleeping. He believed that 'capital' allowed no time for education, intellectual activity, social functions and social inter-course and the 'free-play of bodily and mental activity'. According to Marx, 'Capital cares nothing for the length of life of labour power and would shorten the life of labourers in the same way that farmers rob the soil of fertility' (1961, pp. 264–5). But with an average working week for manual workers in Britain of less than forty-three hours it is apparent that the demands of capital have been success-fully resisted.

When the marginal value of work time increases steeply there may be good economic grounds for employing more workers and more machines for shorter hours rather than operating a smaller amount of capital equipment for longer time periods. An important question for the future may be how far this process should be continued, and whether, in particular, it may be better to employ a larger work force and more capital equipment for very short periods (judged by present standards) rather than to have a large number of people permanently unemployed. The important distinction between current pressures determining the length of the working day and the situation relating to much shorter work periods is that with future reductions in the length of the working day there may be a more obvious clash of interests between the potentially un-employed and those who are at work and that the market structure will not take account of the low utility of time for those who are wholly unemployed. It may be presumed that the utility of work time is reasonably constant over the present length of the average working day. Utility may perhaps fall after about four hours for those who would prefer not to return to work after lunch but it is unlikely that the decline is of the same order as that which would occur if the working day was extended. Most people (or so it is assumed in this argument) would prefer to work rather than to be unemployed even if they were given unemployment pay that was equivalent to the amount of wages that they could have earned. If these propositions are true then some degree of work-sharing or 'overmanning' might add to human happiness even although it appears to reduce economic efficiency.

Let us suppose that in the near future technological development (such as the adoption of a much higher degree of automation of industrial processes) means that the labour force employed by manufacturing industry is reduced, and that there is no alternative source of employment available. There may still be some choice between producing a given output with a smaller capital and labour input but a larger consumption of time and using more capital and labour for a shorter time period. In our example (given the assumption that total sales of the product will not increase), adoption of the new technology, which reduces the man/machine hours input requirement from 800 to 80, must involve some reduction in manpower unless the time input is reduced to less than one hour. The combination that would minimise private costs, given an eight-hour day maximum constraint, would be ten workers and ten machines operating for eight hours. But it is possible that a less efficient mixture of inputs, such as twenty men and twenty machines working for a four-hour day might increase welfare. The cost of the extra machines might be more than offset by the gains in welfare received by workers.

Figures 4.1 and 4.2 represent the marginal utilities of work and leisure activities respectively for workers in an industry that has recently enjoyed a technical improvement that enables the output of each worker per unit of time to be increased. The 'work' and 'leisure' utilities are not necessarily on the same scale. It is assumed that all workers have the same preferences and that the utility and disutility they receive is on the same scale (i.e. that interpersonal comparisons of utility can be made). Workers receive a positive but constantly declining utility from work up to OH_3 hours; beyond this point work is a disutility. OH_4 represents a full period of twenty-four hours. Similarly in the 'leisure' diagram, Figure 4.2, it is assumed that the marginal utility of leisure falls constantly. Following

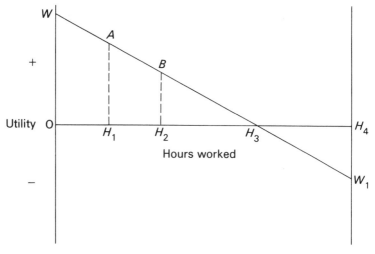

Figure 4.1

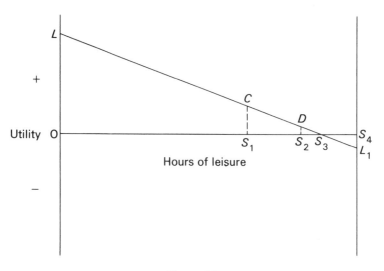

Figure 4.2

the treatment already developed in this study, the utility obtained from work relates to the pleasure or displeasure received from the work activity itself and does not include any utility connected with wage payments received. Two situations can be compared with the use of these diagrams: the intensive use of capital equipment with a longer time input and a smaller labour force; and the 'work-sharing' situation with more workers and machines and a smaller time input. For simplicity it can be assumed that the choice to be made is between one worker and one machine operating for OH_2 hours, the second worker being unemployed, and two men with two machines working for OH_1 hours $(= \frac{1}{2} OH_2)$. It is also assumed that both men receive identical incomes in both situations, since, if one worker is employed for OH_2 hours, half his share of the value of the product will be transferred by the state to pay benefits to the unemployed worker. Given these assumptions it is apparent that the welfare of the two men would be greater if the work-sharing alternative was adopted. If one man worked for OH_2 hours, the total utility from work $OWBH_2$ would be less than $2(OWAH_1)$ — the total utility obtained if two men worked for OH_1 hours. The total utility from leisure time if both men were employed for OH_1 hours a day (and where $S_1S_4 = OH_2$ and $S_2S_4 = OH_1$) would be $2(LDS_2O)$. This is greater than $LCS_1O + LS_3O - S_3S_4L_1$ which is the total leisure-time utility with one man working OH_2 hours and the other unemployed. The leisure-time utility gain from moving to the work-sharing situation would be $CDS_2 S_1$, whereas the loss would be $(DS_3 S_2 - S_3 S_4 L_1)$, which is clearly smaller than the gain. This conclusion, that more workers and a smaller time input would increase welfare, would apply generally, given our assumptions, except for some rather unlikely utility curves.

In a situation similar to our simplified example, an omniscient authority would need to compare the value of the losses from providing the extra capital equipment with that of the gains to the workers arising from the choice of the work-sharing alternative. In conventional cost–benefit analysis in a real-world situation, the 'cost' of unemployment would probably be represented by the money value of unemployment benefit and the issue would be complicated by the way in which the product was distributed. There is little doubt that workers in an industry using an established technology would resist any work-sharing designed to provide employment for additional workers, whether this was carried out by using a shift system with existing capital equipment or, as in our model, by using more capital equipment with a smaller time input. It would not be possible, in the real world, to p.... on the benefit from the reduced payment of unemployment benefit exclusively to those workers who had to· work for shorter hours and to accept a lower income. But where a technical improvement increased the output of workers so that higher wages could be paid to a smaller number of men, workers might agree to work shorter hours and enjoy a smaller increase in total wages in order to preserve jobs. Economists should not automatically condemn the work-sharing, reduced time-input solution even though it is inefficient when measured by the criterion of the relationship of the input of resources to the output of goods.

It is true that there may be better solutions than work-sharing to the problems created by labour-saving technological improvements, and these should be tried out before a policy of work-sharing is adopted. In the long run there may be alternative forms of employment available for displaced workers and in this case the arguments for work-sharing are greatly weakened. The greater use of automation in manufacturing industry is expected to reduce the demand for labour in the future, but it would be wrong to assume that no alternative work can be found. Since human wants and capacity to consume are almost unlimited, the only finally binding constraints preventing the development of new jobs for displaced workers are shortages of raw materials and the lack of suitable skills. There is no reason, for example, why there should not be a new development of labour-intensive craft industries producing high-quality furniture, pottery and other specialised consumer goods. There is some evidence that this may already be happening. But there will be some displaced workers who cannot acquire new skills and will be unemployed if work-sharing is not adopted. It would also be more efficient to bring in work-sharing by means of shift systems so that 'surplus' capital equipment is not required. In our example, production costs would clearly be lower if ten machines were installed and operated by successive four-hour shifts of ten workers instead of using twenty machines with twenty workers employed simultaneously for a four-hour period. Another traditional solution to the new technology problem is, of course, to take advantage of reduced costs and lower prices in the hope that sales will be increased sufficiently to make it possible to retain most of the labour force. It is also likely that the machines of the new technology will require a larger labour input in their production than did the less sophisticated machines that they replaced. International competitiveness will also be affected where one country adopts work-sharing while others do not.

The reduced-time-input, work-sharing method of dealing with technical development is therefore a 'last-resort' solution. Nevertheless there are circumstances in which work-sharing might be justified. These are: when the cost saving from the new technology is insufficient to allow a significant reduction in the price of the product; when the demand for the product is inelastic; when there is no alternative employment for displaced workers; and when the technological improvement enables the wage paid to workers to be maintained or increased even for a shorter working period.

3. TYPES OF TECHNOLOGICAL CHANGE

Technological development has been classified by Pigou and Hicks according to the likely effect on the distribution of the product. The three categories as described by Hicks (based on the original analysis of Pigou, 1960) are 'labour-saving', 'capital-saving' and 'neutral' innovations (1963). Hicks defines capital-saving innovations as those that raise the marginal product of labour more than that of capital; labour-saving technical changes cause a more than proportional increase in the marginal product of capital; and neutral technical changes have an equal effect on the marginal products of both labour and capital. But this is not necessarily the most helpful classification for all purposes and there is a possible confusion in its application that is illustrated by Heertje's (1977) account of the types of technical change, which reverses Hicks' definition of labour-saving and capital-saving innovations. Hicks admits that it is not easy to find examples of capital-saving inventions but argues that 'wireless is, of course, the standard case' (1963, p. 123). While it is true that radio may enable messages to be carried with less capital equipment than is required for telegraph services, it is an oversimplification to classify the development of radio as a pure capital-saving technical development since the main use of radio has not been to replace the telegraph but to provide entirely new services that were not previously available at all.

An alternative classification of technical change may be more useful when we are concerned with the effect on the use of time rather than with that on the distribution of the product. Five categories, including capital saving and labour or time saving may be distinguished although some innovations may overlap the classes, which are not mutually exclusive. The categories are raw-material saving; new products; better quality products; capital saving; and labour saving. Labour-saving developments, as has already been argued, may alternatively provide the opportunity for time savings.

Raw-material-saving innovations enable a larger output to be obtained for a given input of raw materials. Thus the technique of blowing jets of powdered coal into the furnaces of coal-fired electric power stations may produce more energy per ton of coal (taking into account the inputs required for the powdering process) than would burning large lumps of coal. Raw-material-saving innovations do not necessarily involve increasing output per unit of time and, as will be argued later, the distinction between this type of technical change and other types may be relevant to a discussion of what is meant by changes in productivity. Some innovations do not enable an existing good or service to be produced more efficiently but make possible the production of some entirely new product or service. If 'wireless' could originally be thought of as a simpler, capital-saving version of the telegraph, it is apparent that the development of television was neither labour nor capital saving but a means of producing a new service that previously did not exist. Whether or not this type of 'new product' innovation can be said to create new wants is a philosophical issue that it is not particularly rewarding to pursue. Presumably some of our ancestors in Tudor times would have liked to have watched the defeat of the Armada or the latest play from The Globe in their own homes, but the impossibility of having such wants fulfilled may have prevented them from being formulated except in fairy stories.

Some technical developments may make it possible to purchase a better-quality version of goods and services that were already available. Usually these innovations will also replace manual labour. Thus machines used during road construction can produce a better compacted surface than could be achieved if only hand tools were used so that, although it is likely that some workers will be displaced, use of the machines may be justified even in countries where the cost of the replaced labour is less than that of operating the machines. (The preferences of workers for being employed, discussed in the last section, ought also to be taken into account where welfare maximisation is the agreed objective.) In practice, quality-improving technical changes may be confused with quality changes that result not from the use of a new technology but from the choice of a superior raw material or from an increase in the raw-material, labour or time input.

Despite Hicks' difficulty in finding examples, capital-saving improvements do occur where less costly capital equipment, combined with the same mixture of other inputs, can produce the same output (or an increased output with a larger raw material input and the same labour and time inputs). Present-day electronic hand calculators will perform all the functions that were carried out by much more elaborate mechanical calculators (plus many additional ones) at approximately one-fifteenth of the capital cost. (The fraction would be even smaller if allowance was made for inflation.) A worker who used a mechanical calculator costing about £250 for simple arithmetical processes five or ten years ago could now carry out the same calculations with capital equipment costing only about £15. Even the development of electronic calculators is not a pure capital-saving innovation since the calculation time may be slightly shorter so that there is a small labour-saving or time-saving element. The labour-saving factor becomes much more important for those using the many functions that mechanical calculators could not provide.

Some of the main issues relating to labour-saving or time-saving innovations have already been discussed in the last section. The development of electronic calculators and computers provides an interesting and rather different example of the problem of choosing between replacing labour and reducing the length of the time input. The amount of calculation and data storage and retrieval required in the operation of a process of manufacture and distribution may be fixed in relation to output. Where these processes have been transformed by labour- or time-saving innovations but the process of manufacture remains unchanged, the opportunity to expand sales of the product may be very limited (since the cut in total production costs caused by the fall in labour or time input required for data processing may be too small to have any significant effect on price). If there is only a fixed amount of work to be done then an innovation such as the development of calculators and computers can lead only to either shorter working periods or a reduced labour force, or both. Hicks' possibility of liberating resources to make more of the product will not apply. Where an innovation in one part of the total process of manufacture does bring about a significant reduction in costs and a consequent increase in the demand for the product then, of course, 'bottlenecks' caused by the existence of processes where there has not been any technical development can be removed by employing more capital and labour. But any labour displaced from the improved process may not be suitable for employment in an unimproved process. Clerks who are replaced by a computer may not be capable of operating machines on the factory floor.

4. TIME AND PRODUCTIVITY

Consideration of the time input into the production of goods and services raises some issues about the nature of productivity. Productivity will normally be held to have been increased when output is raised more proportionately than any increase in the quantity of inputs. It is usually assumed that increases in productivity are desirable because scarce resources are used more economically. But the real-world situations may be a little more complicated than this simple judgement implies and it may be that some forms of productivity improvement are more to be welcomed than others. In a competitive market, productivity increases will be measured by their effect on costs. If a new machine costs less than the labour that it replaces then it will be used. We have already seen that this procedure will not necessarily maximise welfare where the displaced workers remain unemployed. Another obvious possibility is that there will be other external costs (besides the creation of unemployment) that the profit-maximising firm will fail to take into consideration. The new machine may produce some environmental pollution that, for the community, more than offsets the productivity gain. As there is an extensive literature on external disbenefits, and as most governments are now increasingly ready to take action to control pollution, this issue need not be pursued any further in a study concerned with problems of time.

If the market solution can go wrong because external costs and benefits are ignored, there is also a possible error that can result from state planning. It is possible for the managers of an industry not dominated by the profit-maximising motive to follow some such 'efficiency' objective as maximising output per manhour. Output per manhour figures are often quoted as measurements of the relative levels of productivity achieved by different production units in an industry or by the parts of an industry located in different countries or for comparisons over time. But it is apparent that relating output only to the labour input, with time held constant, may be an exercise in sub-optimisation. There will, of course, be many situations in which output per manhour of input is a good indication of productivity levels, but it is obviously dangerous to measure only two inputs. A high output per hour of labour employed might be achieved by making a wasteful use of raw materials or by employing an excessive amount of capital equipment. The use of a computer system can again be used as an example. A small firm could employ a computer to maximise the output of accounts or stock control documents in relation to time and labour inputs, but the use of the computer would reduce productivity if its manufacture and operation used up more scarce resources than those that it replaced. This type of reduction in productivity would not occur in an efficient profit-maximising organisation since the purchase, maintenance and use of the capital equipment would be found to cost more per unit of output than the replaced labour and time input.

But there is a less obvious way in which an apparent increase in productivity might be shown to be of questionable desirability. As has already been argued, labour-saving innovations may also be regarded as time saving. A machine that enables a worker to transform some raw material into a finished product five times as quickly as before may be used to reduce the labour force to one-fifth of its previous size or to increase output fivefold or for some mixture of these objectives. Previously we have been concerned with the implications of decisions to reduce the size of the manpower input and the loss of welfare suffered by those who become unemployed. At first sight, a technological innovation that makes possible such a large increase in output that the entire labour force can be retained, or even expanded, and that does not create any additional pollution, would seem to be an unmixed blessing. The events of the Industrial Revolution in Britain (although they do not fulfil the requirements about pollution) are usually seen as technical changes that led to the output of much cheaper products, the large-scale expansion of markets and the rapid growth of the labour force required by manufacturing industry. The factor that is ignored in welcoming all increases in productivity resulting from labour- or time-saving innovations is the effect on the consumption of raw materials. A technical development that enables raw materials to be turned into a finished product more quickly does not increase productivity in the same way as does an innovation that makes it possible to produce more ouput per unit of raw material with all other inputs remaining constant.

At the macroeconomic level, the debate about economic growth is now well established, and the arguments of those who see raw-material shortages placing strict limits on growth, and eventually leading to economic decline, are well known, as also are those of economists who take a more optimistic view. There is also widespread concern about the future world supply of petroleum and, to a lesser extent, of some other essential raw materials. But developments in individual industries that enable the transformation from raw material into finished product to be made more quickly are not, perhaps, often seen in relation to the consumption of the raw-material input. The supply of some raw materials is virtually inexhaustible so that the depletion problem does not arise. A process that enabled 'fixed' nitrogen to be extracted from the air or sodium chloride from the sea at a faster rate than before is unlikely to lead to any depletion problems. We would be able to consume more nitrogen-based fertilizers and more salt per time unit, and there would be no future penalty. But other innovations may enable us to consume products based on raw materials that are in limited supply more quickly. It may be argued that a technical change that makes it possible to consume more today but less tomorrow increases productivity in only a rather special and limited sense. The range of choice may be widened by the innovation, and in so far as present are preferred to future satisfactions (an issue discussed more fully in chapter 7) wealth can be said to have been increased. But in the long run a more rapid transformation of depletable resources into finished consumer goods may be regarded as a means of shifting consumption in time rather than as a way of increasing total wealth. The situation is most straightforward with raw materials that are used relatively unprocessed, and an illustration can be used that also relates to some of the other choices already described in this chapter.

Suppose that new coal-cutting machinery is developed that enables coal in a particular Yorkshire colliery to be cut and brought to the surface at double the rate per time unit that was possible with existing plant. The new machinery requires the same number of workers to operate it as did the equipment it replaces. Various choices could be made. Half the seams in the colliery could be closed. If the displaced miners were found alternative work – on, for example, improving housing and the environment in their area – that paid them the same wage and gave them at least equal satisfaction to that obtained from working in the colliery, then useful labour saving would have taken place and the colliery would be able to show a meaningful productivity increase measured in tons of coal produced per man shift. It must also be assumed that the new technology machinery is not so much more costly than the replaced equipment that the gains from reducing the labour force are completely offset. If there was no alternative work for the redundant miners (or if it yielded much less utility than mining) then the innovation might increase productivity but reduce welfare. A second choice would be to shorten the length of each shift so that output and the size of the labour force remained constant. This would be less profitable for the Coal Board but would be likely to increase welfare, since most miners would presumably consider themselves better off if they were able to work a shorter day for the same salary. Productivity would appear to increase if it was measured in relation to a fixed time input but not if it was related to the variable-length shift. The third alternative, however, represents the choice that is relevant to the discussion in this section. This is that the full workforce would be retained with the same length of shift, so that output would be doubled in relation to relatively short time periods. Suppose that the colliery had sufficient coal resources to last for fifty years at the rate of extraction that applied before the technical improvement was made. After the new machinery was installed, productivity would increase if output was related to the man shift, to a month or to or year. But over a fifty-year period output would remain the same, since after the first twenty-five years, when it was doubled, output would then fall to zero for the remaining twenty-five years. Total productivity might still be held to have increased if the labour that would have been required in the pit at the slower rate of extraction was used for some other productive purpose when the colliery became exhausted after twenty-five years of operation using the improved technique. But maybe some words other than 'productivity increase' should be found to describe the kind of technical change that merely makes it possible to consume more today and less tomorrow.

5. DOMESTIC LABOUR-SAVING EQUIPMENT

Families in all reasonably affluent countries have to make choices about how much labour-saving equipment they will use in the home. Continual technical change makes the choices more complicated. As with industrial capital equipment, labour-saving domestic appliances may equally well be regarded as yielding time savings. They enable time to be transferred to a preferred use, such as from washing clothes to attending a coffee party. Domestic equipment may also increase the utility obtained from carrying out housework. Even if a vacuum cleaner does not reduce the time required to remove the dust from the floor of a room, a housewife (or househusband) may find it more pleasant to operate the cleaner than to sweep with a broom. As with capital equipment in industry, domestic equipment may also be regarded as less attractive to operate. Some people may dislike the noise of a dishwasher or be confused by the complexities of an electric sewing machine.

Suppose that a rational 'economic person' who was free to fix the length of his working day and who did his own housework had reached an equilibrium position in relation to the choice between work and leisure where the marginal utilities of work (including the utility received from wages in this case) and leisure were equal. This would mean that there were no existing goods or services that could be acquired with the earnings from extending his working day that would compensate him for the loss of utility resulting from substituting work time for leisure time. If a new or improved labour-saving domestic appliance was developed, he would need to review his position to ensure that he still had the optimum work and leisure mix. The simple model developed here examines the problems in terms of the single currency of time. Suppose that the technical change was the development of a new dishwasher that was quicker to load, had a larger capacity and was cheaper than existing models. Let a and b represent the number of standard time units required for washing up by hand or with the machine respectively so that, assuming that $a > b$,

$$a = b + (a - b)$$

where $(a - b)$ is free time that can be allocated to some new activity if the dishwasher is purchased. If (to make the analysis simpler) it is assumed that the worker would buy the machine entirely by hire-purchase and that his decision relates to a time horizon that does not go beyond the repayment period, so that the total average cost of operating the machine per working day is Y, then if his marginal wage rate is W the worker would need to work Y/W extra units of time per day. If the utilities of washing up by hand, of operating the dishwasher, of paid employment (excluding any utility derived from the earnings) and of the preferred activity for which the extra leisure time could be used were U_1, U_2, U_3 and U_4 respectively, then the man would buy the dishwasher if

$$U_1 a < U_2 b + U_3 \frac{Y}{W} + U_4 \left[a - \left(b + \frac{Y}{W} \right) \right].$$

The different utilities obtained from the alternative activities are equivalent to a system of weights applied to the use of time. The utility measured is the average utility per time unit for the whole increase or reduction in the 'lump' of time allocated to that activity. In the case of paid work and possibly of the preferred activity it represents 'averaged' marginal utility in so far as the utility of these activities will be influenced by the time already spent on them. In particular, of course, the length of the existing working day will affect the utility received from any further period at work. None of the utilities is marginal in the strict sense of the term since the decision about buying domestic equipment involves reallocating indivisible periods of time.

Where the householder cannot choose to work a little longer in order to pay for the improved piece of domestic capital equipment, then the problem becomes the normal one of maximising utility from the allocation of a fixed money and time budget. If utility was maximised before the innovation became available then the householder would have to compare the utility obtained from being able to transfer time from housework to the most preferred alternative activity (or activities) with the utility lost from sacrificing whatever good or service or reduction in savings was necessary in order to buy and operate the improved domestic equipment.

In the case of a dishwasher it is possible to estimate some actual figures and to deduce an implied value for time savings. According to a study in *Which?* made in July 1978 prices, a dishwasher would cost about 16p a day to operate (including the cost of depreciation) and would save one hour a day in washing-up time. A worker paid £2 an hour would therefore only need to work an extra five minutes a day to pay for the dishwasher. If washing-up time using the dish-washer was cut from seventy minutes a day to ten minutes, if we assume that the utility received per unit of time from both methods of washing up was the same and since the utility received from the 'preferred activity' must by definition be greater than that of wash-ing up, the decision maker would have to rate the utility of work at a very low rate in order to prefer the 'no-dishwasher' situation. The value of 16p an hour for time saving from a generally disliked activity such as washing up is very low and is much below the value usually put on transport time savings.

It would involve considerable research to determine why relatively few people in Britain fail to take advantage of this relatively cheap form of time saving, and do not own dishwashers. But there are a number of possible explanations. Domestic appliances cannot be bought on a completely deferred payment basis and the initial capital payment required may create a problem. Many people may be unaware of the *Which?* figures or may not believe that the per-formance of dishwashers is as good as the result that can be achieved when washing up by hand. People cannot always add a small amount of time to their working day. Relatively poor people who could not choose to work longer would have to surrender goods or services yielding a high utility in order to buy the time saving that a dish-washer can give. Some people may not have any strongly preferred alternative activities or may already have ample leisure time so that time saved from washing up would have no great value. Finally, washing up may not be carried out by the wage earner himself so that it would involve some altruism for him to work longer hours in order to save time for someone else, even if it was a person about whose welfare he was concerned. Nevertheless, the analysis suggests that if Britain enjoys any economic growth at all, dishwashers could soon become as common as washing machines or refrigerators.

6. DO-IT-YOURSELF OR PROFESSIONAL LABOUR

The discussion of the use of labour-saving domestic equipment assumed that housework was unpaid. If this were not so then a market solution would be found to the use of this equipment in the same way as in profit-maximising manufacturing industry. The use of washing machines and vacuum cleaners involves paying for capital equipment that will reduce the hours of unpaid labour required. The do-it-yourself movement represents the opposite tendency whereby unpaid labour is used to replace paid professional work. As with domestic equipment, a simple model expressing all costs in terms of time can be used to analyse the choice between the use of paid labour and doing it yourself. Again it is assumed that the utility produced by the existing time budget has been maximised and that the decision maker is free to extend his working day (or to work overtime or to take on an additional part-time job) as a means of paying for outside labour to carry out the decorating or other household improvements that might alternatively be completed on a do-it-yourself basis. Additional assumptions are that the potential do-it-yourself worker can produce work of similar quality to professional labour and that the wage earner will undertake the home improvement himself.

Let t_1 be the time taken to complete some household improvement project using professional labour, measured in hours, c represent the hourly cost of professional labour (including overheads, taxes and profits averaged over the working period), t_2 be the time required to complete the project by do-it-yourself labour, and w be the marginal hourly earning power of the householder. It is assumed (slightly unrealistically) that the cost of raw materials is the same for professional and do-it-yourself labour and that the householder already possesses the necessary capital equipment required for the home improvement project. The unweighted time consumption comparison would then be between t_2 and $t_1 c/W$. For anyone with average hourly earnings it is likely that, very approximately,

$$t_2 = \frac{t_1 c}{W}$$

or that the extra work time required would be approximately equal to the time needed to complete the do-it-yourself task, although with experience t_2 would decrease. The hourly cost of professional labour will be inflated by the overheads and profit content, and, if decorators or builders are paid wages near to the national average, then the total cost will be above average earnings so that the householder will need to do more extra hours of work than t_1, the time taken by the professional decorators. But since do-it-yourself workers may take longer to complete a home improvement scheme than professional workers, the two time periods may be approximately equal.

It is apparent that below-average earners will have to work for longer periods to pay for home improvement projects, and will therefore be more likely to do the work themselves, whereas for high wage earners the opposite is true. This would suggest that only below-average wage earners should practise do-it-yourself home improvment, but the conclusion may be changed when the utilities obtained from carrying out the different activities are taken into consideration. It is very likely that the marginal utility of extra paid work will be considerably lower than the average utility per time unit obtained from undertaking do-it-yourself activities. This means that if, for the average-earnings worker, $t_2 = t_1 c/w$, when the relative utilities, U_1 and U_2, are taken into account then

$$U_1 t_2 > U_2 \frac{t_1 c}{w}.$$

For higher wage earners the inequality

$$t_2 > \frac{t_1 c}{w}$$

can be made into the equation

$$t_2 = \frac{t_1 c}{w} + t_3$$

by adding the extra free time, t_3 (which is equivalent to $t_2 - t_1 c/w$), that would be available if the paid-work option was chosen. Even for these high earners, however, the higher utility of do-it-yourself work compared with paid work might offset the presumably high utility of the extra free time so that

$$U_1 t_2 > U_2 \frac{t_1 c}{w} + U_3 t_3$$

even although

$$U_3 > U_1.$$

CHAPTER 5

Time and Transport

For my part I travel not to go anywhere but to go.
I travel for travel's sake. [R. L. Stevenson]

1. INTRODUCTION

During the last twenty years or so, the field of study connected with the economics of time that has attracted most attention is almost certainly that of the value of transport time savings. This book itself was developed from an interest in this particular topic. The act of transportation involves moving goods and people from one geographical location to another, but the main product of any improvement in transportation is nearly always a reduction in journey or transit times. The most important benefit resulting from the majority of new investments in transport projects is a saving in transport time that can be transferred to some alternative and preferred activity. In a developed country like Britain it is already possible for physically fit people to travel from virtually any location to any other location. There are relatively few sites that are physically inaccessible and those that cannot be reached are mostly parts of cliffs, mountains or small islands, which only the exceptionally adventurous have any desire to visit. The distribution of goods is not quite so universally possible, but it is usually only in the case of a new development of some mineral resource that transport facilities are entirely lacking. When it is suggested that transport facilities are inadequate the most usual meaning is that existing services are too slow. The main purpose of the development of the high speed train and of supersonic aircraft, and of the construction of new bridges and roads, is to enable people and goods to be transported more quickly than was previously possible. Sometimes transport investment produces greater comfort for human travellers or reduces the risk of damage to goods traffic, but speed is its most usual and most important product.

If transport investment in more extensive infrastructure or in new technology yields transport time savings, then the value of those savings is clearly a matter of considerable interest. Judgements on whether an investment will be worthwhile or on which of a number of alternative investment projects should be preferred may depend upon the value of the resulting time savings. The value of transport time savings may also be a necessary piece of information for those who are trying to make forecasts relating to such matters as the future demand for transport, the modal split of demand between alternative forms of transport and the demand for shopping or recreational activities at particular geographical locations.

In some cases the problem of evaluating transport time savings is not dissimilar to that of any private sector firm when it has to estimate the demand for a new or changed product. Where time savings can, in effect, be sold in the market then any evaluation mistakes will soon be revealed. If a quicker electric rail route replaces a diesel engine service, or a high speed train operation is introduced, then the railways will be able to sell the service directly, finding out what the demand is and testing different price strategies. Similarly, the fare surcharges on the supersonic Concorde services could be adjusted if the pattern of demand indicated that the value passengers placed on the journey time savings was under- or over-estimated. But road space is not marketed in Britain and so there is no direct data on the value that people attach to reduced journey times. If the estimates of transport time-saving values used are wrong, then there could be a major misallocation of resources, with either too much or too little new road building and improvement. (This somewhat oversimplifies the situation since the road building programme is not wholly determined by the level of the estimated rate of return.) When the time-saving values recommended by the British Department of Transport are used, about 80 per cent of the benefit received from an investment in a typical trunk road is represented by the value of these time savings (Department of the Environment, 1976, para. 5.13). (The other items are changes in vehicle operating costs and in accident rates.) Since road and bridge investment is made in the public sector, the ultimate criterion may be regarded as the improvement in social welfare. This means that the interests of all those who gain or lose as the result of a reduction in journey or transit times should be taken into consideration. This is of particular importance in considering the value of time savings made by people travelling during working time.

As the literature on transport time savings is so very extensive, it would be impossible to attempt an adequate survey of all the issues covered in the space of one chapter of this study. The dis-cussion ranges from highly theoretical papers to reports of empirical evidence relating to particular types of travel time (e.g. Beesley, 1965; Quarmby, 1967; Dawson and Everall, 1972). One of the major issues is how far it is necessary to compromise by accepting figures that have a less than perfect theoretical basis. This is an area where actual figures have to be used in real-world investment decisions and where it is not possible to wait for all theoretical difficulties to be solved. If the usual assumption of economic analysis that individuals are the best judges of their own interests is accepted, then there must be a very large range of different time-savings values. People hurrying to catch a train or a plane, a man who is late for an important appointment; and young lovers travelling to a brief meeting might all put a very high value on a travel time saving. The value of a time saving that allowed a costly consignment of export goods to catch a container ship and avoid a three-week wait for the next ship could be very considerable. Even a small reduction in the time required for a replacement part to reach a mine or factory where some essential equipment has broken down might bring a valuable increase in production. On the other hand, a family going for a ride in the country, like Stevenson's voyager, 'for travel's sake' might not put any value at all on the potential time savings provided by a road improvement on their route. A reduction in the journey time of a lorry taking goods to be stored in a distribution warehouse that did not lead to any improved utilisation of the vehicle or any reduction in the driver's wages would have very little value. (If the driver preferred driving to 'killing time' at his depot the saving might even have negative value.)

Time-saving values used to guide investment or planning decisions must, it is apparent, relate to average values based on a high degree of aggregation. Unless the investment appraisal is to be very pro-longed and costly only a very few general classes of traveller, and flows of traffic, can be considered. Just how many classes of trans-port should be distinguished is a major issue, which will be discussed in this chapter.

Even if it is accepted that the consumers' own preferences should be considered rather than those that planners and decision makers might be tempted to impose on them, it is still possible to question the methods by which preferences are revealed. It is a familiar problem of cost–benefit analysis that 'willingness-to-pay' measurements are influenced by the size of people's income. Other things being the same, richer people will be willing to pay more for a given time saving than will their poorer compatriots. Whether time-saving values should be adjusted to allow for income differences is a debatable issue that depends on what value judgements are made. If we believe that the incomes that people receive reflect the value of the contributions they make to the economic well-being of the community, then it would seem to be logical to allow them to use this income to buy transport time savings. On the other hand, it can be argued that the present distribution of income does not represent either an economic or any other kind of optimum and that all men's time should be regarded by society as being of equal value. This is not just a matter for philosophic speculation but could affect the allocation of transport investment because income levels may be strongly associated with different classes of transport user or different areas. The average train passenger is likely to have a higher income than the average car traveller, who in turn (in Britain) is considerably richer than the average bus passenger. The average level of income varies in different parts of Britain and this would be reflected in differences in average time-savings values.

Another problem discussed in this chapter is that of the value of very small or very large transport time savings. There may be benefits equivalent to scale economies in the use of transport time savings so that their value does not increase linearly with size. If a saving of sixty minutes is valued at 240p it does not necessarily follow that a one-minute time saving would be valued at 2p or a three-hour time saving at £7.20. The smaller time saving might have a very much lower unit value because it could not be used to undertake any new, preferred activity. Standard consumer theory, on the other hand, suggests that the marginal utility of transport time savings must eventually start to decline. The debate about the size and unit value of transport time saving has concentrated mainly on the problem of small savings as these are more commonly found, especially in road investment appraisal.

Another problem that has not been solved satisfactorily is that of the value of the benefit of time savings relating to the transit of goods. The literature on the evaluation of transport time savings has dealt almost exclusively with the transportation of people, and very little attention has been given to the benefits that society may derive from reducing the time that consumer goods, partly finished goods and raw materials spend in transit.

A last problem relates to the relationship of the value of time savings to different modes of travel. Empirical evidence suggests that the average traveller would receive different amounts of utility from the same time period spent travelling by different transport modes. All other things being equal they would therefore value a reduction in journey times in a less preferred mode more highly than the same reduction in the journey time in a more favoured transport mode. Since richer people tend to travel in the preferred modes of transport, the 'income' and 'mode preference' factors will work in opposite directions. Richer travellers will be prepared to pay more for a given travel time saving in a particular mode but they will travel by a mode that has a relatively high utility so that the ability to transfer time to an alternative activity will have less value than it would if they were travelling less pleasantly. Ten minutes saved from a journey made in pouring rain on a motor cycle would have higher value for most people than the same time saving made when travelling as a passenger in a chauffeur-driven Rolls Royce.

2. WORK-TRANSPORT TIME SAVINGS

One important group of travellers that can be distinguished when making estimates of the value of travel time savings consists of people making journeys during their working day. This group includes salesmen and commercial travellers, all workers travelling to any kind of meeting away from their work base, those making journeys to provide services or repairs away from their own office or workplace, and workers such as bus and lorry drivers who are paid to provide transport services. People engaged in 'work' travel will normally be paid for the travel time period as though it were part of the working day. Self-employed people would be travelling at a time when they would normally be at work. Commuters travelling to or from their normal workplace are excluded from the work-travel category. In the 1972/3 *National Travel Survey* carried out by the Department of the Environment (1975) it was found that 11 per cent of the mileage covered by passengers was completed 'in the course of work'. In the 1975/6 survey the equivalent figure was 10 per cent (Department of Transport, 1979a).

Discussion relating to the value of work-travel time savings has been relatively limited. A recent book devoted entirely to a study of the value of travel time savings (Bruzelius, 1979) has virtually nothing to say about 'work' time savings. The reason for this comparative neglect is that there is an easy solution to the problem of finding a value for these time savings. If the time taken by work journeys is reduced then the extra time can be used productively at work, and if wages paid reflect the value of the worker's product then the wage rate can be used to represent the value to the employer of the work time saving. Some writers have pointed out that the use of wage rates (or earnings) as a measurement of the value of work time savings may not be wholly accurate. Wages may not reflect productivity very closely, some time savings may not be used productively and the preferences of the worker himself are ignored. But for the practical purpose of feeding figures into investment appraisals or forecasting calculations it is usually agreed that wage rate or earnings figures are more suitable than any available alternative. In this study, however, the main concern is to examine the underlying reasons why time savings are valued rather than to provide practical recipes for making the evaluation, and so the valuation of work time savings is investigated a little more fully.

If work-time journeys are shortened and if the time saved can be used productively, then society will gain the total value of the increased production. Suppose that for each one of a group of workers the total working day is fixed at K minutes and that this is made up of t_1 minutes doing productive work and t_2 minutes travelling, so that

$$t_1 + t_2 = K.$$

If the value of the product per minute of productive work was x and the total value of one day's product from one worker was V_1 then

$$xt_1 = V_1.$$

If wages were a fixed proportion, a, of the value of the total product then the wage rate per minute, W_1, would be

$$W_1 = \frac{aV_1}{K}$$

and profits per minute of productive work, p, would be

$$p = \frac{(1-a)V_1}{t_1} .$$

The total value of the product per worker per day could be written

$$(W_1 + p)t_1 + W_1t_2 = V_1 .$$

Now suppose that work-travel time was reduced from t_2 to t_3, and that

$$t_3 - t_3 = t_4 ;$$

then, assuming that all the saved time was used for productive work, the total daily product per worker would be increased to

$$x(t_1 + t_4) = V_2.$$

The new wage rate would be $W_2 = aV_2/K$ if profits per minute of production time remained constant. The workers would gain $K(W_2 - W_1)$ per day and the employers would gain pt_4.

This analysis could be expressed in words by stating that the main part of the benefit from the work time saving is the extra output produced by the worker when time is transferred from travelling to productive work. But the more detailed analysis does bring out two points that have usually been ignored in discussions on the value of work time savings. Firstly, the total gain from increased productivity may be more than the wage paid to the worker since there is presumably also some profit element that will accrue to the firm. Secondly, the whole gain does not necessarily go to the employer. The wage paid for the travelling time must be met from the total yield of the productive work period so that, although the fixed proportions of profit and wages assumed in the model may not apply in the real world, it may happen that some of the extra product is passed on to the workers. This distributional point does not affect the total money value of work time savings but it could influence the size of the time savings. Workers' cooperation may be necessary to achieve full work time savings even when transport facilities are improved, so that the degree of incentive to shorten work-time journeys may not be without significance.

If the assumptions that there was a fixed working day, including work travel, and that the time saving was used for productive work are changed, a rather different situation could exist. Suppose that the productive working day was fixed and work-travel time added to this. Then if the travel time was reduced the worker would merely have a shorter working day. The total product per twenty-four hours would remain the same, and if the worker successfully demanded that his share of the product must not be reduced (wage rates per minute being adjusted upwards to allow for the shorter total working day) then the employer would not be any better off while the worker would only gain the benefit from transferring some travel time to leisure time. If workers reduced their working day by the length of the travel time saving and wage rates were not adjusted, then the firm would gain but workers would lose income and the net gain to society would, as before, be the difference between the utility of travel and the alternative use made of the travel time saving. In these circumstances it could be argued that work time savings should only have the same money value per unit as reductions in commuting time. The situation is analogous to some forms of technological development discussed in chapter 4. A reduction in essential work-travel time of, say, thirty minutes could mean that the same output (from one worker) could now be produced in 510 minutes instead of 540 minutes. If the employing firm was able to save the half-hour's pay (which might well be at overtime rates) then it would regard the change as an increase in productivity. Thirty minutes of labour would be available for some productive work. If, however, no such work was available then the gain to the employers would be offset by an equal loss to the worker and, as argued, the net gain to society would be represented by the benefits to the worker of using the time saving for some alternative non-paid-work activity.

The position of transport workers is different from either of the cases discussed. Moving goods or people is productive work so that a shortening of journey times could mean increasing productivity from a fixed working day. If a bus or lorry can complete more journeys when travelling speeds are increased, then the productivity of the vehicle and driver are increased and output will grow. The effect is the same as where a transport time saving can be used productively by the firm, but in the case of the bus or lorry driver there will be no alteration in the type of work undertaken. The value of the time savings of goods vehicles is discussed more fully in section 4.

Changes in output may be the most important result of work time savings but if we are concerned with their total effect on welfare then the reactions of the workers involved must also be taken into account. When the length of the working day remains constant and the time saving is used to increase output, then the worker may prefer his work activity to travelling or vice versa. In the absence of research in this area it is impossible to say whether (discounting any earnings effects) the average worker would prefer to spend longer in work travel and less time at his main job or more time at work and less time travelling. Individual reactions would no doubt vary widely in very different circumstances. An overworked schoolteacher teaching at two separated parts of a school might welcome the journey between them and be sorry if the travelling time was shortened. But an electrician carrying out repairs at several sites might dislike constant delays in traffic and be glad to spend more time at his trade. It can be assumed that workers would normally gain more utility from allocating time to a non-paid-work activity than they would from using it in work travel. In the transport worker's case, where more journeys were possible in a given time, the worker would continue with the same work activity and should experience little change in utility.

This discussion has dealt with only three possible situations and several others could be found, as, for example, where self-employed people or executives whose remuneration does not vary directly with the hours worked use travel time savings to shorten their working day. There are forms of travel, such as long-distance rail journeys, where it is possible to undertake some types of work activity. It has been shown that work travel savings are by no means homogeneous, and that wage rates or earnings do not always give an accurate guide to the money value of the time savings. The kind of work undertaken by those who have to do much work travel is often of a kind where it is difficult to measure the productivity of short extra periods spent at work.

3. COMMUTER AND 'PURE LEISURE' TIME SAVINGS

The journey to and from work is one of the most important forms of travel. In the 1975/6 *National Travel Survey* (Department of Transport, 1979a) commuting accounted for 23.0 per cent of all mileage undertaken by travellers in the sample. This was the most important journey purpose, the next major category, 'other personal travel', accounting for 21.0 per cent of mileage. In the Multi-national Project survey of time budgets, the average times spent travelling to and from work ranged from 38 minutes in Jackson, USA to 89 minutes in Lima–Callao, Peru (Szalai, 1972). (See chapter 6 for details of this survey; the figures do not agree with those in table 6.7 which are averages for all those in the sample, including non-commuters.)

If people are persuaded by the promise of wages to exchange leisure time for paid work, and if the marginal wage rate is equal to the marginal value of leisure, then it might seem that the value of a small increase in leisure time caused by a reduction in commuting time should be closely related to the marginal wage rate. But this is not the case. The difference in utility between work and leisure is not necessarily the same as that between time devoted to the journey to work and time used for some leisure or non-paid-work activity. But there is a more important difference between the value of commuter time savings and marginal wage rates, which follows from the, usually unstated, value judgement that is used as the basis of valuation.

If a worker agrees to work an hour's overtime then he will produce a product for his employer and receive a payment as a form of compensation (even if he obtains positive utility from the work activity). But a commuter whose journey to work is made quicker receives all the benefit himself and the value of the time saved is notionally based on what he would be willing to pay to be able to transfer time to some other preferred activity. But there are other possible cases for evaluation. Society might decide that it was the duty of the state to provide the best possible transport infrastructure and services and that workers should be compensated if they are delayed when travelling to or from work. In these perhaps unlikely circumstances, marginal wage rates, less the marginal utility of the work activity, might be an appropriate basis for valuing commuter time savings.

On the normal assumption that the commuter, who benefits from time savings made on his journeys between his home and work, should pay for them, the value of the savings is likely to be below marginal wage rates. Each commuter can, in theory, be seen as trading the money cost of his journey to work against reductions in journey time. Many factors will affect each individual commuter's evaluation of the amount of utility that he will gain if he is able to transfer time from his commuting journey to some preferred activity. A great deal of the literature on transport time-saving evaluation deals with attempts to measure these values and to find some reasonably acceptable averages that can be used for investment appraisal and in aiding planning decisions. Various models have been constructed to explain user's choice of transport and to link this with time-saving values. As there is no theoretical basis for using any single proxy to represent the value of commuter time savings, values have been commonly based on empirical evidence.

The most common approach to attempts to measure commuting (and other non-work) time-savings values has been to find out what travellers were willing to pay for faster travel in situations of choice. Beesley was a pioneer of this approach in Britain and worked out some of the basic methodology in his account (1965) of the choices made by civil servants travelling to the former Ministry of Transport offices in London. Subsequent research has shown that, as might have been expected, the utility of travel time varies with the mode of transport. In Britain, travellers appear to prefer car travel to rail travel and to obtain more utility from rail travel than bus travel. All other things being the same, a saving in car travel time would therefore be valued less than a saving in rail travelling time, which would in turn have a lower value than a similar reduction in bus journey times. Empirical evidence also suggests that people travelling by public transport value reductions in the time involved in walking to a bus stop and in waiting for a bus at a higher rate than that applied to reductions in in-vehicle time. This is also presumably likely to apply to walking and waiting and in-vehicle time for rail travellers. There may well be other differences in the valuation of commuter-travel time savings (and of other travel time savings) that have not yet been revealed by the empirical evidence. A ten-mile car journey that took thirty minutes driving at a steady 20 mph might be preferred to a journey of the same length where the average driving speed was 30 mph but that also involved a ten-minute wait in a traffic jam. Similarly, a slightly slower continuous train speed may be preferred to a journey taking the same overall time where the train travels faster but is also stopped by signals. Travel-time utilities will vary not only between modes but also within modes as comfort and travelling conditions vary. The utility of commuter travelling time is often reduced by the overcrowding of public transport that may occur at peak travel times.

Empirical evidence on commuter and on other non-work travel time savings has mainly related to these differences in travel-time utilities and there has been little consideration of the part of the total value of these savings that comes from the alternative activity for which the savings can be used. Reductions in travel-to-work times will only have any value if there is some alternative activity available that is more attractive then travelling. A man who had nothing but unpleasant chores waiting for him at home or a lonely person without any leisure-time interests might even put a negative value on a reduction in commuting time. But the main concern in estimating commuting time-saving values is whether there are large groups of people having different average values. Probably the only grouping relating to the alternative use of the time savings that could be considered in actual investment appraisal is that which depends upon income. The value of commuter (and other non-work) travel time savings is obviously likely to be associated with income when a willingness-to-pay measurement is used. Even if the gain in utility from being able to transfer ten minutes from commuting to playing with his children is the same for both Mr Richman and Mr Poorman, the rich man may be willing to pay more money to make the transfer possible, since the alternative use for the money may yield less utility to him. But it may also be the case that Mr Richman's command of extra market goods raises the utility of his alternative use of the ten minutes above that obtained by Mr Poorman.

A particular feature of commuting time savings is that they occur on days when the 'stock' of time available for non-paid-work activities is relatively small. Time savings cannot be transferred from one day to another but must normally be consumed when they are made. The exact time when some new 'free' time becomes available can be varied by rearranging other non-paid-work activities, but it would be impracticable to move free time from a holiday or a weekend to a working day. Since work will consume about eight hours of a working day and other non-paid activities must also be undertaken, time that can be freely allocated to preferred activities will be relatively scarce and its marginal utility is likely to be higher than that of travel time savings made on non-working days. This argument applies not only to commuter travel but also to time savings in travel for other purposes on working days. It is apparent, however, that commuting time savings are likely to be much the most important and regular source of freely allocable time on working days. Some of the time-saving values found in surveys relating both to commuter and other non-work-time travel, all recalculated to 1968 prices, are shown in Table 5.1.

As well as 'willingness-to-pay'-based studies, some research on travel time-saving values has been carried out with measurements based on variations in house prices. It seems reasonable to assume that people take the time and money costs of travelling to their workplace into consideration when deciding where to live and that the consequent variation in the demand for houses in different areas should be reflected in house prices (if many other variables remain constant). People can afford to pay more for their houses when the money costs of travelling to work fall, and vice versa. Workers may therefore trade off travel costs against house prices. A study made by Wabe (1971) of house prices and the value of travelling time in the Greater London Council area produced an estimate that a one-minute reduction in travel time to Central London added £20–38 (1968 prices) to the price of a house. The estimated value of journey-time saved (or a reduction in the equivalent distance from the centre) was 62.25p per hour. The figures relate to travel by rail (British Rail and the underground services).

One theory that has been put forward about commuter behaviour is that people have a constant or stable time budget that they are prepared to use for the journey to and from work. This would suggest that, as travel facilities improve and speeds are increased,

TABLE 5.1
Commuter and other non-work time-saving values (1968 UK prices)

Name of survey and locations	Year of data collection	Travel mode	Value of time savings per hour per person
Quarmby:			
Leeds, UK	1966	Car/Bus	7–25
Beesley:			
London, UK	1963	Public transport	12–19
		Car	12–25
LGORU:	1967/8	Average of bus, train, car	43
Leeds, UK			22
Leicester, UK			84
Liverpool, UK			39
Manchester, UK			32
Lee and Dalvi	1966	Car	66
		Public transport	40
Edinburgh Study	1969	Rail	41
		Car	59
Solent Travel	1970	Hydrofoil	34
Study		Hovercraft	39
Dawson and Everall:	1969	Small car	26
Italy		Medium car	53
		Large car	119
Hensher and Hotchkiss:			
Sydney, Australia		Ferry	17

Source: Jennings and Sharp (1976).

people choose to live further from their work. The theory receives a certain amount of empirical support from the Multinational Project data. Workers in some of the more affluent countries, with faster transport facilities such as cars and electric trains at their disposal, spent nearly as long travelling to work as did those in countries where walking or cycling is more common. The average commuting time (averaged over a seven-day week) for all locations in the Multinational Project was 28.9 minutes, with a standard deviation of 7.9 minutes. The range was from 16 minutes in Osnabrück, West Germany, to 41 minutes in Kazanlik, Bulgaria, and in Györ and district, Hungary (Szalai, 1972).

In theory it is likely that there will be fairly rigid limits to the time that people will be prepared to spend commuting, as the marginal utility of residual leisure time increases, but within that constraint there is no reason why there should not be considerable variation with individual choice and circumstances. People working in the centres of large conurbations may be compelled to travel a long way to work unless they are either able to buy very scarce and expensive inner-city housing accommodation or are prepared to live in uncongenial inner-city suburbs. Those working in smaller isolated towns can usually enjoy much shorter work journeys whether their preference is for living in a suburban or a rural locality. The main element of truth in the 'constant commuter travel time' hypothesis seems to be that people have often chosen to lengthen their work journey rather than to enjoy shorter travelling times when any improvement in transport facilities has made it possible to achieve faster journey times. Research by Warnes (1972) suggested that the average distance of commuting journeys in North West England increased by 0.9 per cent per year during the period 1921–66. An estimate by Beesley and Dalvi, quoted by Warnes, indicated that commuting distances for male workers in Britain had grown by 1.1 per cent per year between 1951 and 1961 (cited by Das, 1978). Table 5.2 shows the distribution of journey-to-work times for the *National Travel Survey* samples in Great Britain in 1972/3 and in 1975/6. These figures show that there was some variation in

TABLE 5.2
Commuting journey times, GB, 1972/3 and 1975/6

Time (minutes)	No. in sample 1972/3	No. in sample 1975/6	% 1972/3	% 1975/6
Less than 15	3700	5124	36.9	38.1
15 and less than 30	3550	5098	35.4	37.9
30 ” ” ” 45	1645	2085	16.4	15.5
45 ” ” ” 60	601	632	6.0	4.7
60 ” ” ” 90	421	417	4.2	3.1
90 ” ” ” 120	70	67	0.7	0.5
120 and over	30	27	0.3	0.2
Total	10,017	13,450	99.9	100.0

Source: Department of the Environment (1976); Department of Transport (1979a).

commuting times although about 90 per cent of commuters in the samples did not spend more than forty-five minutes on their journeys to and from work. The evidence suggests that there was some reversal of the trend towards longer commuting times. In 1972/3, 11.2 per cent of the sample spent forty-five minutes or more commuting, while in 1975/6 this figure had fallen to 8.5 per cent. A chi-squared test was carried out on the assumption that the two surveys could be treated as random samples, and it was shown that the calculated χ^2 value was 57.4, so that the association between the sample data and the distribution of journey times was significant at the .05 level ($\chi^2_{.05}$ 6d.f. = 12.6).

Apart from the suggestion that people allocate a fairly fixed amount of time to commuting, there is a more general hypothesis that states that individuals have a fixed time budget for all travel purposes. The accuracy of this hypothesis is of some practical importance as some models used to predict the demand for transport have assumed that individuals have a stable travel time budget. There are no very convincing theoretical arguments that support the fixed travel time budget hypothesis, apart from the possibility, already noted, that people's commuter-travel time budget may be relatively stable in relation to technological change. This may also apply to general travel time. Individuals may make longer or more frequent 'pure' leisure-time journeys, keeping total travelling time relatively constant, when average journey speeds are increased. Work on the effect of road improvement or new road building has shown that some new traffic flows are usually generated by the improved facilities. There is, however, no theoretical reason why the time allocated to travelling should not be affected by such factors as changes in the cost of transport or in income levels.

The Multinational Project figures show a smaller variation for total travel time (average time = 70.7 minutes, standard deviation = 14.1 minutes) than for commuter travel time (average time = 28.9 minutes, standard deviation = 7.9 minutes) but this would be expected with greater aggregation. The range for total travel time, from 39 minutes in 100 districts in West Germany to 90 minutes in Callao, Peru, was quite considerable (Szalai, 1972). In *Expenditure of Time and Money on Travel* (1979), Tanner argues that there is no theoretical reason why either the time or money budgets allocated to transport should remain constant. His analysis of time-series data showed that both the time and money spent on travel in Britain increased between 1953 and 1979. Tanner was also able to make use of *National Travel Survey* data classified by household income groups and residential density. An analysis of this data showed that the time spent travelling increased with income but did not vary consistently with residential density. The *National Travel Survey* data are reproduced in Table 5.3. These figures show that the time spent travelling by car increased with income, over the whole income range, for people in the 1975/6 *National Travel Survey*. This increase in travelling time was not offset by any fall in

TABLE 5.3
Travel time and income, GB, 1975/6

| Household income £ per year | Travel time, minutes per person per day | | | |
	Public transport	Private transport	Walk/ cycle	All modes
0–749	8	6	20	34
750–1249	7	9	22	38
1250–1499	6	11	22	38
1500–1999	7	14	24	45
2000–2499	7	17	28	51
2500–2999	5	21	22	48
3000–3999	6	24	22	52
4000–4999	7	28	21	55
5000–5999	8	30	21	59
6000–7499	8	33	23	64
7500 and over	7	41	22	70
All	7	23	22	53

Source: Department of Transport (1979a); contained in Tanner (1979).

the time spent travelling by public transport, or walking and cycling, so that total travel time also increased with income. (These findings should, perhaps, be compared with those based on time-series data that have shown that the demand for bus public transport tends to decline with an increase in car ownership.) Linear regression equations were estimated for the private transport and 'all mode' data. The equation for the regression of daily travel time on income for private transport was

$$Y = 7.98 + 0.00369X$$

while that for 'all modes' was

$$Y = 36.92 + 0.00373X$$

where Y represents daily travel in minutes and X is household income.

It would require considerably more research to be able to explain fully this relationship between income and time spent travelling in Britain. If travelling was exclusively a means to an end, part of the 'package' of activities that must be undertaken in order to enjoy a preferred activity such as swimming or eating out, and if the only change was a reduction in journey times caused by the greater availability of private transport, then it might be expected that more time would be allocated to the preferred activity itself. As was shown in DeSerpa's theoretical analysis, a relaxation of the minimum travel time required to take part in an activity would enable this time to be used elsewhere. But it is unlikely that a reduction in existing travel times would be sufficiently large to enable a consumer to undertake some new activity that itself required a travel-time input. If the only effect of an increase in income was to allow an individual to buy faster travel to the locations for existing work and leisure activities then the probability that he would increase his total travelling time would be low.

There are several possible explanations of the apparent positive association between travelling time and income in Britain. The possession of a car is likely to have an important influence on time allocation. Although the fall in journey times for existing activities may be relatively small, the journey-time input required for potential new activities may be reduced very considerably. Visits to friends or to the countryside, which might require an impossibly large time input if public transport was used, may now become possible. But this would suggest a stepped relationship between income and total travelling time, with a proportionately large increase in travelling time when a family can afford to run a car and, perhaps, another step for those households that move from the one- to the two-car level. Further increases in total travel time may result if a growth in income enables a household to use a car more fully although, even with inflated fuel prices, the short-run marginal cost of car operation is low. The money marginal costs of car travel, for a car averaging 30 miles per gallon, would be currently below the cost of much bus or rail travel even with a 1.0 car occupancy rate. (The cost of travel on a well-used, relatively low-priced bus route in Leicester in 1980 was about 6.8p per mile. Fuel costs for a car consuming 0.033 gallons of petrol per mile at a price of 150p per gallon would be 5.0p per mile.) It may also be the case that an increasing income encourages people to undertake new activities, requiring market good inputs that they could not previously afford, and also demanding some travel-time input. Finally, the assumption that travel time has a low utility and is a kind of 'inferior good' activity that richer people will replace by some preferred use of time when they can afford to buy quicker methods of transport, may not always be true. Some people may regard travel as an end in itself, so that it is equivalent to a normal good, and they will thus tend to increase their purchases when their income grows.

There are, however, undoubtedly many circumstances in which travel is regarded as what may be described as an 'inferior activity' and when an increase in income will result in the partial substitution of some preferred activity (such as spending longer at home before starting a commuter journey) at the cost of buying a quicker but dearer form of transport. Most empirical work on time-savings values shows that there is a strong positive association with income levels. The *National Travel Survey* statistics may only reflect the relationship between travel time and income over specific income ranges. The Multinational Project results show the lowest average travel time allocation in one of the richest locations (West Germany) and the highest allocation in what was probably the poorest location (Peru). The special effect of car ownership may disappear at very high income levels. Models used for forecasting car ownership make use of the empirically observed phenomenon of a 'saturation level' of cars per household or per person beyond which car ownership is unlikely to grow. Current estimates of the saturation level for Britain range from 0.4 to 0.6 cars per person.

In his study of the constant travel time budget hypothesis, Goodwin (1978) concluded that the assumption of a stable travel time budget should not be used as a modelling tool. The degree of stability that is found to exist, Goodwin argued, may result from 'a balancing out of counteracting forces' (p. 374) including such variables as different costs and incomes. Goodwin also put forward as an alternative hypothesis the argument that the total time allocated to travel will increase as time or money costs fall, or as incomes increase, but subject to the constraint of a maximum acceptable allocation of about ninety minutes (on average) per day.

There are several categories of non-work, non-commuting travel time. The relative importance of the main categories is shown in Table 5.4. It is likely that there are some considerable differences between the average travel time-savings values for travellers in these different journey purpose categories. Education travel or travel to school or college and 'escort' travel (mainly the carriage of schoolchildren by parents), which will normally cover the same route each day, may yield very little utility so that the value of being able to transfer some travel time to an alternative use would be relatively high. The position of these travellers is similar to that of commuters. 'Shopping and personal business' journey time (which includes travel to hairdressers, banks, libraries, meetings and church services) may also have a relatively low utility and high time-savings value. Trips to restaurants, to visit friends and to watch sport or to be

TABLE 5.4
Purposes and importance of non-work travel, all transport modes, GB, 1975/6

Journey purpose	% of journeys	% of mileage
Education	10	4
Shopping and personal business	28	16
Eating and drinking	3	2
Social	15	18
Entertainment and watching sport	4	4
Day trips and sport participation	7	10
Holidays	1	10
Escort and other	5	4
All purposes except journeys to and from and in course of work	73	68

Source: Department of Transport (1979a).

entertained may, on average, be regarded as more pleasurable, especially as they are more likely to be made in the company of other people. The average car occupancy for 'eating and drinking' trips according to the 1975/6 Survey was 1.99, while that for 'entertainment and watching sport' was 2.30. The two main parts of the composite category 'day trips and sport participation' might be expected to have different average time-savings values. Travel to and from active sporting activities is a necessary part of the total package of time that must be allocated to this form of recreation and it is likely that a reduction in the required journey time would be welcomed and given some positive value. Pure pleasure trips, however, may be an end in themselves. Where travel itself is the chosen activity (as, for example, on a Sunday afternoon 'run into the country') and where there would be no gains to be obtained from the ability to transfer some of this time to an alternative activity, travel time savings could have zero or even negative value. But negative time-savings values are, perhaps, unlikely, since people travelling by private transport need not increase the speed of their vehicle even when the opportunity for faster travel is provided. It is difficult to generalise about holiday travel. Some people may plan their holiday journeys as part of the holiday, and regard them as a pleasurable activity. But most holiday travellers would probably put a high money value on time savings made on long, congested holiday trips.

The amount of time allocated to travelling depends on a complex interaction between free choice and necessity. One important influence on the travel-time choices that are available is the decision by individuals about where they will live. This decision will itself be influenced by attitudes towards travelling time. In Alonso's model attempting to explain residential location (Alonso, 1964) he assumes that households spend their income on a house (or the land on which it can be built), on commuting and on all other goods. Commuting costs consist of both money costs and time costs, and, all other things being the same, house prices might be expected to fall as generalised travelling cost to a central business district increases. But in the real world many complicating factors may confuse the relationship between house prices and generalised commuting costs. Even where a central business district does attract large numbers of workers, there may also be other important centres of employment that are not situated in city centres. Modern industrial development has largely taken place in areas on the fringe of dense city development. Many inner-city areas, from which it would be possible to commute to the central business district at low money and time costs, offer a very poor environment. The growth of large towns and conurbations in Britain has often produced a situation in which inner-city industrial workers must travel further out to reach factories while central business district workers live in outer suburbs and travel through the industrial belt and the inner city to their workplace. Thus in Birmingham, people living in the inner-city suburbs of Aston, Lozells or Washwood Heath may work at local factories or travel away from the city centre to the Tyburn/Gravelly Hill and Witton/Perry Bar industrial areas while many central business district workers travel from Sutton Coldfield or places even further from the centre of the conurbation. A more efficient residential pattern (in terms of minimising journey-to-work times) may emerge as industrial workers demand an improved residential environment and as inner-city areas are rehabilitated. There is some evidence that house prices in conurbations are influenced by the availability of quick public transport facilities, such as a commuter rail link, and thus reflect the time costs of commuter travel.

Even if a family was to choose where to live by following the single objective of minimising the travel time of the whole household, it might find that quite complicated calculations were necessary.

A site that minimised commuting time might very well involve long journeys to school and for shopping, recreation and social life. If the previous arguments of this chapter about the different levels of utility obtained from travelling for different purposes are correct, then it would be necessary to attach different weights to the time costs of travel for each main purpose, and to those of journeys made by different modes.

The figures in Table 5.5 give an analysis of *National Travel Survey* data according to journey purpose and the type of area in which respondents lived. The general picture given by these figures is that

TABLE 5.5
Average journey times (minutes) for different purposes by type of area, GB, 1975/6

Journey purpose	London	Provincial conurbations	Towns over 100,000 population	Towns 3,000– 25,000	Rural areas	All
			Area			
To and from work	29	22	21	19	20	21
In course of work	37	48	33	37	34	36
Education	20	17	16	17	19	17
Shopping and personal business	19	16	16	16	17	17
Eating and drinking	18	14	16	14	16	15
Social	29	23	22	19	23	22
Entertainment and watching sport	29	23	21	16	21	22
Day trips and sport participation	35	38	32	30	31	32
Holidays	81	84	71	69	79	75
Escort and other	15	15	14	13	16	15
All purposes	25.4	21.4	20.4	19.4	21.7	21.0

Source: Department of Transport (1979a).

average journey times for most purposes were longer in London and the provincial conurbations than they were in small towns and rural areas. People living in towns with a population between 3,000 and 25,000 had the lowest average journey times for all purposes except journeys made during the course of work and journeys to places of education. People living in London had the longest average journey

Time and Transport

times for all purposes except 'journeys made during the course of work', 'day trips and sport participation', 'holidays' and 'escort and other'. In each of these cases the longest average journey times were enjoyed (or suffered) by people living in provincial conurbations, except for escort journeys, which were longest in rural areas. These data are highly aggregated and it is not easy to explain some of the differences. It is perhaps surprising that even 'shopping and personal business trips' were on average slightly longer (in time) for Londoners than they were for people living in country areas. There must, of course, be many inhabitants of conurbations who are closer to banks and shops than are country dwellers, but there must also be many residential areas, such as large estates in big cities, that are not very near to shopping areas or other amenities. The Survey figures relate to journey times and it may be that people in rural areas and small towns can make faster journeys either because they are more likely to use private transport or because roads are less congested. People who live in the country but work in towns will, of course, have longer journeys to work than town-dwellers, but this is presumably offset in the calculation of average figures by the number of people who are able to make short journeys to local farms and other rural workplaces. Different comparisons might result if separate averages were calculated for 'commuter belt' country and for wholly agricultural areas.

4. SOME PROBLEMS OF TRANSPORT TIME-SAVINGS VALUES AND INVESTMENT APPRAISAL

As has already been argued, the main benefit produced by investments in transport services is usually a reduction in journey times. Except in the case of the development of previously untapped mineral resources or the provision of roads for new housing estates it is very unusual for transport investment in a developed country to make transportation possible for the first time. In the average trunk road investment appraisal in Britain, carried out according to the techniques developed by the Departments of Transport and of the Environment, 80 per cent of the benefits represents the value of time savings and 20 per cent consists of the estimated value of reducing accident rates.

The Departments of Transport and of the Environment have estimated a number of time-savings values that they use themselves in the assessment of motorway and trunk road investment projects and that can be used for evaluating local authority road and other transport investment projects. The time-savings values of people travelling during the course of their working day (this category includes both businessmen travelling to meetings and bus and lorry drivers) are valued according to average earnings plus National Insurance and pension contributions and an allowance for those overhead costs of employers that vary directly with the hours of labour employed. Information supplied to the Leitch Committee on Trunk Road Assessment (1978) suggested that these additions amounted to 31.3 per cent of gross wages. This valuation of working time is based on the assumption that a reduction in 'work' journey times would enable the time saved to be used productively and that the grossed-up earnings is the best available measure of the value of the increased production. Average values are estimated for passengers and drivers in each type of vehicle (and also for rail and underground travellers) using national figures. Thus the same values are assumed for both high- and low-wage areas. Travel for all other journey purposes is described as non-working time and two standard time values are used for travellers in all types of vehicle. These are 'in-vehicle' and 'waiting' time. The values are based on empirical evidence that suggests that the average willingness-to-pay value placed on non-work time savings amounts to approximately 25 per cent of average wage rates. It was decided by the Ministry of Transport that, as a matter of policy, a standard 'equity' time value should be applied to the non-work time savings of all citizens. The time values are increased annually in proportion to growth in the gross domestic product. The 'official' time values, in 1979 prices, are shown in Table 5.6.

These time-savings values are based on a number of different, and sometimes conflicting, assumptions about the appropriate basis for valuation. The working-time-savings values relate to the benefits received by the employer (or to the increase in money income that a self-employed worker might be expected to receive if he could use a travelling time saving for productive work activity). The interests of the worker, who might prefer travelling to being at work, are ignored. Thus the valuation is not based on willingness-to-pay measurements, although it is likely that there would be a high degree of correlation between these and earnings-based values since willingness to pay for travel time savings is usually strongly influenced by income. The effect of using the 'official' values would be to attach high estimates to the value of benefits on roads with a high proportion of cars containing drivers and passengers travelling during the course of work. This consequence does not follow in

Time and Transport

TABLE 5.6
Time-savings values estimated by the
Departments of Transport and of
the Environment (1979 prices)

	Value (p. per hour)
Working time	
All workers	393.4
Car drivers	411.2
Car passengers	328.8
Bus passengers	272.9
Rail passengers	440.4
Underground passengers	400.0
Bus drivers	276.8
Bus conductors	270.6
HGV occupants	300.0
LGV occupants	258.4
Non-working time	
In-vehicle time	55.4
Walking and waiting time	110.8

Note: The non-working-time values are 'resource' values adjusted to allow for the
influence of indirect taxes and subsidies.
Source: Department of Transport (1980).

practice, however, as national average percentages of working- and non-working-time travellers are assumed to apply to all roads and no attempt is made to measure the actual proportion of people travelling 'during the course of work' on the routes being considered for new investment. In some cases national average traffic composition figures are also used, a procedure that means that investment decisions will be mainly determined by the size of the total traffic flow, all vehicles counting equally. In their report, the Leitch Committee (1978) recommend that those using the COBA road investment appraisal computer programme should be allowed to vary the assumed national proportion of working to non-working people in cars. The Report cites evidence from the Birmingham area that some traffic flows have been observed to contain up to 50 per cent of 'working cars' instead of the national average figure of 17 per cent. The sensitivity tests carried out for the Committee showed, as might be expected, that a change in the work/non-work proportions from 17:83 to 30:70 would have a significant effect on the ranking of the benefits received from alternative road-investment schemes. If a willingness-to-pay measurement of transport time-savings values was adopted, and if surveys were made on the routes being considered for investment, then it is likely that investment in roads in high-income areas, like the South East of England, would yield a relatively high rate of return.

The use of standard 'equity' values for non-work time savings is presumably based on the value judgement that increments of time 'saved' from non-work travel should be given the same value for all people, irrespective of their incomes. All people have only twenty-four hours to 'spend' each day of their lives, and for most people many of these hours are committed to working, sleeping, travelling to work and other essential activities. Therefore, it can be argued, the freedom to reallocate some time to a preferred activity should be regarded as being of the same value, on average, for all people. The amount of pleasure that can be obtained from being able to transfer ten minutes from travelling to carrying out activities at home may be unrelated to income levels. On the other hand, it can be argued that unacceptable income inequalities can be corrected through the tax system, and that there is no particular reason why rich people should be denied the right to 'buy' quick transport in the same way as they can buy high-quality food or large houses. The supply of market goods available to people with large incomes may mean that they obtain a high marginal utility from increments of freely allocable time. High earnings may result from working for long hours so that time savings have a high money value.

The Leitch Committee recommended that the use of equity non-work time-savings values should be abandoned. This recommendation was linked with the proposal that separate values should be attached to commuting and to other non-work or 'pure' leisure travel time savings. The Committee believed that the use of a single equity value for all non-work time savings is 'inconsistent with the general philosophy of cost benefit analysis' and that it is absurd that 'high income car commuters, say on the M4 into London or in the neighbourhood of Birmingham, should be attributed the same time saving values as holiday makers in the country' (1978, p. 102). The Committee believed that commuting time-saving values are closely linked to earnings levels, whereas pure leisure values would have to be found from further research on the behaviour of travellers. Although the 1978 *Highway Economics Note* still gave a single value of non-working time for all travel modes, it stated that 'the Department no longer adheres to the principle of equity value of non-working time. Where local income distribution differs from the national average, and where sufficiently reliable data about the incomes of travellers exist, appropriate values may be adopted' (Department of Transport, 1978, para. 4). However, the 1980 revision of *Highway Economics Note* still contains only one value for in-vehicle non-working time and states that this reflects 'the Department's continued adherence to the equity principle' (Department of Transport, 1980).

If higher values were allocated to the time savings of commuters but the weighted average of commuter and pure-leisure time-savings values was kept constant (and equal to the present value given to all in-vehicle non-work time savings) then the average yield from road investment would not change. At present, a standard travel-purpose composition is assumed for all roads (for cars it is assumed that 16.7 per cent of all mileage represents work journeys and that the remaining 83.3 per cent covers all other non-work activities). The use of separate time values for commuter traffic would not affect the ranking of investment projects unless figures of the actual commuter traffic on different roads were available. Presumably if the actual commuter traffic percentage figures were used then the use of national average work-travel percentages would also be abandoned. The obvious effect of these changes would be that roads carrying large commuter or work flows of traffic would show a higher rate of return and thus attract a larger share of investment capital.

The Leitch Committee's belief that commuting time values are close to the values of working time suggests, however, that the present empirically determined average values used for all non-working time savings are too low. If the value of commuting time savings was assumed to be 227p per hour in 1976 prices (75 per cent of the 1976 car driver time-saving values adjusted to remove overheads) and the 1975/6 average travel-purpose figures for car drivers and passengers are used (65.4 per cent pure leisure, 34.5 per cent commuting), then pure-leisure time savings would have to be given a negative value of −64.6p per hour if the weighted average value was to be kept constant at 36p per hour. If pure-leisure time-saving values were to remain at about the same level as the present figure for all non-work savings, but much higher values were used for commuting time, then, of course, the rate of return shown by all road investment would increase. If actual travel-purpose data were used, investment would be diverted from holiday routes towards urban roads carrying heavy flows of commuter traffic. New lanes might be added to the London end of the M4 motorway while nothing was done to remove the summer traffic jams around Indian Queens in Cornwall. But the use of substantially increased commuter time-saving values without a corresponding downward adjustment of pure leisure values would also mean that investment would be directed towards roads with a high proportion of car traffic rather than to those routes with heavy flows of lorries. The Department of Transport time-saving values per vehicle (using resource values where applicable), in 1976 prices, were:

'Average' cars	131.3p per hour
'Working' cars	418.8p per hour
Heavy goods vehicles	213.6p per hour
Bus (PSV)	898.8p per hour

The ratio of vehicle time values, taking an 'average' car as 1, was therefore 1:3.190:1.627:6.845 ('average' car; 'working' car; goods vehicle; bus). If a commuter's time was valued at 75 per cent of working time, and the proportion of commuters in each type of vehicle was assumed to be equal to those found in the 1975/6 *National Travel Survey*, then the ratio for 'average' car, 'working' car, heavy goods vehicle, public services vehicle and 'commuting' car would become 1:1.995:0.997:6.683:1.685. It was assumed that the 'average' car would contain 28.4 per cent of commuters, but the Department of Transport figure of 17.8 per cent work travellers was retained. (The 1975/6 *National Travel Survey* showed that 23.2 per cent of car mileage was for work purposes.) The 'average' car value was thus:

$$(.178 \times 418.8) + (.284 \times 361) + (.538 \times 69.1) = 214.2$$

The *National Travel Survey* estimate of 30.1 per cent of bus travel stages being 'to and from work' was used with the Department of Transport assumption of an average load of 15.8 passengers. Average bus time was thus:

Driver and conductor	=	191.0p
Working passengers	=	58.8p
Commuting passengers	=	705.6p
Other passengers	=	385.2p
Total		1431.6p per hour

The 'average' car, 'working' car, goods vehicle and bus ratio, using the revised 1979 figures, was 1:2.88:2.16:7.03.

The treatment of the time savings of goods vehicles in road-investment appraisal in Britain is not entirely satisfactory. At present the benefits measured are the earnings of drivers and other occupants and changes in vehicle operating costs. Although the Department of Transport has developed a formula for measuring the effect of increased speeds on operating costs, including capital costs, its adequacy may be questioned. The formula used for measuring operating costs for heavy goods vehicles (1979 prices), where C is vehicle operating costs in pence per kilometre and V is speed in km per hour, is

$$C = 14.76 + \frac{82.26}{V} + 0.000227V^2 .$$

This formula assumes that, except at very low speeds, most of the cost of operating vehicles does not vary with time and that some part of fuel and maintenance costs increases with speed. Speed increases can yield either positive or negative benefits, and the average net influence of this item in road investment appraisal is zero. Suppose that on a haul of 200 km the journey speed was increased from 40 km/hr to 50 km/hr and then to 66.6 km/hr, giving two successive time savings of one hour. The first hour saved would be valued (for its effect on vehicle operating costs only) at 41.4 pence and the second hour at −5.8 pence. In some cases even a small time saving may bring a large cost saving or a significant increase in vehicle availability. A time saving that just enabled a lorry to return home to base instead of staying away overnight would not only bring about a significant increase in vehicle availability but would also save the cost of overnight maintenance for the driver. The reduction of maximum driving hours from ten to eight in accordance with the EEC directive will alter the point at which this cost discontinuity occurs and will also tend to produce more journeys where time savings will have a high value. It is difficult to believe that the savings in vehicle occupants' wages (valued at 178p per hour in 1976 prices for heavy goods vehicles) represents, on average, the only net benefit from reducing vehicle journey times.

A study of the allocation of goods traffic in the West Midlands (Sharp, 1970) showed that many firms were prepared to pay higher rates in order to enjoy speedier deliveries. In some cases, such as when goods are stored in a warehouse, slightly quicker deliveries may not benefit either the consignor or the consignee. But if stock-holding is reduced or if the consignor receives payment more quickly, then there will be benefits available. At an interest rate of 15 per cent, the charges on a consignment worth £10,000 amount to just over 17p per hour. Some consignments are of partly finished goods moving between factories, and the speeding-up of these flows of traffic is equivalent to an increase in productivity (in relation to time) inside one plant.

An approach that would allow for all the benefits of reducing the journey times of goods vehicles to be counted would be to measure the value of the extra work that could be performed as the result of a time saving, minus the marginal cost of the increased mileage. The situation is illustrated in Figure 5.1. In Figure 5.1

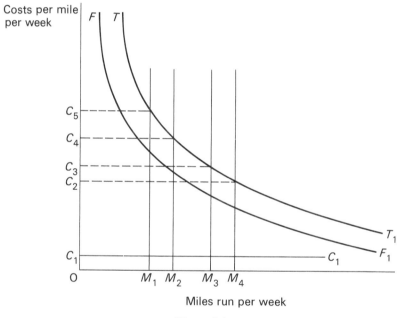

Figure 5.1
Fixed and marginal costs of vehicle operation

FF_1 represents the fixed costs of operating a lorry, C_1C_1 is marginal costs and TT_1 measures total cost. Suppose that before a road improvement OM_3 miles can be run each week. Drivers' hours regulations will in practice affect the use of vehicles and impose limits on achievable daily and weekly mileage. If road improvements cut journey times so that OM_4 miles could be run by a vehicle each week, then total costs per mile would fall from OC_3 to OC_2. Suppose that a reduction in permitted driving hours reduced the weekly mileage, before the road improvement, from M_3 to M_1. Then it is apparent that the same absolute reduction in journey time would bring a larger fall in costs (from OC_5 to OC_4) because of the increasing slopes of the fixed cost and total cost curves, which take the shape of a rectangular hyperbola. A constant percentage increase in speeds or fall in journey time would give a constant reduction in costs per week (or per day) as the smaller increase in mileage, at lower weekly mileages, is offset by the larger fall in costs per mile.

The gains from reducing the journey times of goods vehicles can be illustrated by using actual costing data. The figures in Table 5.7 are based on *Commercial Motor* estimates of vehicle operating costs in 1979. It is assumed that vehicles are driven for forty hours a week so that the average original speeds for vehicles running 1000 miles and 500 miles per week would be 25 mph and 12.5 mph respectively. The new speeds giving one hour's time saving for the different weekly mileages would be 25.64 mph and 12.82 mph. Weekly mileages could therefore be increased to 1025.64 and 512.82. The 'earnings per mile' figures represent the *Commerical Motor* recommended minimum charges per mile assuming weekly revenue-earning trips of 1000 and 500 miles. The figures include an allowance for general overhead expenses and for profits. But they may also be regarded as representing an estimate of the value of transport services to consumers. Although the figures are cost-based, it can be assumed that customers would be willing to pay at least these amounts for their goods to be carried; if this were not so the road haulage industry would become unprofitable and start to contract. Since no allowance is made for consumer surplus, the charges represent a minimum estimate of the value of the work done by goods transport. A reduction in journey times would make it possible to cover a greater distance without breaking the constraints of maximum drivers' hours. The extra running would involve some increase in variable costs, but if this marginal cost is deducted from total charges then the result is an estimate of the value of each additional mile of transport work completed. The same net benefit figure may be calculated from a general model. If the original average vehicle speed is s and the fixed drivers' hours per time period (assumed to be one week in this discussion) is x, then the total mileage per week is xs. If the new speed yielding one hour's time saving is s^1 this is given by

$$xs = s^1(x - 1)$$

TABLE 5.7

'Increased output' value of one hour's time savings for heavy goods vehicles (1979 prices)

Gross vehicle weight Tons	Total earnings per mile p	Running costs per mile p	Net value of increased output p	Estimated Department of Transport value of speed increases 1979 p
1000 miles per week base				
14.0	71.08	28.09	1102.31	413
16.5	73.57	28.82	1147.43	413
17.0	80.00	32.63	1214.61	413
22.5	84.04	34.25	1276.66	413
26.0	86.83	35.62	1313.08	413
32.0	106.13	41.97	1645.13	413
500 miles per week base				
14.0	102.83	28.09	958.17	440
16.5	106.81	28.82	999.83	440
17.0	114.31	32.63	1047.14	440
22.5	120.15	34.25	1101.24	440
26.0	123.77	35.62	1130.08	440
32.0	153.50	41.97	1429.81	440

and

$$s^1 = \frac{xs}{x-1}.$$

If the fixed cost per week is F, then at the slower speed the cost per mile, C_1, is

$$\frac{F}{xs} = C_1$$

and the cost when the average speed increases (C_2) is

$$\frac{F}{xs^1} = C_2.$$

The gain from the time saving of one hour is therefore

$$\text{Gain} = (C_1 - C_2)\, xs^1.$$

For a 14-ton vehicle originally running 1000 miles a week, with forty hours driving time and fixed costs of 42990 pence per week, the value of an hour's time saving is thus given by

$$\text{Gain} = (42.990 - 41.915251)\ 40 \times 25.641$$
$$= 1102.31\text{p}.$$

This is equivalent to the gains from running an extra 25.641 miles calculated by the method used in Table 5.7.

This analysis assumes that the increase in average speed does not impose any extra cost on the vehicle operators, apart from the marginal cost of running additional mileage. If the increase in speed over the previous mileage did involve extra fuel consumption, then a further deduction should be made from the gross benefit figure to allow for this factor. But for most vehicles fuel costs are greater than real marginal resource costs because of the large tax context. This tax may be considered to represent payment for the use of the road track. According to the Department of Transport estimates for 1979/80, the revenue from fuel tax and vehicle excise duty for all goods vehicles over 3.5 tonnes gross vehicle weight exceeded track costs by a ratio of 1.1:1 while the comparable ratio for vehicles under 3.5 tonnes GVW was 3.0:1 (Department of Transport, 1979b). 'True' marginal costs, however, represent only a part of track costs; the capital costs and some maintenance costs do not vary with mileage. For many vehicles the fuel tax payment may therefore exceed marginal road wear costs.

The report of the Leitch Committee (1978) made some references to the problem of the value of the time savings of goods vehicles. The report quotes, without comment, the opinion of the Department of Transport that the effect of any allowance for carrying loads more quickly would be insignificant. It was assumed by the Committee that the Department of Transport's operating cost formula adequately represents the 'capital saving' result of reduced journey times. The result of increasing the allowance for capital savings included in the operating costs formula by 30 per cent was then shown to have an insignificant effect on cost–benefit ratios. But this sensitivity test does not deal with the more basic criticism that the Department of Transport's formula is itself quite inadequate as a measurement (together with personal time savings) of the total resource costs of goods vehicles. The Leitch Committee research team also estimated the effect of doubling the value of time for goods vehicles on the net present value/cost ratios for a sample of road-investment projects. The average NPV/C ratio for the twenty-five sample schemes was 0.38 and it was calculated that doubling goods vehicle time values would increase average ratios by 0.287.

It is not clear why the report concludes that 'even if the Department's values for both vehicles and drivers were too low, no very serious bias would be introduced into the appraisal process' (Leitch Committee, 1978, p. 102). A serious undervaluation of the time savings of goods vehicles could alter the ranking of the NPV/cost ratios for alternative road schemes with different proportions of goods vehicle traffic. The report did, however, argue that 'we would expect, *a priori*, that there are indeed wider benefits that COBA does not adequately take into account'.

The figures in the last column of Table 5.7 show estimates of the value of time savings of one hour for heavy goods vehicles (now classified as 'other goods vehicles') following the Department of Transport method of calculation. The Department's 1976 prices figures were increased by 20 per cent a year (more than the actual rate of inflation as measured by the index of retail prices) to make them comparable with the 1979 *Commercial Motor* figures. The 'output' figures were between 2.5 and 3.9 times those based on the Department of Transport 'personal time-savings values plus changes in operating cost' technique. If the Department's operating cost formula is applied to vehicles running at 25 mph the figures show that 85.3 per cent of operating costs (excluding personal time savings) were assumed not to vary with reductions in journey times while 2.2 per cent of costs increased with vehicle speed. When occupants' time savings are included, the figures become:

	%
Not varying with journey time	54.0
Varying inversely with vehicle speed	44.6
Increasing with speed increases	1.4

If the time savings of goods vehicles was to be valued on the basis of what consumers would be willing to pay for the extra output that becomes available when journey times are shortened, then the question arises whether a similar measurement should be used for the time savings of cars and buses. The position of buses is in some ways comparable to that of lorries. The transport service they produce is sold in the market and drivers are subject to maximum driving hours regulations. The organisation of urban stage bus services may make it easier to use a second crew to extend daily mileage, but the hourly demand for passenger transport is more rigidly determined than is that for goods traffic. The gap between the Department of Transport's 'personal time-savings values plus changes in operating cost' valuation and a 'net value of extra output' measure is probably much smaller for buses than it is for lorries, however, and, as the estimates below show, the 'official' value may even be higher. This is because the 'official' bus time-saving values include the value of time savings for passengers as well as those representing the driver's and conductor's wages, whereas the lorry measurement ignores any benefits obtained from speeding the delivery of consignments. The 'official' value of an hour's time saving for a bus running 600 miles a week (with a speed increase from 24.135 to 24.754 km/hr), using 1979 prices for the personal time-saving component, would be approximately 1018 pence. The 'net value of output' measurement of an hour's time saving that made it possible to produce an extra 15.6 vehicle miles (25 km) of output from a bus (using the same crew) would be 980 pence. Stage buses are likely to have a lower weekly mileage than lorries (thus increasing the overhead cost per mile), but the effect of this would be offset by the smaller increase in mileage available from a given time saving.

There is no drivers' hours constraint affecting the use of private cars and they do not have any earning capacity. It will only be in relatively few cases that a journey time saving will be used to run extra miles in a car. The total stock of cars is unlikely to be reduced as a result of journey time reductions, whereas time savings that make it possible to obtain more output from buses and lorries will lead eventually to a reduction in required fleet size. (This resource saving for buses and lorries might be partially offset if the extra annual mileage involved adopting shorter replacement periods.) A personal time-savings value plus changes in operating cost measurement is thus satisfactory as an indicator of the value of reductions in car journey times.

The argument on lorry and bus time-saving values needs, perhaps, to be summarised. Regulation of drivers' hours means in practice that the use of many goods vehicles is also limited to a maximum number of hours per day. In these circumstances the value of a journey-time reduction is equivalent to the extra output obtainable from the vehicle (within the drivers' hours constraint) less the marginal cost of the extra mileage. The lower the drivers' hours limit (while the assumption that this also determines vehicle use holds), the higher will be the unit value of time savings. The Department of Transport vehicle operating cost formula, in which about 85 per cent of operating costs is not reduced when journey times fall, does not make adequate allowance for the value of extra lorry output (which would represent a real saving in resources when lorry fleet sizes were reduced). The difference between the 'official' time valuation per lorry and the 'extra output' valuation is considerable, the latter ranging from 250 per cent to 390 per cent of the Department's figures for the vehicles shown in Table 5.7.

In the discussion so far it has been assumed that the unit value of all time savings is the same irrespective of size. But this is a matter of dispute and Mishan (1970), Tipping (1968), Heggie (1976) and others have argued that small time savings have a lower value per minute. This contention is based both on theoretical considerations and on empirical evidence. A distinction needs to be made between work and non-work time. The main value of work time savings, even when allowance is made for the preferences of the worker himself, comes from the value of the work that can be performed with the extra time available at work. It is apparent that isolated very small time savings may not lead to any increase in output. A business executive may not be able to make a productive use of an extra two minutes in his office and it is very unlikely that a few minutes' time saving for a lorry driver or a commercial traveller could be used productively. On the other hand, it can be argued that if there is a minimum time saving that can be used productively then some workers may have already accumulated a lump of 'unproductive' time saving and that an additional saving may make the whole of this time productive. Suppose that savings of thirty minutes were worth 2p each but time savings of less than thirty minutes were valueless, and that existing travellers were randomly distributed between all the possible ranges of holdings of 'non-productive' savings (which it is assumed are not measured in units of less than one minute). Then an additional one-minute saving would be worth nothing to all the travellers with a 'stock' of less than twenty-nine minutes 'non-productive' saving, but all travellers with twenty-nine minutes' saving would value the extra minute's saving at 60p and the average value of the saving for all affected travellers would be 2p. The assumption of continuous small reductions in journey time is, however, somewhat unrealistic. The accumulation of a 'usable' lump of time savings would normally only be possible on long journeys. Savings made on different days cannot be accumulated. Routes used by commuters and other urban traffic seldom benefit from a number of separate small improvements. The 'accumulation' argument only seems to be applicable, therefore, to small improvements made on routes used predominantly by long-distance traffic. These are the routes that are much more likely to enjoy major improvements leading to large time savings.

There is a stronger case for believing that the unit value of time is constant for non-work time savings. Time saved from commuting journeys, for example, does not need to be used for any particular productive purpose in order to have value. Travellers might put the same unit value on time savings of a few minutes made on the journey home from work as they would on much larger time savings. Spending time at home doing 'nothing in particular' may be considered preferable to using the same time on a commuter journey. For non-work journeys, where the preferences of the traveller, rather than the value of lost output, determine time-saving values, it might be expected that small time savings would have more value on shorter journeys. A five-minute time saving on a six-hour journey to Cornwall, representing a 1.4 per cent fall in total journey time, might have less value than a similar saving on a forty-five-minute work journey where the time saving would be equivalent to 11.1 per cent of the original journey time.

Empirical evidence on the relationship between the value of time savings and their length is limited and does not provide any very clear picture. Some work by Thomas and Thompson (1970) based on a choice between toll and free roads suggested that there may be some increase in unit value with the length of time saved, but the effect of income was more important than that of the amount of time saved. From a study of commuters in Vancouver, Heggie (1976) concluded that the value of time savings is a non-linear function of the amount of time saved and that, when the effect of journey length is removed, the unit value is a function of the square of the amount of time saved. A study of commuter's 'willingness to pay' by Hensher suggested that 'as the amount of travel time saved increases, an individual is prepared to pay more, for any trip length to save a unit of travel time' (1976, p. 170). The amount that a commuter would pay was proportionately less, for the same unit of time, as trip length increased. Bruzelius (1979) has criticised the models used by Thomas and Thompson, Heggie and Hensher, and cast some doubt on their conclusions. He does not, however, altogether deny the possibility that small time savings may have a lower unit value, although he argues that individuals can adjust their behaviour to take advantage of future time savings.

Neither the behavioural studies of Thomas and Thompson and Hensher, nor Heggie's study of attitudes, measures the value to employers of saving work time. But, as it has been argued, this is the area in which there is the strongest theoretical reason for believing that smaller time savings should have lower unit values. The official attitude towards the issue has been based on the argument that it would be administratively difficult to give two values to small time savings in road-investment appraisal. However, two values are already used and adoption of the Leitch Committee's recommendation on commuter time would mean that three values could be used (as well as possible local variations in the former 'equity' value of pure leisure). A feasible reform would be to attach leisure or commuter time-saving values to small work time savings of under ten minutes.

The evaluation of small time savings has clear implications for investment appraisal. If small time values were reduced then the rates of return on isolated urban or rural road improvement schemes would fall while those on large-scale investment projects, such as new motorway building or rail electrification schemes (if an equivalent investment-appraisal technique to that used for road projects was adopted), would remain constant. The large-scale projects would then become relatively more attractive. A study of an actual urban road-investment appraisal in Leicester (the investment has now been carried out) showed that the total time saving over the whole improved network would not be as much as three minutes for any vehicle. If time savings of two minutes or less resulting from this investment project were devalued to 25 per cent of the full-time value, then the estimated first-year rate of return would fall from 19.7 per cent to 5.3 per cent.

CHAPTER 6

Time and Leisure

If all the years were playing holidays,
To sport would be as tedious as to work;
But when they seldom come, they wish'd for come.
[W. Shakespeare]

1. INTRODUCTION

In this chapter some alternative definitions and descriptions of leisure time are examined and are related to the approach adopted in the study. Some figures of hours worked in Britain are then examined and simple statistical tests are used to measure the relationship between hours worked and the level of earnings. A study is then made of some time budgets that show how samples of people in Britain and in a number of other countries allocate their stock of time between alternative activities. Finally, some of the problems that may arise as a result of a growth in the amount of 'free' leisure time available are considered.

2. DEFINITION OF LEISURE

As was shown in the chapter on travel time, it is possible to divide time into only two categories, work time and non-work time, and all non-work time is sometimes described as leisure time. But this, as the arguments in chapter 2 and other earlier chapters have implied, is an extremely crude and not very logical division. Work in this context presumably means work for which some form of money payment or reward is received. But there are many activities, such as washing dishes, growing vegetables or mending a puncture, that can equally well be regarded as work. A peasant farmer who at first grows crops for his own family to eat, but then at some stage decides

122

to market his produce, will be doing very much the same kind of work whether he is operating in a subsistence or a market economy. In some developing countries, and in some earlier periods in the history of developing countries, a mixed economy in which people work partly for the market and partly for their own consumption has been common. For many years it was customary for the lead miners of Derbyshire to spend part of their time mining lead ore to sell and another part working on small-scale farming for their own direct benefit and that of their families. The position of people today who use part of their non-paid-work time to build an extension to their homes or to grow tomatoes is not very different. This argument suggests that even the work and non-work division of time is not founded on a logical basis. The phrase 'paid work' has generally been used in this study to cover work for which a money reward is received. Although this form of work is not essentially different from other work activities it does have a special importance in the economies of developed countries that justifies its separate consideration.

If some non-paid-work time can be used for work activities, then it is apparent that to describe all time periods when people are not earning a money income as 'leisure time' would be extremely misleading. It has generally been recognised in discussions relating to leisure time that people are not free to allocate all the time that is not devoted to paid work to what can properly be called leisure activities. We have to eat and sleep and may feel strongly obliged to undertake at least some household chores. For a period in Britain, as in other Western countries in the eighteenth and nineteenth centuries, leisure was considered to be virtually the exclusive possession of one social class. The ordinary working men and women, farm workers, servants and factory hands were thought of as the labouring classes who had little if any entitlement to leisure. Leisure was a special activity for the 'leisured classes' who, if they took part in any form of work activity, whether paid or unpaid, did so for pleasure rather than from any economic necessity.

In his general theory of the economics of time, DeSerpa argued that the essential nature of leisure was that the time consumption constraint is ineffective and that when people choose to allocate more time to the consumption of goods than is required then these become 'leisure goods' (1971, p. 834). In *The Price of Leisure* (1970), Owen develops the definition of leisure as time spent in consumption, consumption time itself being defined as 'time devoted to activities which are, at the margin, primarily carried on for their

own sake rather than for the control over financial or other resources
which the activity might yield' (p. 3). According to Owen, this
definition excludes paid work, housework, do-it-yourself repairs and
commuting time but includes sleeping and eating time. Owen dis-
cusses an alternative definition of leisure time as 'free time' that
could be devoted to 'recreation and non-productive contemplation',
but points out that this leads to difficulties because people may
choose to spend more than the bare minimum of time required in
such activities as eating and sleeping. Vickerman, in his book *The
Economics of Leisure and Recreation* (1975), is mainly concerned
with planning to meet recreational needs and he has a much wider
definition of leisure as any activity that can take place in leisure
(or non-paid-work) time. His definition would include the journey
to work and shopping and, presumably, housework and do-it-yourself activities. In his study, however, Vickerman excludes travel
time, because it does not all take place in leisure time, shopping,
because of its 'special nature', and 'non-active leisure and personal
activities' for convenience. Vickerman also has an interesting sub-
division of leisure time into three categories: recreation, pleasure
and social activities. He uses the term 'recreation' to cover organised
activities such as entertainment, sport and eating out. He also sub-
divides recreation into market recreation, where the primary activity
is commercially marketed (cinema, professional sport), and non-
market recreation, which is not sold in 'saleable units'. 'Pleasure'
in Vickerman's classification relates to activities that are not organised commercially, such as walks in the country and holidays, while
he defines social activities as 'essentially involving people and not
places' (1975, p. 4), the primary purpose being to visit friends
rather than the location where the activity takes place. In discussing
Owen's definition of leisure, Vickerman stresses that the main
characteristic of what he terms recreation is that a goods input is
required.

    There are undoubtedly different areas of human activity and
there is no reason why some economists should not choose to
concentrate their studies on one of those areas. Vickerman and
Owen are both quite correct in pointing out that 'leisure activities'
have been comparatively neglected as a separate branch of study
by economists. But attempts to find a sound theoretical basis for
classifying activities do not appear to have been very successful.
Vickerman may be justified in choosing certain activities that are
particularly relevant to his study of the demand for recreational
facilities and for travel, but, as has already been argued, his apparent

inclusion of all non-paid-work activities as being leisure activities is difficult to defend. A category that includes every activity from listening to Bach to unblocking the drains is not very meaningful. Vickerman's recreation, pleasure and social activity classification also presents some difficulties. Many people visit their local pub to meet friends rather than to quench their thirst. Is this therefore market recreation like eating out (which may also be motivated by the desire for companionship rather than food) or is it a social activity? Holidays, trips into the country and visits to friends all require some market goods inputs.

Owen's definition of consumption activities as those primarily carried on for their own sake illustrates what is perhaps the main difficulty in classifying human activities. This is to reconcile a classification based on economic factors with one that reflects psychological realities. Owen's concept of 'consumption time' activities that are carried on for their own sake and 'work' activities that are undertaken for the sake of monetary reward oversimplifies the complex realities. Even the qualification 'at the margin' does not make the association acceptable. Of course a great deal of paid work is carried out mainly in order to earn a money income, but there are also many cases where this is not the controlling motive. In a television programme dealing with technological development and the demand for labour in British industry, which was broadcast in August 1979, a former worker in a glass works said with great vehemence that he loved his work so much that he would have carried it out just for 'board and lodging'. There is no reason to believe that this man was unusual except perhaps in having thought out his position so clearly. No doubt if people were asked why they went out to work the great majority would answer that they needed to earn a living. But the fact that work is an economic necessity does not mean that it may not also be an end in itself, and, as was argued in chapter 2, it may often be the case that people would choose to go on working even if the economic necessity was removed. Similarly, some non-paid-work-time activities may be carried out primarily for their own sake even if there is also some indirect benefit to be derived. People may grow vegetables or decorate their homes primarily because they enjoy those activities. Being able to eat the vegetables or enjoy looking at a differently patterned wallpaper may be only secondary considerations. Owen's rather amusing implication that contemplation suddenly turns into work if it becomes productive could be justified on economic but not on psychological grounds. It is often only in retrospect that we can say whether an activity is, or is not, productive. An artist may obtain intense satisfaction from the activity of painting a picture. Even if he subsequently sells the picture it seems rather odd to argue that its production was a 'work' activity primarily motivated by the desire to have command over financial resources.

The other implication of Owen's definition, which is that people will allocate time to non-productive activities only if they want to carry them out for their own sake, is much more generally true. But even here there is the complication of those activities like a visit to the dentist that we only undertake for the indirect benefit that they will yield. Also, as has already been argued in this study and as Owen himself suggests, it is sometimes necessary to spend 'free' time on activities that yield little or even negative utility because time can be neither saved nor destroyed.

It is possible to develop a classification of activities based either on economic factors or on psychological motivation but to combine the two can lead to a confusion of overlapping categories. An 'economic' classification could ignore motivation and be based on the effect of the activity on the supply or consumption of goods and services. Those activities that, directly or indirectly, lead to the output of some good or service could be classified as being productive. These could be subdivided into those where the product is marketed and those where it is not. The first category of productive activities with marketed products would include all paid work and travel to, from and in the course of work. Productive activities with non-marketed products (or activities producing products that will be consumed by the producer or his family) would include housework, do-it-yourself activities, gardening to produce fruit or vegetables, keeping animals or poultry as a source of food supply, education, and child care. Consumption activities could be subdivided into those involving measurable marginal costs and those that require market goods inputs but for which marginal costs per (short) time period are very low or zero. The first subcategory would include eating, pleasure travel and visits to the hairdresser. The second would include sleeping, most forms of sport and walking for pleasure. Finally, some activities could be classified as neutral in that there is no product of goods or services and no discernible consumption of resources. An example already cited in this study would be that of nude swimming from a beach directly adjacent to the bather's house. Nude sunbathing in one's own garden (without the benefit of any form of mattress to lie on!) would be another example. But these examples are somewhat limited and there is very little difference between these 'neutral' activities and those, like going for a walk, that demand the market input of shoes and clothes but that would normally have a very low marginal cost.

This 'economic' classification is, however, by no means without its difficulties and there are several awkward cases. Non-productive activity could subsequently become productive if the output or service was sold. Playing tennis presumably becomes productive as soon as spectators pay to watch the game. As has been noted by other writers, 'productive consumption' is not easy to classify. Travelling to work or attending a lecture both involve consuming services but are classified as being productive because their ultimate purpose may be to enable production to take place. But eating and sleeping have been classified as forms of consumption although, to some extent, these are also necessary prerequisites of any productive activity.

Possibly more satisfactory, and more useful in explaining changes in human behaviour, is the psychological classification of activities, which has already been partly developed in chapter 2. The basic distinction is between the direct and indirect utility that may be obtained from an activity. All activities will yield some direct utility or disutility. Normal human beings must have some reaction to all the activities in which they engage. The utility may be very low and we may be indifferent between a number of alternative activities but it is difficult to think of any situations in which taking part in an activity does not have some direct significance. There may be some activities that do not give us any particular pleasure or cause us any distress but this does not mean that they do not have a ranking on our subjective 'utility scale'. There will be some activities that give us greater pleasure and others that we find more distasteful. On a continuous scale running from positive to negative values, some time must be ranked zero. An activity that gives us neither pleasure nor displeasure can still be ranked and may be relevant in our attempts to allocate our time so that positive utility is maximised (or, for some unfortunate people, disutility is minimised). Apart from the direct utility or disutility that all activities produce, some will also yield an indirect utility. Apart from the pleasure or pain produced by the activity itself, there will be some effect on the utility to be received in another time period. This indirect utility is most likely to be positive, though there are some important instances where it may be negative.

Leisure activity may now be said to occur when only direct utility is produced, while work time can be extended to include all activities that produce indirect utility. This very broad category of work can be subdivided into work where the indirect utility takes the form of money payments (this has been called 'paid work' in this study) and unpaid work, where the direct utility is the production of some specific good or service. The distinction is significant not just because the paid-work activity coincides with what economists normally define as work but also because money income can be used for a large number of different purposes (including saving) whereas the other forms of indirect utility only serve certain specific purposes. A home-grown cabbage is not of very much use except as a contribution to the dinner table. The unpaid-work category would include housework, do-it-yourself improvements and repairs, child care and personal hygiene. In unpaid work the consumer uses time, plus one or more of the inputs of market goods, services produced by other people and his own labour in order to produce a good or service or to be able to enjoy some other activity in the future. This definition would include such activities as visits to the hairdresser as unpaid work since the benefit of having short or well-groomed hair is produced.

When both direct and indirect utility are produced it need not necessarily be the case that obtaining the indirect utility is the main reason for undertaking the activity. This has already been argued in the case of paid work. But it is quite possible that do-it-yourself activities, gardening, cooking and child care, for instance, may sometimes provide a direct satisfaction that is more highly valued than the 'end-products' of newly papered rooms, immaculate gardens, pots of jam or clean children. It is also possible that the same activity can provide only direct utility in one situation but both direct and indirect utility in another. Eating is the most obvious and important example. Since we must eat in order to be able to do anything else, some basic consumption of food will produce the indirect benefit of keeping us alive and will also produce some immediate pleasure or displeasure from the act of eating. But it would clearly be absurd to allocate all eating time to the 'unpaid-work/indirect utility' category. Some eating is not necessary for survival and time may be allocated to eating that provides only direct satisfaction and that is therefore a pure leisure activity. Since human beings are complex creatures, motivation for activities may vary and in allocating such activities as amateur sport to the 'leisure-time/direct utility' category it is assumed that this represents the motivation of the majority of people, but not necessarily of all participants. It is possible to be persuaded to play football because of the indirect utility that will result from pleasing one's workmates by making up a works team. We may play tennis with a beginner for the sake of friendship or out of a sense of duty, rather than because of any direct satisfaction to be derived from the tennis itself. The very important activity of sleep also creates certain problems. Since the basic purpose of sleep is to refresh and recreate our minds and bodies it is primarily an activity yielding indirect benefit and is certainly not a leisure activity. But, as is the case with eating, some surplus sleep time (in so far as this is physiologically possible) may be chosen because the direct utility (which is presumably zero, unless one can rely on very pleasant dreams) is greater than that of any alternatively available activity. Some prisoners develop the ability to sleep away part of their sentences. Sleeping, even if it yields zero utility, may be preferred to the negative utility that might result from merely sitting thinking or from talking to an uncongenial companion.

But it would not be profitable to extend this discussion of the complexities of human behaviour and the main points of the discussion are summarised. All activities yield some level of positive or negative utility. The chief characteristics of pure leisure activities is that they must be undertaken 'for their own sake' because they produce only direct utility. All activities that produce some indirect benefit that will be enjoyed in a future time period may be classified as relating to work or non-leisure time. Paid work is a special case of work activity. Activities producing indirect utility are not always undertaken primarily in order to enjoy this future benefit. The direct benefit resulting from work activities (and particularly that which may be yielded by paid work) should not be ignored in economic analysis. Activities, such as smoking, that produce direct utility but a probable future disutility must be placed in the leisure category. They are not likely to be undertaken in order to suffer the disutility. The ancillary 'package' activities discussed in chapter 2 must logically be classified as work activities but the most important example, travel time, is discussed in chapter 5.

3. TIME DEVOTED TO PAID WORK IN BRITAIN

In the previous section the utility provided by different activities has been discussed as though it were constant over all time periods. This, of course, is not the case and the marginal utility obtained from an activity will eventually start to decline as the time allocated to its pursuit increases. The ninety-first minute spent watching TV may yield less utility than the ninetieth minute. It has been argued that paid work commonly yields a positive direct utility and that in what is probably a not unimportant minority of cases the indirect utility, or pay, received may not even provide the main motive for working. But the direct utility of most work will decline as the length of the working day increases and workers may require larger payments to compensate them for the growing difference between the direct utility of extra work and that of the preferred alternative pure-leisure or 'unpaid-work' activity that might be enjoyed. In chapter 2 it was argued that basic wage rate increases (as opposed to increases in overtime rates) are more likely to lead to a decrease than to an increase in the length of the working day. In this section some figures of recent trends in average hours worked in Britain are examined, and they are related to changes in earnings.

The long-term trend of average hours worked, including overtime, appears to be falling in Britain for both men and women manual workers, although the movement is not even and hours actually increased slightly between 1975 and 1978. The figures for the period 1956–78 for full-time men and women workers are shown in Table 6.1, from which it can be seen that the hours worked by both men and women have declined by about 10 per cent during the period 1956–78. The total hours-worked figures were then compared with earnings figures for the same period. The average earnings during the October survey period for each of the twenty-three years, for the same group of industries and for manufacturing industries only, were adjusted to allow for price increases as measured by the Index of Retail Prices. No allowance was made for changes in tax rates. The revised earnings figures were adjusted to December prices in each year, with 15 January 1974 = 100. According to these calculations, real average weekly wages for full-time male manual workers in manufacturing and other industries increased by over 1 57 per cent during the period 1956–78, from £25.92 to £40.89 (both figures in 1974 prices). The wages of full-time manual women workers increased by just over 178 per cent (from £13.75 to £24.50) in the same period. The figures for the increase in real wages for manufacturing industry only were:

Full-time men   = 155 per cent increase (£26.75–£41.51)
Full-time women = 182 per cent increase (£13.44–£24.52)

The (linear) correlation coefficients for real earnings and total hours worked for the twenty-three years were then calculated for

TABLE 6.1

Average weekly hours, including overtime, for full-time adult employees in manufacturing and certain other industries, GB, 1956–78

Year (Oct)	Men aged 21 and over (hours)	Index 1956 = 100	Women aged 18 and over (hours)	Index 1956 = 100
1956	48.5	100.0	41.3	100.0
1957	48.2	99.4	41.0	99.3
1958	47.7	98.3	41.0	99.3
1959	48.5	100.0	41.4	100.2
1960	48.0	99.0	40.5	98.1
1961	47.4	97.7	39.7	96.1
1962	47.0	96.9	39.4	95.4
1963	47.6	98.1	39.7	96.1
1964	47.7	98.3	39.4	95.4
1965	47.0	96.9	38.7	93.7
1966	46.0	94.8	38.1	92.2
1967	46.2	95.2	38.2	92.5
1968	46.4	95.9	38.3	92.7
1969	46.5	95.9	38.1	92.2
1970	45.7	94.2	37.9	91.8
1971	44.7	92.2	37.7	91.3
1972	45.0	92.8	37.9	91.8
1973	45.6	94.0	37.7	91.3
1974	45.1	93.0	37.4	90.6
1975	43.6	89.9	37.0	89.6
1976	44.0	90.7	37.4	90.6
1977	44.2	91.1	37.4	90.6
1978	44.2	91.1	37.4	90.6

Sources: Department of Employment (1978a, 1979a).

each of the groups of workers and industries. The results are given in Table 6.2. These figures suggest a strong negative correlation between average earnings and average hours worked, and show that the strength of the relationship is not affected by the exclusion of workers in the service and other non-manufacturing industries. It would, of course, be dangerous to base any arguments about a causal relationship between hours worked and earnings on these estimates of correlation between figures in two time series. The decrease in average working hours was unlikely to have been brought about entirely by the free choice of the workers themselves. If the number of hours worked is influenced by the level of industrial activity and by changes in the organisation of industry, it is apparent

TABLE 6.2
Correlation between real earnings and hours worked for male and
female manual workers

	Coefficient of correlation	
	Full-time men	Full-time women
Manufacturing and other industries	−0.92	−0.86
Manufacturing industries only	−0.92	−0.86

that it cannot be wholly determined by workers' responses to changes in real earnings. Nevertheless, the figures do appear to give some support to the argument in chapter 2 that increased average earnings are likely to reduce the supply of hours of labour in Britain and in other similar countries. But the attitude of workers to hours worked is discussed more fully after a few more figures have been examined.

Linear regression equations were fitted to the adjusted earnings and hours data, with hours worked as the dependent variable (Y). The results for all industries were:

$$\text{Men} \quad Y = 55.26 - 0.26X$$
$$\text{Women } Y = 44.72 - 0.33X.$$

For manufacturing industries only, the equations were very similar:

$$\text{Men} \quad Y = 56.17 - 0.30X$$
$$\text{Women } Y = 44.77 - 0.34X$$

It could be argued that changes in earnings might take some time to have an effect on hours worked and so equations were fitted to the 'all industries' data with a one-year lag for the hours-worked figures. The effect of introducing the lag was very small, the revised equations for all industries being:

$$\text{Men} \quad Y = 55.18 - 0.27X$$
$$\text{Women } Y = 44.44 - 0.32X.$$

As would be expected from the nature of the trends, all the equations show hours worked declining with increases in real income. It is perhaps surprising that the rate of decline is greater for full-time women workers than it is for male workers in both cases. If the average hours worked were mainly determined by earnings, and if the 1956–78 linear relationship continued to apply for the next twenty or thirty years (two very large assumptions), then it would be possible to predict future average hours given further assumptions about the growth in real average earnings. The average weekly hours for full-time men in the year 2000, assuming real average earnings growth rates of 1 per cent, 2 per cent and 3 per cent would be 42.0, 38.8 and 34.9 hours respectively. The equivalent figures for women workers, on the same assumptions, would be 34.6, 32.2 and 29.2 hours. But other factors, such as the rate of technological development, will also have a strong influence on the average length of the working week. If the length of the working week continues to fall, the attitudes of workers to a further decline might change significantly.

A cross-section of average hourly earnings and hours worked by manual workers in seventy-eight industry groups (including construction, transport, service industries and government services as well as manufacturing industry) was studied. The figures were contained in the *New Earnings Survey* and related to April 1978. The earnings figures in the time series included overtime earnings but the effect of overtime payments was removed from the cross-section figures. As overtime rates are likely to be higher than normal hourly rates, the inclusion of overtime would tend to raise the level of average hourly earnings so that industries with high overtime hours (and consequently high total hours) would also have high average earnings and a positive association between earnings and hours worked would be generated. With overtime hours removed there was, however, very little variation in weekly hours. Nevertheless, the correlation coefficient was calculated for the seventy-eight industry groups for male workers and a rather weak negative correlation of $r = -0.41$ was found to exist. A linear regression was fitted to the adjusted hourly earnings and weekly hours data for male manual workers and the equation was estimated to be:

$$Y = 41.95 - 0.01X$$

where Y is average hours worked and X is average hourly earnings (in pence).

When actual hours worked, including overtime, are examined, it is apparent that there is very considerable variation in the length of the working week both within and between highly aggregated industry groups. Table 6.3 shows the percentage of full-time male manual workers falling into the modal group for total weekly hours worked, the percentage working more than sixty hours a week and the average hours overtime found in the Department of Employment sample for April 1978 (Department of Employment,

TABLE 6.3
Variation in length of working week, full-time male workers, April 1978

	SIC Order	% with total hours in modal class of 38–40 hours	% working over 60 hours per week	Weekly hours of overtime
I	Agriculture, forestry, fishing	33.7	9.8	6.8
II	Mining and quarrying	23.3*	6.1	6.5
III	Food, drink, tobacco	21.1	10.5	8.6
IV	Coal and petroleum products	42.6	5.3	5.9
V	Chemicals and allied industries	33.5	7.0	6.4
VI	Metal manufacture	36.7	3.9	5.6
VII	Mechanical engineering	29.8	3.8	5.9
VIII	Instrument engineering	33.2	2.1	5.0
IX	Electrical engineering	33.8	3.1	5.1
X	Shipbuilding and marine engineering	30.9	8.1	7.4
XI	Vehicles	38.7	2.3	5.3
XII	Metal goods n.e.s.	30.1	3.7	5.7
XIII	Textiles	28.8	4.0	5.5
XIV	Leather, leather goods and fur	–	–	–
XV	Clothing and footwear	53.9	0.3	2.3
XVI	Bricks, pottery, glass, cement etc.	22.9	8.1	7.6
XVII	Timber, furniture, etc.	37.4	3.1	4.5
XVIII	Paper, printing and publishing	28.0	5.8	6.1
XIX	Other manufacturing industries	26.1	4.0	5.7
XX	Construction	33.6	6.5	5.8
XXI	Gas, electricity and water	42.0	5.0	5.1
XXII	Transport and communications	24.5	12.2	9.0
XXIII	Distributive trades	33.4	4.3	5.1
XXIV	Insurance, banking, finance and business services	21.8	6.7	5.8
XXV	Professional and scientific services	40.2	4.2	5.2
XXVI	Miscellaneous services	39.9	4.0	4.0
XXVII	Public administration and defence	42.5	4.4	4.7

*Modal class = 36–38 hours per week. Standard Industrial Classification, 1968.
Source: Department of Employment (1979a).

1979a). The figures relate to twenty-six out of the twenty-seven major 'Orders' of the 1968 Standard Industrial Classification. Leather, leather goods and fur is omitted from most tables of the *New Earnings Survey* data because of the small number in the sample. The figures show that even when industries are classfied into the highly aggregated groups of the Orders of the Standard Industrial Classification, considerable differences in actual, as opposed to normal basic, working hours remain. The percentage of workers working the 'modal' week of 38–40 hours ranged from 53.9 per cent for clothing and footwear to only 21.1 per cent in the food, drink and tobacco group of industries. Mining and quarrying were unique in having a different modal working week of 36–38 hours. The highest percentages working more than sixty hours a week were 12.2 per cent in transport and communications and 10.5 per cent in food, drink and tobacco, while the industries with the lowest percentages of workers in this category were clothing and footwear (0.3 per cent) and instrument engineering (2.1 per cent). Weekly hours of overtime ranged from 2.3 in clothing and footwear to 9.0 in transport and communication.

The relationship between the average hours of overtime worked per week and average hourly earnings (with the influence of overtime pay removed) is of some interest. All other things being the same, it might be expected that workers in industries with low basic hourly earnings would be more willing to work overtime than those with higher hourly earnings. The marginal utility of extra money income would be higher for lower-paid workers (this argument assumes that the 'normal' working week without overtime is of approximately the same duration for both groups of workers) and this should make an exchange of paid-work time for non-work time relatively more attractive. This factor would be partly, but probably not fully, offset if, as is likely to be the case, overtime rates for workers with higher basic rates of wages are higher than the overtime rates for lower-paid workers. However, the overtime statistics of Table 6.3 do not support this hypothesis. Workers with lower basic hourly wages do not have longer average overtime hours. There is rather a weak positive correlation (of about $r = +0.2$) between basic hourly earnings and hours of overtime. Four of the six industry groups with the lowest average hourly earnings (excluding the influence of overtime payments) are also amongst the six groups with the lowest average hours of overtime. These four industry groups are miscellaneous services, distribution, public administration, and clothing and footwear. Professional and scientific services, which is also amongst the six 'lowest earners', has the eighth lowest average overtime hours. The remaining member of the 'low-earners' group – agriculture, forestry and fishing – had noticeably lower average basic hourly earnings than any other group and relatively high overtime hours of 6.8 (the unweighted average overtime hours for all twenty-six Orders was 5.79).

As is so often the case in economics, issues become complicated as soon as the world of theoretical analysis, with its mathematical models showing the effect of changing a single variable, is changed for the real world to which our statistical data relate. In that real world there are a number of factors that determine the length of the working week and the supply of hours of manpower. The model in which individuals are seen as surrendering leisure time and undertaking work in order to enjoy the utility of a money income is very incomplete. The length of the average working day, or week, in different industries may be determined by both demand and supply factors. It is obvious that hours are likely to be influenced by the level of activity in particular industries. Since it may be difficult to reduce the size of the labour force and almost impossible to reduce wage rates, a fall in the demand for an industry's product may well result in a drop in average hours worked. In the first place, overtime working may be eliminated and then short-time working instituted. To some extent, then, workers may work for the hours that are available to them and inter-industry differences merely reflect varying levels of economic activity. The price mechanism cannot easily be used to reduce the total supply of labour into a particular industry. A second demand factor may be called 'organisation'. There are some industries, such as road haulage, shipping and the operation of oil rigs, where workers cannot easily be replaced by another shift at set intervals of time and where long hours may therefore be required. In this case the price mechanism of high overtime rates can be used to ensure a supply of workers willing to work for long working days (or weeks or months).

The supply position has already been largely covered by earlier discussion. Workers will undertake paid work partly for the sake of the utility provided by the work itself and partly in order to obtain a money income. If average hourly rates of pay are increased then it seems most likely that (all other things being the same) the total hours worked will fall. If overtime rates are increased then hours worked will increase. But the different levels of utility yielded by different occupations, or by the same occupation in different industries or in different firms in the same industry, mean that the reaction to a given change in overtime rates may be far from uniform. Workers in some firms, or in some specific jobs in those firms, may be much more ready than others to extend their working hours. Thus a small firm, which could not enjoy technological scale economies that were available in its industry, might nevertheless be able to provide its workers with a happy environment where they obtained a high utility from work and they might easily be persuaded to extend the length of their working day.

Non-manual workers, according to the Department of Employment surveys (1978a, 1979b), enjoy both shorter average working hours and higher average hourly earnings than manual workers. In 1976 the average hourly earnings for all male manual workers was 141.0 pence (excluding the effect of overtime) and the average weekly hours worked were 43.3 (including 5.4 hours overtime). The equivalent figures for male non-manual workers were 210.6 pence and 38.5 hours (including 1.3 hours overtime).

Trade Union Congress spokesmen are currently making out a case for a shorter basic working week and they have argued that it is unjust that non-manual workers should have shorter working hours. It is a feature of current debates about many aspects of the British economy that arguments relating to equity and to efficiency are often employed together. It is difficult to see why egalitarian considerations should apply to hours worked any more than to earnings. If it is unfair that non-manual workers are on average employed for shorter hours than manual workers, then it is perhaps equally unfair that workers in the mining and quarrying industry should earn an average of 221.8 pence per hour (plus overtime) while the equivalent earnings for those employed in agriculture, forestry and fishing were only 127.8 pence (in April 1978). This is not to argue that there must be sound economic reasons why non-manual workers should work for shorter hours than manual workers. It may be true that intellectual effort cannot be sustained for such long time periods as physical work, but only a limited amount of non-manual work demands such effort. As is undoubtedly the case with wages, hours of work may still sometimes be determined by convention and custom rather than by any discernible market forces.

The campaign by the unions for a shorter working week suggests that the marginal utility of work is low and that there is a strong demand to enjoy more non-paid work and pure-leisure time. But the issue is complicated. Overtime work is voluntary, but average overtime worked by male manual workers in April 1978 was equivalent to an addition of about 15 per cent to a basic forty-hour working week. Individual unions are mostly seeking increases in hourly wage rates at the same time as shorter hours and it is not clear how far there is a real desire to achieve shorter basic working hours even at the cost of some loss of income (or at the cost of a smaller increase than might otherwise be obtained). One advantage of a shorter basic working week is, of course, that more working time will attract higher overtime rates. Some union leaders wish to see work shared more evenly in a time of high unemployment but this wish may not be shared by all their members.

In discussing union attitudes towards the length of the 'normal' working week it is important to remember that there may be wide varieties of opinion. If it is true that the direct utility obtained from the work experience is important, then attitudes towards working hours might be expected to vary between unions in different industries. Some large unions may represent workers who find little pleasure in their work, but many other workers may have no strong desire to increase the proportion of their time that is allocated to non-paid work and pure leisure activities. The *General Household Survey* of 1971 (Office of Population Censuses and Surveys, 1973) examined, amongst many other things, people's feelings of job satisfaction. The general results, on a percentage basis, are shown in Table 6.4. This 'job satisfaction' was not exactly equivalent to

TABLE 6.4
Job satisfaction of working persons aged 15 or over, GB

Degree of job satisfaction	% of sample in category
Very satisfied	52.4
Fairly satisfied	36.4
Neither satisfied nor dissatisfied	5.6
Rather dissatisfied	3.6
Very dissatisfied	2.0
Total	100.0

Source: Office of Population Censuses and Surveys (1973).

either direct or indirect utility as these have been defined in this study. It did cover the reaction to the job itself, which is similar to any direct utility concept, but it also included satisfaction with the wages received. This is not, of course, the same as the utility yielded by the money earnings. Nevertheless it is interesting to note the wide variation in the degree of satisfaction, and that more than half the sample were very satisfied with their jobs. Amongst those who were not 'very satisfied' with their jobs, the main reason was pay for 31.5–43.2 per cent of the sample in each 'satisfaction' category. But if all the other reasons (such as 'dissatisfied with organisation', 'did not like the kind of work', 'physical working conditions', etc.) are added they outweigh the importance of pay. Pay was a much more important reason for dissatisfaction with men (38 per cent for all satisfaction categories) than it was with women in the sample (23 per cent of all satisfaction categories). The degree of job satisfaction was also classified by socioeconomic group, which reflects major types of job. The results are shown in Table 6.5. The chief point of interest in these figures, as far as this study is concerned, is the relatively high degree of job satisfaction expressed by people in the lower-paid jobs such as agricultural work and personal service. It is surprising that 57.9 per cent of unskilled manual workers were highly satisfied with their jobs whereas only 44.4 per cent of skilled manual workers put themselves into this category. It is normally assumed that satisfaction in a job increases with the degree of skill employed, but in this case it may be that skilled manual workers were particularly dissatisfied with their pay.

4. THE SCARCITY OF PURE-LEISURE TIME

It has been shown in the previous section that the average length of the paid working day in Britain has fallen, and the trend has been similar in other Western countries. It may therefore seem surprising that a well-known book about the use of leisure time has argued that time is becoming increasingly scarce. The main theme of Linder's *The Harried Leisure Class* (1970) is that 'economic growth entails a general increase in the scarcity of time' (p. 27). Linder's book is a mixture of useful insights and applied common sense with a rather puzzling use of economic analysis and some occasionally confused arguments. It is no doubt true that many people today feel harassed and would claim to live their lives 'at a faster rate' than people in the past. But it is, of course, untrue to say that time has become more scarce. Life expectations have increased, there are still twenty-four hours in the day and most people in Western countries now have more time to allocate to various non-work activities. If a factory worker or agricultural labourer of the mid-nineteenth century could be transported to our times he would be very surprised to be told that leisure time is scarcer today than it was in the 1850s. The phenomenon that Linder is discussing is an increase in the demand to use leisure time for many new activities. Linder rightly links this new demand to increasing affluence. As more market goods have become available and as personal transport facilities have been transformed, so

TABLE 6.5

Job satisfaction by socioeconomic group

Socioeconomic group	% in satisfaction category					Average score
	Very satisfied	Fairly satisfied	Neither satisfied nor dissatisfied	Rather dissatisfied	Very dissatisfied	
Professional workers – self employed*	64.6	29.0	4.1	1.5	0.8	4.7
Personal service workers	63.8	29.9	4.5	1.3	0.4	4.5
Agricultural workers						4.5
Employers and managers (large establishments)	59.5	32.8	3.5	3.0	1.2	4.5
Unskilled manual workers	57.9	29.9	6.3	3.7	2.3	4.4
Intermediate non-manual workers	56.0	35.2	4.2	3.2	1.5	4.4
Senior non-manual workers	55.5	33.8	5.4	3.5	1.9	4.4
Employers and managers (small establishments)	55.2	36.0	5.0	2.8	1.0	4.4
Farmers – self-employed*	52.3	36.6	5.6	3.8	1.6	4.3
Foremen and supervisors	50.4	36.1	6.9	2.6	4.0	4.3
Non-professional self-employed	48.5	34.6	9.2	3.1	4.6	4.3
Farmers – managers						4.2
Semi-skilled manual workers	47.1	41.0	5.8	3.8	2.3	4.3
Professional workers – employees	45.3	42.4	5.7	5.4	1.2	4.2
Skilled manual workers	44.4	41.5	6.8	4.6	2.7	4.2

*Small sample numbers

Source: Office of Population Censuses and Surveys (1973) Introductory Report.

more attractive activities have become available. Scarce non-paid work and pure-leisure time become more precious as more attractive and competing ways of using it are made available. But Linder's development of what he presents as a firm economic law, that increased affluence must lead to the use of more market goods in consumption and to a greater demand for time (an increased scarcity of time in Linder's analysis), is questionable.

Linder argues that when the 'yield' of working time increases, the yield on time devoted to other activities must be raised. Consumption time becomes more productive, according to Linder, when it is combined with more consumption goods, which are defined as 'the definite end products that are combined with time in an attempt to create material or spiritual well-being' (1970, p. 28). Linder's argument that when the yield on working time increases 'the yield from time in consumption must be increased to create an equilibrium between the yield on time in different sectors' (p. 28) is based on a number of assumptions that do not hold in the real world to which his analysis is supposed to apply. We cannot easily extend or contract our working day by small amounts, but in so far as this is possible an increase in the marginal yield of working time could lead to more time being allocated to paid work rather than to any changes in the yield of non-paid-work activities. In practice, time must be allocated in large discontinuous 'lumps', often between 'packages' of activities. Linder does not explain what he means by 'yield', but presumably this can be interpreted as the sum of the direct and indirect utilities produced by an activity. This utility may also be discontinuous. We may obtain a very high utility from ten minutes spent in an activity, while the utility of an eleventh minute might be zero or even negative. The assumption that the utility produced by an activity will, at some point, start to decline continuously as further increments of time are used in its pursuit may be useful in theoretical analysis but it is dangerous to apply it to the behaviour of people in the real world. If the utility of activities is not a continuous function of time, then the marginal utility of all activities will not be exactly equal, and a change in the utility of the activity will not necessarily involve a reallocation of time between all other activities or, as Linder suggests, a corresponding change in all other activities' utility levels.

The falsity of Linder's law can also be demonstrated by taking illustrations that might apply in the real world. The utility of paid-work time can increase either because work becomes more attractive or because higher wages are paid. In the first case, if we have a friendlier boss or better working conditions we might be ready to work for a slightly longer period, but if this opportunity is denied us then the improvement is just a bonus to enjoy. It will not affect the utility we obtain from other activities and it will not be necessary or possible to increase that utility. But Linder's analysis appears to equate the yield of work with the wages or payment received. In this case it is certainly likely that some of the increased earnings may be used to buy market good inputs that will increase the utility obtained from non-paid work or pure-leisure activities. But there is no 'iron law' to make this inevitable. The extra income may be saved or given away or it may be forgone through a reduction in the worker's hours that keeps his money income constant. It is extremely unlikely that the new income will be spread over all non-paid work or pure-leisure activities so that there is an exactly corresponding increase in utility in each case. If I start to earn an extra £10 a week, I may decide to have a more expensive holiday or pay to have my house redecorated. Some of my leisure activities will almost certainly remain unaffected. I will not necessarily feel compelled to increase the utility that I obtain from watching TV or reading the life of Dickens, even if I knew how to achieve these ends.

In a development of his argument, Linder suggests that there are inferior activities that are analogous to the inferior goods of consumer theory and that will receive a reduced allocation of time when the incomes of consumers increase. These inferior activities are those where utility cannot be increased easily by increasing the money spent on market goods inputs. Two examples given by Linder are the pleasures of eating and of sex. Again, the general conclusion that it is likely that more time will be devoted to activities requiring expensive market goods inputs when people become more affluent is probably correct and this result was shown as a possibility in the analysis of chapter 2. But there is no inevitability about this and the analogy with inferior goods is inexact. Inferior goods are those for which most consumers believe that there is a superior substitute. Preferred activities may continue to yield more utility than previously excluded activities however many market goods inputs are added to them. The position will vary according to the starting point before the income increase. Very poor people may find that many new activities become available and attractive when their income rises, but relatively well-off consumers may wish to make little change to their pattern of activities if they receive still more income. Linder does not distinguish very clearly between undertaking new activities and spending more money on existing ones. His examples are curious and interesting. Eating for pleasure is very much an activity of an affluent society. There are few restaurants, except for tourists, in the poorer parts of the world. The evidence of the time budgets discussed in the next section suggests that people in the more affluent countries spend more time on eating than do citizens of poorer places. Nor does Linder produce any very convincing evidence to show that the time spent on 'free' sexual activity is reduced when people become richer. As part of the discussion on sex he argues that fewer men now have time to keep a mistress! But this particular activity has never been very common amongst poor people. Neither the mill workers of Elizabeth Gaskell's novels, nor the farm labourers of Charles Kingsley's *Yeast* had the resources to pay for this form of extra-marital sex. Indeed it might be argued that a mistress (or a gigolo) is a market good input to the activity of sex that is only available to the wealthy.

This example of keeping a mistress is, however, interesting because it illustrates a possible development of Linder's arguments. How different the position of the 'leisure classes' of Victorian and Georgian society is from that of the 'millionaire class' of today (the term 'millionaire' is used here, as in chapter 2, to describe people who have ample unearned income to buy all the market goods inputs they might desire) is debatable. But what has happened in this century is that many workers also enjoy significant amounts of leisure and have sufficient wealth to choose activities requiring market goods inputs. It is these people whose problems Linder describes and who may indeed become harried if they try to put in too many leisure activities as well as having to spend time in paid or unpaid work. For the majority of people in Western countries the time available for leisure activities has become more, not less, plentiful. At the same time, as Linder has argued, the growth of affluence has provided people with a wider choice of more attractive activities. But although the amount of time that a worker of today can allocate to leisure activities is greater than it was for his predecessor of 100 years ago, it is much less than the time available to the leisured classes who had no need to undertake any paid work. An increase in real income may make it possible to substitute new activities for old ones or to use more expensive inputs for existing activities (which need not be pure leisure activities). In the latter case the time spent in the activity may remain constant. If we move to a more luxurious house or, to use Linder's own example, buy more expensive golf clubs, it does not necessarily mean that we shall spend more time indoors or playing golf. 'Living in a house' is not normally regarded as an activity in its own right, so that in the case of the more expensive house it is not clear that the benefit to the consumer could be attached to any particular activity.

There are some ways in which, as Linder points out, modern developments do reduce the quantity of leisure time, but these usually represent the difference between a gross and a net increase in available time and seldom involve an absolute decrease. Linder argues that many market goods need maintenance and that this reduces free time. This is of course true, but it is not very likely that, as Linder suggests with his swimming pool example, maintenance time will be so great that the good can never be used for its intended purpose. It may well happen, however, that people underestimate maintenance time, and find that the total package of time required for some new activity is greater than they had imagined. Thus, owning a horse involves much more time than is devoted to the enjoyment of riding it. On the other hand, maintenance activity may itself yield considerable utility. A young man may enjoy taking his motor bike to pieces, and the maintenance of a garden is an end in itself for the dedicated gardener.

In the past, both the leisure classes with their unearned income and prosperous people engaged in the more well-rewarded economic activities enjoyed cheap and abundant service labour. Their successors today may have to use much more of their own time in looking after their houses and gardens, in cooking, and in maintaining equipment. Domestic servants, gardeners, chauffeurs and valets still exist but they are only available to people who are relatively high in the scale of affluence. This does not mean that total leisure time has decreased, only that it may be distributed a little more evenly. The successors of the domestic servants who used to work very long hours and who had virtually no holidays (except such once-a-year occasions as 'Mothering Sunday') now enjoy a forty-hour week in factories and shops. In modern societies, as Linder points out, people are more dominated by 'the clock'. As was argued in chapter 2, the necessity to undertake activities at fixed times does limit individual choice very considerably. The existence of fixed working and shopping hours does not mean, however, that total leisure time is reduced, though it does make the task of allocating time optimally more difficult.

The main problem of leisure time today for people at work is, then, that there are more activities that can be chosen and that the process of choice is difficult. With more choices to be made it is likely, as Linder argues, that some people will make the wrong choice (though much of Linder's analysis suggests that people do not have much choice, being compelled to choose activities requiring ever more costly inputs). But it is very dangerous for the economist to become involved in judging the choices made by others. If we are happier living an 'unhurried' life, in which we spread out our time over relatively few activities and leave a few gaps in between, other people may have different tastes and enjoy crowding as many activities as possible into their day. A general concern in Britain today is that people may soon have too much rather than too little non-paid work and pure-leisure time, and this issue is discussed in section 6 and chapter 8.

5. TIME BUDGETS

The study of ways in which people spend their time has developed into a major area of research. Surveys have been carried out in many countries, usually under the supervision of sociologists rather than of economists, and time budgets have been constructed. The earliest time budget studies were largely concerned with the division of time between work and leisure. Workers' movements at the beginning of the present century were pressing for a 'three by eight' day of eight hours sleep, eight hours work and eight hours leisure. Most pre-Second World War studies took place in Britain, the USA and the USSR; in more recent times many large-scale studies have been completed.

The most ambitious international study has been the Multinational Comparative Time Budget Research Project (reported in Szalai, 1972), which was carried out under the auspices of an international committee in 1965–6. The survey covered fifteen areas in twelve countries. In some cases the investigation related to a particular town, in others data from up to 425 different communities were aggregated. The places included in the survey, with reference letters that will be used in the tables, were:

B 425 communities in Belgium
BU Kazanlik, Bulgaria
CZ Olomonc, Czechoslovakia
F Six cities in North-East France
WG1 100 electoral districts in West Germany (Federal Republic)
WG2 Osnabrück, West Germany

EG Hoyerswerda, East Germany (Democratic Republic)
H   Györ and district, Hungary
P   Callao and parts of Lima, Peru
PO Torun, Poland
US1 44 towns of at least 50,000 people in the USA
US2 Jackson, Michigan, USA
R   Pskov, USSR
Y1 Kragujevac and two neighbouring villages, Servia, Yugoslavia
Y2 Maribor and six neighbouring villages, Slovenia, Yugoslavia.

The original data, collected in diaries, related to ninety-six activity categories, but in most of the analysis these were reduced to thirty-seven categories, which were themselves divided into nine major groups. Some of the brief descriptions of the categories are not very revealing, and 'American English' rather than 'English English' is used. The activity 'marketing', for example, covers 'purchasing of everyday consumer goods and products' (presumably mainly food-stuffs) whereas the separate activity of 'shopping' included 'purchasing of durable consumer goods', administrative services, repair services (such as laundry and electrical repairs, presumably carried out by someone else outside the home) and 'waiting in line' or queueing to obtain goods or services. In Table 6.6 the descriptions contained in the report of the Multinational Project have sometimes been changed to make them as informative as possible to British readers. The time spent on activities was averaged over all days of the week so that, for example, a group spending an average of seventy minutes on Sunday in 'religious practice and attending religious ceremonies' would be shown as allocating ten minutes a day to this activity. People often do two things at once and some-times an arbitrary distinction had to be made between 'primary' and 'secondary' activities. The respondent's description of his be-haviour was the criterion used. As is stated in the report, 'There was no other satisfactory way to decide . . . whether a person is watching TV while eating or eating while watching TV' (Szalai, 1972, p. 36).

Table 6.6 shows the unweighted average time spent on the thirty-seven main activities (with some group sub-totals) by respondents at all fifteen locations. The group totals were averaged from the fifteen area averages in the report, and do not necessarily agree exactly with the averages shown in this table because of rounding errors. It is apparent that the classification could be varied and that it must, to some extent, be arbitrary. The division of shopping into

TABLE 6.6

Unweighted average times allocated to 37 main activities,
Multinational Project, 1965-6

Activity	Average time per 'standard' day (minutes)	
1 Main job (including travel during workday)	258.7	
2 Second job	3.9	
3 Regular work hours and time at work before and after work activity	10.9	
4 Travel to and from work	28.9	
Total work		302.1
5 Cooking	56.5	
6 Housework (cleaning, dishwashing)	56.4	
7 Clothes washing and upkeep	29.1	
8 Shopping for 'everyday consumer goods'	17.8	
Total housework		159.7
9 Gardening and animal care	14.5	
10 Shopping for 'durable consumer goods', taking goods for servicing	7.9	
11 Other repairs at home, heating water and miscellaneous home duties	20.2	
Total other household obligations		42.4
12 Baby and child care	17.9	
13 Playing and talking with children, medical care and babysitting	11.4	
Total child care		29.3
14 Personal and medical care inside and outside home	55.3	
15 Eating, inside and outside home	84.4	
16 Sleep	478.0	
Total personal needs		621.5
17 Travelling with children, to shop or meet personal needs	19.8	
18 Travel for pleasure or to study	17.5	
Total non-work travel		37.4
19 Study including homework and 'political or union training'	16.7	
20 Take part in religious organisations or in worship	3.5	
21 Take part in political activities or those of other organisations	5.1	
Total study and 'participation'		25.3
22 Listen to radio	8.5	
23 Watch TV at home	58.7	
24 Watch TV outside home	2.5	
25 Read newspaper	15.7	
26 Read magazine	4.5	
27 Read books	11.1	
28 Attend cinema	5.1	
Total mass media		105.5

Table 6.6 *continued*

Activity	Average time per 'standard' day (minutes)	
29 Social activities at home	14.7	
30 Social activities outside home, visit pub, cafe	23.5	
31 Conversation, including phone conversation	15.6	
32 Take part in sport and physical exercise	2.6	
33 Excursions, hunting, fishing, walking	15.9	
34 Attending a sports event, dancing, show, night club	3.8	
35 Visit theatre, concert, opera, museum or exhibition	1.4	
36 Nap or rest (not sleep) and relaxing, thinking, planning, doing nothing	23.3	
37 Miscellaneous leisure − hobbies, knitting, dressmaking, artistic creation, making music, singing, listen to records, writing private letters	17.7	
Total leisure		116.9
Total 'free time' (18–37)		264.7
Total travel (4 + 17 + 18 + travel at work)		70.7

Source: Calculated from figures contained in report of the Multinational Project in Szalai (1972).

two categories (each in a different group) might not be recognised by all housewives. The distinction between visiting a restaurant to eat and visiting a cafe for social activities must often be blurred in practice. Visiting a theatre (at any rate in Britain) is not necessarily a more 'cultural' activity than attending the cinema, watching TV or reading a book. The definition of 'leisure' (activities 29–37) is very narrow and many writers would include all activities 18–37 (these are described as 'free time' in the survey) plus perhaps some eating time as well as parts of other activities such as playing with children. On the other hand, what is rather quaintly described as 'ladies work' (confection, needlework, dressmaking, knitting, etc.) in the full ninety-nine-category classification might well be removed from the leisure-time classification.

The averages are in some cases unrealistic in that they are affected not only by taking an 'average' or extended day but also because there must have been many respondents who did not participate at all. While everyone must sleep or eat they need not go to the theatre or opera, so that the 1.4 minutes per day spent in that activity is not a very meaningful statistic. Those who did visit the theatre during the survey period must have allocated a block of at least 200 minutes, or 29 minutes per 'standard' day, to that activity.

As might be expected, the variation between the amounts of time allocated to the activities differed considerably between activities. Some measurements of dispersion are given in Table 6.7. The variance tends to fall with increasing aggregation and is generally lowest for the more basic activities. The six activities where the standard deviation between locations was the lowest percentage of the mean were:

Sleep	4.6%
Personal care	13.6%
Main job	16.2%
Eating	16.6%
Cooking	19.5%
Housework	22.2%

The activities showing the biggest variation, according to this measurement (in descending order), were:

Religion	98.8%
Gardening	91.7%
Magazine reading	80.0%
Second job	76.9%
Entertainment	76.3%
Reading book	67.6%

The 'minority' activities, which were hardly followed at all in some locations, not surprisingly show the biggest variation. The 'gardening and care of pets' activity variance was partly caused by the exceptionally high time allocation of forty-nine minutes at the Maribor, Yugoslavia location. (The average time allocation at the Yugoslavian location, Kragujevac, was only six minutes.)

It would go beyond the scope of this book to carry out a detailed discussion of the reasons for inter-location differences in time allocation. Some may represent genuine differences of choice between different cultures. Others, such as the zero times recorded as being allocated to religious activities in communist countries, may be influenced by the local political situation. Other differences reflect participation-rate differences rather than time-allocation differences. Thus the working hours shown are strongly affected by the number of workers in the sample and particularly by the number of women in full-time employment, which varied from 30 per cent at the Peru location to 92 per cent at Pskov in the Soviet Union. Differences are

TABLE 6.7

Variation in average time allocated to different activities, Multinational Project, 1965–6

Activity	Standard deviation (minutes)	Standard deviation as % of mean	Range, with extreme locations	
			Minutes	Code
1 Main job	41.9	16.2	200–338	P–BU
2 Second job	3.0	76.9	0–11	BU–YZ
3 Other work	6.3	57.8	4–25	B,WG2,P–BU
4 Travel to work	7.9	27.3	16–41	WG2–BU,H
5 Cooking	11.0	19.5	39–76	BU–Y2
6 Housework	12.5	22.2	36–78	BU–EG
7 Washing	8.4	28.9	12–45	BU–P
8 Day-to-day shopping	5.0	28.1	10–27	R–CZ
9 Gardening	13.3	91.7	2–49	P–Y2
10 Durable goods shopping	4.8	60.8	3–18	WG1–US1
11 Other household	5.4	26.7	6–27	P–CZ, Y2
12 Basic child care	6.2	34.6	9–32	BU–F
13 Other child care	4.1	36.0	5–18	B–PO
14 Personal care	7.5	13.6	44–71	B–CZ
15 Eating	14.0	16.6	65–106	CZ–P
16 Sleep	21.8	4.6	418–510	BU–WG1
17 Personal travel	8.3	42.6	4–34	WG1–PO
18 Leisure travel	4.4	25.1	11–28	EG–P
19 Study	8.8	52.7	6–38	WG1–R
20 Religion	3.5	98.8	0–11	BU,EG,R,Y1–US2

21 Organisations	2.6	51.0	2–12	F,WG1,P-EG
22 Radio	4.6	54.1	3–20	US2–BU
23 TV at home	22.9	39.0	14–99	BU–US2
24 TV outside home	1.5	60.0	0–6	Y2–PO
25 Read newspaper	4.3	27.4	10–25	P–UŠ2
26 Read magazine	3.6	80.0	1–13	BU,H,Y1,Y2–WG2
27 Read books	7.5	67.6	2–29	P–R
28 Cinema	3.4	66.7	1–15	EG–PO
29 Social – at home	8.0	54.4	4–29	R–Y1
30 Social – outside home	10.4	44.2	8–42	BU–Y1
31 Conversation	5.6	35.9	8–28	R–Y1
32 Active sports	1.7	65.4	0–6	Y1–US1
33 Outdoor activities	9.4	59.1	2–39	US1–WG1
34 'Entertainment'	2.9	76.3	2–14	CZ,EG,PO,Y1,Y2–BU
35 Cultural events	0.9	64.3	0–3	Y2–B,R
36 Resting	13.9	59.7	9–63	US1–P
37 Other leisure	6.9	39.0	9–36	H–Y1
Total 'free' time	35.8	13.5	200–311	H–Y1
Total travel time	14.1	19.9	39–90	WG1–P

Note: The range given is from the location with the smallest average time allocation to the one with the largest for each activity. The 'locations' column gives the countries in each of the two categories. The key to the abbreviations is given on pp. 145–6. In cases where more than one location fell into the 'lowest' or 'highest' time-allocation category, all locations have been shown. Thus the entry for reading magazines indicates that the average time allocation ranged from one minute in Bulgaria, Hungary and both Yugoslavian locations to thirteen minutes in Osnabrück.

Source: Calculated from figures contained in report of the Multinational Project in Szalai (1972).

reduced considerably when only employed men and women are considered. Some of the differences, such as the relatively small amount of TV watching in Bulgaria and the large amount of 'resting and doing nothing' in Peru, may reflect economic factors, and were predictable. The Peruvian figures support the argument, developed from Linder's study in the last section, that the demand to use leisure time will be positively associated with the supply of available market goods inputs.

The six most important activities, measured by the unweighted average amount of time allocated to them by people in all locations in the Multinational Project, are shown in Table 6.8. These six

TABLE 6.8
Six main time-consuming activities.
Average of Multinational Project figures

Activity	Unweighted average time allocation	% of total 1440– minute day
Sleeping	478.0	33.2
Main job	258.7	18.0
Eating	84.4	5.9
Watching TV	58.7	4.1
Cooking	56.5	3.9
'Housework'	56.4	3.9
		69.0

Source: Based on Szalai (1972).

activities absorbed, on average, 69 per cent of each twenty-four hours. The activity of sleeping, according to these figures, occupies about one-third of our lives. If the total 'package' of time required for each final consumption activity was measured, then relative rankings might change and eating, in particular, would become more important. Thus if time spent cooking, cleaning dishes (estimated at one-half of the 'housework' time) and doing food shopping was added to actual 'eating' time the total would become 186.9 minutes or about 13 per cent of each twenty-four hours. This total does not include time taken travelling to food shops. The very considerable amount of time allocated to TV watching is of interest. This is the only 'pure-leisure' activity included in the 'top six' of time consumers. Since TV has only been developed on a large scale in the last thirty years it is apparent that it has had a very considerable impact on the use of leisure time. An analysis of the Multinational Project data by Robinson and Converse (1972) has shown that time spent watching TV declines as the educational level of people rises in the United States and West Germany, where the ownership of TV sets has reached saturation point. In Balkan countries, with a relatively low rate of ownership of sets, however, the time spent in viewing increased with the educational level of respondents.

The project data did not include any earnings or income figures, but some 'background' information was obtained relating to such indicators of affluence as possession of a car, a telephone, and both a radio and TV set. If the United States is chosen as representing a country with high income levels and a high availability of market goods, then it is of some interest to compare the time allocation of two US locations with the average figures for all fifteen locations. The differences from the averages (which include the US figures) for the main groups of activities are shown in Table 6.9. The extra

TABLE 6.9

Differences between US and all-locations average time allocation (minutes)

	US1	US2
Work	−36.1	−43.1
Total housework	−17.7	−18.7
Other household	+2.6	+2.6
Child care	+2.7	+1.7
Personal needs	−1.5	−2.5
Non-work travel	+12.6	+16.6
Study and 'participation'	+2.7	+0.7
Mass media	+28.5	+34.5
'Leisure'	+6.1	+9.1

Source: Based on Szalai (1972).

time spent in non-work travel and in 'mass media' activities seems to have been gained at the expense of paid-work time and housework (mainly dishwashing and cleaning) rather than by replacing other leisure activities. As might be expected, the US time allocations to the 'resting' or 'doing nothing' activity were much below the all-locations average. There is no evidence to support Linder's suggestion that eating time would be reduced with increased affluence. The three locations with the lowest average eating times were Olomonc, Czechoslovakia (CZ), Torun, Poland (PO), and Pskov, USSR (R), while the three locations where the respondents spent the longest average times eating were France (F), Belgium (B) and Osnabrück, West Germany (WG2). Table 6.10 shows the level of ownership of a telephone, bathroom, television and radio set and a car by respondents in the six locations. The three locations allocating most

TABLE 6.10

Ownership of facilities and consumer durables in relation to time allocated to eating, 1965

| Facility or good | % owning facility or good | | | | | |
| | Location | | | | | |
	CZ	PO	R	F	B	WG2
Telephone	12.4	15.8	5.5	3.7	27.1	13.3
Bathroom	58.0	NA	40.8	63.6	50.9	80.6
TV and radio	70.1	53.6	46.5	62.1	67.3	74.3
Car	15.2	4.3	1.9	64.7	55.2	45.0

Source: Report of the Multinational Project in Szalai (1972).

time, on average, to eating (France, Belgium and West Germany 2) also tend, with some exceptions, to have the highest ownership of goods and facilities.

It is unfortunate that there was no British location in the Multinational Project. A time budget study carried out in Reading in January–March 1973 by the Centre for Sample Surveys (Bullock *et al.*, 1974) cannot be compared directly with the Multinational Project figures as the classification of activities was different. The respondents in this survey were divided into the three categories of men, working women and non-working women. The results were given separately for all respondents and for respondents who took part in the activity. Table 6.11 shows the time allocation for all respondents in each category, converted to a minute basis for comparison with the Multinational Project data. The figures were averaged over a seven-day week. It is difficult to make meaningful comparisons with the Multinational Project figures because of the different classification of activities, the later date of the Reading survey and the separation of figures for men and women. The working hours for men of 284.4 (including travel) is not very different from the fifteen-locations average for all workers of 258.7 minutes. The Reading respondents were near the top of the 'sleeping time' scale and their TV viewing times of 100.2–139.8

TABLE 6.11

Time allocation in Reading survey, 1973

Activity	Average minutes per day (7-day week), all respondents		
	Men	Working women	Non-working women
Sleep	504.0	513.0	535.2
Work	257.4	216.0	3.6
Work travel	27.0	0.6	0.0
Full-time education	15.0	7.8	0.0
Eating	90.6	82.2	91.2
Drinking (alcoholic)	16.2	7.8	3.0
Casual social	65.4	67.8	88.8
Organised leisure	17.4	19.8	16.8
Private leisure, study	75.6	60.0	81.6
Watching TV	135.0	100.2	139.8
Personal hygiene	40.8	46.2	37.2
Domestic	52.8	175.2	277.2
Child care	6.6	9.6	48.6
Shopping, use of services	15.6	27.0	36.6
Travel	92.4	84.6	57.0
Miscellaneous	28.2	25.2	23.4
Total	1440.0	1443.0	1440.0

Note: Rounding error in original data for 'working women'.
Source: Bullock *et al.* (1974).

were higher than the highest figure for every location (99 minutes in Jackson, USA) in the 1965 survey. As might be expected, working women are shown 'to have a relatively small amount of free time available for recreational activities. This result was also found in some of the detailed analysis of the Multinational Project data.

6. THE PROBLEMS OF LEISURE

Although free time in which recreational and other pleasurable activities can take place is generally regarded as being desirable, nevertheless it is common today to read and to hear references to the problem of leisure. This problem is the opposite of that discussed in section 4, being one of surplus rather than of scarcity. In fact there seem to be at least two problems. One is the expected future shortage of paid work and the consequent surplus amount of leisure time that will become available. Some of the issues relating to the growth of technological unemployment were discussed in chapter 4. The second problem relates to the use that can be made of the growing amounts of leisure time and the readiness with which the economy can be adapted to provide the goods inputs required for recreational activities. These issues, which are fundamental to this study and which relate to the subject matter of several chapters, will be discussed in the final chapter.

There may, in the future, be some blurring of the distinction between paid work and leisure activities. It if turns out that there is a continuous decline in the demand for labour from industry, then one development could be a revival of craft work. The utility obtained from painting, carving, carpentry, making pottery and similar activities may be very high and these may all be undertaken as hobbies as well as for monetary reward. If society cannot provide paid work for people, then attitudes towards craft work may change. Even if much of the product cannot be sold, productive hobbies may be regarded as socially acceptable work. As Jenkins and Sherman (1979) argue, part of the urge to work comes from the 'work ethic', the belief that it is our duty to undertake paid work activity. If the products of manual labour are no longer essential to the survival of society then moral judgements about the need to work for the market may have to be changed. Some of the utility obtained from paid work may be obtained from the feeling that an obligation is being fulfilled. People who now try to earn a living from craft work or who attempt to grow their own food supplies are now often regarded as having 'opted-out' of economic life. If the attitude of society changes, then people may be able to obtain more satisfaction from these peripheral work activities.

Even if the area of 'work' is extended to include activities that were formerly undertaken for pleasure, and if more people follow these quasi-work pursuits, it is likely that the amount of pure-leisure time may continue to increase for the majority of the population. Education and training for the use of this leisure time will therefore become increasingly important. It is sometimes argued that education should be adapted to produce the kind of school-leaver or graduate who is required by industry, or who can make a full contribution to the economic life of the nation. But if there is to be a great contraction in the demand for labour from manufacturing industry then this argument may only be applicable to a part of the population. For the many people who may have no 'mainstream' job at all, or who will only be engaged in paid work for relatively short time periods, it is training for leisure that will become most urgent. The school timetable will have to be adapted to allow more time for music, drama, literature and sport and to include such subjects as camping, sailing, pottery and fishing. There is no fundamental reason why people should not be able to fill their time with reasonably enjoyable and rewarding activities even if large inputs of market goods are not available.

In *The Economics of Leisure and Recreation* (1975), Vickerman was mainly concerned with forecasting the demand for recreational activities, and making sure that rational decisions will be taken. There is a strong econometric element in his research in which he tried to establish relationships between the demand functions for recreational goods, for travel and for leisure time. His prime interest was in the provision of facilities, such as parks, that have all or some of the characteristics of a public good. These are goods that cannot be provided by the market since it is either impossible or undesirable to exclude anyone from enjoying the benefits they provide. Street lighting is a classical (non-recreational) example. It may be difficult to exclude people from parks that are just preserved natural country-side and that are not enclosed. Even if a park is enclosed, it will reduce the benefits that it yields to the community if payment for access is demanded and some people are thereby excluded (unless, that is, the park became so congested that additional visitors would reduce the pleasure of those in the park and would therefore impose a non-zero marginal cost). Vickerman is also concerned with the provision of transport, which is usually an essential ingredient of outdoor recreation. Although cars and coaches can be provided by the market, roads, which have some of the essential characteristics of a public good, are almost always provided by the public sector. Planning decisions are therefore essential in providing for many recreational facilities. Public decisions will also affect the demand for leisure activity and its location in space. A planning decision leading to the building of a new town will create demand for recreational facilities in a new area. For all these reasons, as Vicker-man argues, attempts to measure the future demand for provision for leisure activities, and the location of that demand, need to be made. Vickerman's study contains some interesting data from a survey made in Oxford showing the degree of participation of people in different socioeconomic groups in a number of leisure activities. These figures show that, for example, attendance at a cinema or theatre varied from 6.4 per cent of semi-skilled manual workers in the sample to 37.5 per cent of professional workers, whereas 'club visiting' ranged from 48.2 per cent of non-manual workers to 86.7 per cent of employers, managers and own-account workers.

In *The Price of Leisure* (1975), Owen was concerned with the demand for leisure time in the USA. Compared with Vickerman he concentrates more on the commercial provision of recreational facilities, and he has more to say about wage rates and hours of work. He shows that in the USA average weekly hours of work have fallen considerably (from 58.4 in 1901 to 41.9 – adjusted for vacations and holidays – in 1956) but that the rate of decline has slowed down in more recent years. Owen's econometric analysis included the price of recreation (leisure activities demanding a market input) as an explanatory variable in the analysis of the demand for leisure time and various other innovations. Neither Owen nor Vickerman dealt with the prospect of the disappearance of paid-work opportunities or the possible need to develop people's ability to make use of their growing supply of 'free' time.

7. SHOPPING AND BANKING HOURS

It was argued in section 2 of this chapter that the motivation behind most human activities is complex. Paid work may provide the worker with utility as well as with a wage, and many non-work activities may produce both a direct and an indirect utility. We eat because our bodies need food but also because we enjoy a good meal. Eating to live and living to eat are not mutually exclusive. One important area of activities where motivation is particularly uncertain is the category of shopping and personal business. Some everyday shopping for groceries and other necessities probably yields little if any utility. Housewives in Britain are generally prepared to pay to have their milk delivered to the house and have been alarmed by the suggestion that EEC regulations might result in the abolition of the 'friendly milkman'. But it is equally clear that a great deal of shopping activity is very much more than the last stage in the process of retail distribution. Much non-routine shopping provides considerable direct utility. For retired people and others with an ample supply of leisure time, and for families at weekends, shopping may be undertaken for the direct pleasure that it provides as much as for the need to acquire goods. The shopping case is of particular interest because, as was suggested in chapter 2, it raises the problem of how far the market process can allow people to use their time to provide the maximum amount of utility.

The Shops Acts in Britain (including those passed in 1892, 1904,

1912, 1928 and 1937) were designed to protect shop workers. They introduced compulsory half-holidays, maximum working hours and minimum standards for working conditions. The assumption behind this legislation was that shop workers were suffering from the working of the free market system, being insufficiently organised to prevent exploitation. It may be that today more attention should be paid to the welfare of shoppers. The effect of the Shops Acts is that, except in holiday towns, shopping centres in Britain are usually closed in the evening. Town centres become unattractive and families who might enjoy shopping together can only do so in the crowded conditions of Saturdays. Where evening shopping is possible, as in the USA, it is widely used.

There are two possible approaches to the problem of reconciling the conflicting interests of shop workers and shoppers. If state intervention is deemed necessary, then a large-scale cost–benefit analysis could undertaken to seek to measure the gains and losses to the community that would result from permitting widespread evening or Sunday shopping. It might be possible to estimate the preferences of shoppers by using a willingness-to-pay measurement where evening shopping was more expensive. The preferences of shop workers would be measured by discovering what payment they would require to work outside the normal 9.0 am to 6.0 pm period. It might also be necessary to measure the effect on urban transport and on restaurants and entertainment, and even, perhaps, on the crime rate in towns.

An alternative approach would be to allow more freedom to market forces. Now that shop workers have more effective union organisation, exploitation is unlikely. If the utility of working in shops declines (or the disutility increases) after 6.0 pm, then variations in hourly wages to reflect this factor would compensate those who were prepared to work in shops in the evening. If this resulted in an overall increase in costs then the market would demonstrate whether people were prepared to pay for the privilege of being able to shop in the evening. (It might be difficult to change prices according to the time of the day so that there could be some unfairness if daytime shoppers had to pay more for the benefit of evening shoppers.)

Another area where the interests of workers may now possibly have an undue influence is in the determination of banking hours. The activity of going to a bank, unlike that of shopping, provides little, if any, direct utility for most people. But the closure of all banks during all the time periods when people are free from work is a somewhat extraordinary arrangement. Saturday morning queues at cash dispensers and the use of building societies as substitute banks are just two symptoms of the inconvenience caused by current British banking hours. The reasons for this situation could provide another fruitful area for research. It would be surprising if there was no hourly wage that would induce bank workers to function on a Saturday morning or after 3.30 p.m. It would also seem likely that a bank that did open during times when people were not at work would be able to attract extra customers even if they had to pay higher charges. It may be that bank managements and bank workers' unions, given their present profits and earnings positions, seek to minimise trouble rather than to maximise profits or earnings. There appears to be no way in which customers can influence bank opening hours.

These two areas of shopping hours and banking hours illustrate cases where institutional or legal barriers may prevent people from using their time in ways that would yield them most welfare. Shopping restrictions, in particular, represent a failure to 'colonise' time by spreading 'wakeful activity throughout the twenty-four hours of the day' as has been suggested by Melbin (1978, p. 100).

CHAPTER 7

Present and Future Satisfaction

*This morning Shukhov economized. As he
hadn't returned to the hut he hadn't drawn his
rations, so he ate his breakfast without bread.
He'd eat the bread later. Might be even better
that way.*   [A. Solzhenitsyn]

1. INTRODUCTION

Men have never found it easy to put any part of the Sermon on
the Mount into practice, but perhaps its most difficult injunction
is the command to dismiss all concern for the future from our
minds. Far from removing interest in the questions 'Where will
my food come from? or my drink? or my clothes?' the relative
affluence of parts of the world today has merely lengthened the
list of material concerns that can give rise to anxiety. Most people
are not content if they receive their daily bread. They are also
worried about what they will be able to enjoy tomorrow and in
the much more distant future. Even if it is possible to avoid any
attendant anxiety, we can scarcely escape from the need to make
choices between present and future enjoyment. A prisoner who is
given just enough food each day to keep him alive would appear
to have very few decisions to make. Yet even he, like Ivan Denisovich Shukhov, may have to make a difficult choice between an
immediate or postponed consumption of his daily ration.

When men lived by hunting, their choice, like that of a prisoner,
was confined to that between eating a fixed quantity of food now
or in the near future. Since food decays quickly, it could not be
saved for any distant future, and the amount of food available
would certainly not increase automatically with time. A leg of
deer could be eaten today or sometime in the next few days, but

161

no other alternative choices were available. When men started to farm, the basic 'time of consumption' choice remained but the issue became more complicated because postponing consumption of some goods might bring a bonus. Grain that was not eaten but planted would produce a harvest that might be very much greater than the amount sown. One bushel of wheat today could be exchanged for fifty bushels in six months' time. The simple choice between eating a lump of bread in the early morning or consuming the same bread at midday, which troubled Ivan Denisovich, became more complex when the saved portion of potential food could be made to grow with the passage of time. (The idea of rewards for indirect methods of production was discussed more fully in chapter 4.)

A widening of the time horizon for choices between present and future satisfaction has come about in stages over a long period of history. There have been three main developments, which have, to some extent, all taken place in the same time periods. The basic ability to postpone consumption by storing goods has depended mainly on the growth of technology. During the whole of recorded history it has been possible to preserve some foodstuffs. Genesis records the storing of corn in Egypt during the 'seven years of great plenty', probably in about 1700 BC. Refrigeration through the use of ice and snow dates at least from Roman times, but the development of refrigeration through mechanical means in the nineteenth century (with the first refrigerated ship starting service in 1869) greatly extended man's ability to postpone the consumption of perishable foodstuffs. The growth of wealth meant that there were many other non-perishable goods that might be saved, but most of these were not literally consumed during the process of yielding satisfaction. Furniture and clothes may be gradually worn out by use but few people are likely to choose to postpone the consumption of durable goods that they already possess. Unless it was an antique, whose function was to provide a capital gain rather than to be sat upon, it would be odd to keep a chair in a bank vault. A man who walked naked through today's snows in order to defer consuming his clothes until next winter would generally be considered to be irrational. Durable goods can be saved in so far as their lifetime is extended by careful or frugal use (the largely unused nineteenth-century working-class 'parlour' is perhaps an example of this) but it does not usually make sense to postpone their consumption to a future date. Fuel is an exceptional commodity that can usually be stored but that also loses its ability to provide future satisfaction when it is consumed.

The second important factor affecting the ways in which we can choose between present and future satisfaction has been the development of money. The use of money did not overcome the technical problems of storage. It did not itself make it possible to provide fresh meat in the winter or ice in the summer. But to a large extent it removed the storage problem for individuals. Because money was accepted as purchasing power, and as money could be stored relatively easily, consumption, in a market economy, could be postponed. The man who made and sold a cloak for money tokens could use these to spread out his purchases of food over a period of time. The baker would produce bread and exchange it for a money token at any time so that the cloakmaker would not have to try to store all the bread that a cloak would buy in direct exchange. Suppose that in a primitive economy only two commodities, bread and tunics, were produced. If the rate of barter between loaves and tunics was established, money would not have been needed as a means of exchange. But it would still have been useful as a 'store of value' or promise to provide bread in the future that the wheat growers and bakers, who would only want to buy tunics occasionally, could give to the tunic makers so that their daily need for unstorable bread could be met. In a rather more complex economy, money made it possible not only to postpone consumption but also to move it forward in time. Those with more money than they required for their immediate needs could lend it to people who wanted to consume more today than their income would allow. The lenders would then expect some additional repayment as compensation for making the loan. Loans for consumption, or usury, have been condemned for long periods of history. The payment of interest was actually forbidden in England in 1197, and at other times maximum interest rates were fixed by the state. Even today the occupation of 'moneylender' is not always regarded very favourably. Moneylenders in literature are almost always portrayed as unpleasant people, who were subject to a particularly high risk of becoming murder victims. The reason for this is, of course, that making it possible for very poor people to consume more than they could buy with a subsistence level income, and then demanding repayment plus high interest to be paid out of a future income that has not increased, can be very harmful. Today, in relatively affluent countries like Britain, the 'enjoy-it-now and pay later' facility provided by banks, credit card organisations and hire-purchase arrangements does not meet with social disapproval. It is assumed that the commodities whose availability is put forward in time are not the basic necessities of life, and that future incomes will be adequate to cover repayments. The time-consumption choice is now also very much concerned with consumer durables. Loans that enable a family to buy a house and furniture out of future income are generally regarded as being beneficial.

The development of money has also been important in helping 'roundabout' or capitalist methods of production to take place. The choice between present and increased future consumption became more complicated when tools and then more elaborate capital equipment were required for production. Loans of money made it possible to divert resources into the production of capital equipment, which would not yield any immediate satisfaction, and borrowed money enabled producers to buy the consumption goods they needed immediately while their plant was being prepared to produce its final consumer goods. The ability to create new money or credit, which is not just a token given in exchange for a good or service that has already been produced, has added further complexities to the ways in which the supply of loanable funds is determined. It has also affected the rate of interest, which is the level of the reward that will be received for postponing consumption or of the penalty that must be paid for using other people's resources for consumption or investment.

There are thus several separate, though linked, issues relating to the choice between present and future consumption with which economists may be concerned. It is very unlikely that a family will want to turn its money income into consumption goods (or even consume an income received in kind) at the exact moment in time when the income is paid over. As we have seen, even a prisoner in a labour camp may make decisions about his pattern of consumption. A family will sometimes want to be able to use future income to buy a house, furniture or a TV set today. At other times the family will want to be able to postpone consumption so that they can even-out fluctuations in income and make provision for their old age. Rich people will not want to consume their wealth instantly but will expect it to provide a flow of income for the rest of their lives, and probably for the lives of their descendants as well. At the same time there will be a demand for funds not only from those who want to bring forward their right to consume but also, most importantly, from those who wish to invest in capitalist methods of production.

Discussion of the choice between present and future satisfaction in economic literature has centred around two main issues. Attempts have been made to analyse the behaviour of individual consumers and to try to find a pattern relating individual savings or consumption decisions to a lifetime plan. The influence of changes in the supply of credit or in the level of interest rates on the 'lifetime' allocation of expenditure has been examined. Secondly, the evaluation of alternative investment projects yielding streams of benefits that have different time distributions has been studied. Most of the discussion has been related to the choice of an appropriate discount rate for use in calculating the net present value of the expected returns from public sector investment proposals. These two main themes are discussed in this chapter but they are developed to include the fundamental issue of whether current discounting practices wrongly discriminate against high capital cost projects that produce benefits in the relatively distant future; consideration of the assumption that individuals always prefer present to future consumption; a critical appraisal of Becker's lifetime allocation model; and an examination of some statistics on hours worked and age group.

2. MOVEMENTS OF CONSUMPTION THROUGH TIME

If men knew how to go about it they would try to spend their lifelong ration of time so that it would yield them the maximum amount of happiness. Most 'leisure' activities require some inputs of market goods and services and in chapter 6 the allocation of time to paid-work activity, in order to obtain income that can be exchanged for these inputs, was examined. But the possibility of moving consumption to different points in time, which is our present concern, was not brought into the analysis. The amount of income received from work activity per time period will depend upon the number of hours worked and the rate of pay (or level of profit). Workers may only have very limited control over the former of these and no individual control at all over wage rates. The pattern of earnings over time will vary for different occupations. A professional tennis player may receive a very large income in his twenties that reduces to almost nothing by the time that he is 40. Some professional workers, such as barristers or authors on the other hand, may find that earnings per time unit continue to increase for the whole of their working lives. But, for the average worker, earnings per week will increase up to a point perhaps two-thirds of the way through his career and will then decline. Some British figures are shown in Table 7.1. According to a major American study by Kreps:

TABLE 7.1
Weekly earnings and age groups, UK, April 1979

| | Full-time earnings | |
Age groups	Males £	Females £
Under 18	40.3	36.6
18–20	61.9	48.7
21–24	81.5	59.0
25–29	95.3	67.7
30–39	107.6	68.7
40–49	109.5	67.1
50–59	102.2	64.9
60–64	89.5	59.4
65 and over	79.0	51.5

Source: Department of Employment (1980)

. . . average earnings of different age cohorts observe the same pattern in most occupations. Immediately after entry into the labour force annual earnings are low; higher incomes then accrue to each successive cohort until peak earnings are realised by the age group 45-54. The 55-64 year-old workers, the oldest full-time participants, have incomes significantly lower than the preceding age group. Retirement income is typically less than a third of peak annual earnings. [Kreps, 1971, p. 85]

The need for goods and services is unlikely to vary in the same way as do changes in income. For most households the peak demand for income will come at an early age when a separate home is formed and when it is necessary to buy furniture and a house. The birth and growth of children will bring new demands for market goods. Household income may also fall when children are young and their mother cannot work, so that the pattern shown in Table 7.1 for the individual worker may not be representative of total family income. When children leave home the need for income may fall while total family income could rise. At retirement, earned income may disappear entirely, or be replaced by a relatively small pension. For all these reasons it is apparent that households may wish to rearrange their income flows. Young families will need to borrow against future earnings in order to set up home while households with peak earning capacity may wish to save income that can be spent after retirement.

Even if capital was not required for investment there would still be a need for lending and borrowing. Young people would save for the time when they set up a house, married couples would borrow to buy a house and raise a family and older households would save for retirement. Thus a typical man (with no inherited wealth) might be a saver from the time of starting work at 16 to the time of getting married at 25; he and his wife might then need to be in debt to others, paying off a mortgage loan for the next twenty years, then become savers from the age of 45 to 65 and finally receive back their loans during the period from 65 to the time of their deaths. (In practice, people save for their old age through pension schemes at the same time as repaying mortgage debt.)

It is of some interest to examine a little further the situation in a simple closed economy where lending and borrowing are used solely to transfer purchasing power to different time periods and where loans are not used to produce additional wealth. The existence of interest payments, as will be argued later, not only complicates but also sometimes confuses the analysis. Suppose that the decision-making life of the average citizen is divided into four time periods, t_1 to t_4 years, and that in periods t_1 and t_3 he is able to save, while in periods t_2 and t_4 he and his household consume more than their income and need to borrow. If the sums saved are s_1 and s_2 per year (in time periods t_1 and t_3) while the average consumption 'surpluses' per year are b_1 and b_2 in time periods t_2 and t_4 then, if capital is neither inherited nor left to descendants, it follows that:

$$t_1 s_1 + t_1 s_2 = t_2 b_1 + t_4 b_2.$$

The model can be simplified still further by assuming that the annual savings are the same for both time periods and that average annual surplus consumption or borrowing is also identical in both periods so that $s_1 = s_2 = s$ and $b_1 = b_2 = b$. If it is also assumed that saving is a fixed proportion of income, and thus determined exogenously, then the consumption 'surplus' must be adjusted so that

$$b = \frac{t_1 + t_3}{t_2 + t_4} s.$$

This means that the money available for house purchase (and any other surplus expenditure) in period t_2 and for income during retirement in period t_4 would be determined by the level of earned income and by the relative lengths of the different time periods. If it is assumed that it takes a household twenty years to pay off all mortgage obligations, during which period they remain net borrowers, if an average couple work for nine years before marriage, and if retirement is at 65, then a retirement period of nine years would just exhaust savings where annual surplus expenditure during the 'borrowing' years was equal to annual savings during each of the 'saving' years. Given the assumptions of the model, surplus expenditure on the house and family during period t_2 and spending during retirement (t_4) would need to be reduced if the couple expected to live more than nine years after retirement. Thus a couple living twenty years after retirement would only be able to spend a proportion 29/40 of their savings (or £725 for each £1000 saved) during their 'surplus expenditure' years. A general version of this model would be where there are m savings periods, t_i, with savings of s_i, and n surplus consumption periods, t_j, with b_j excess expenditure over annual income, the sum left to spend during retirement being the residual R. In this case

$$\sum_{i=1}^{m} t_i s_i - \sum_{j=1}^{n} t_j b_j = R.$$

If each household had to balance its lifetime income and expenditure in this way, and if there was a stable population, with approximately equal numbers of households in each age group, then the demand for and supply of loanable funds would balance without the need for a non-zero interest rate. There would be sufficient householders wishing to postpone consumption to meet the needs of housebuyers or those in retirement who needed to consume more than the value of their current production. This situation, far removed from reality as it may be, is perhaps useful in a consideration of that somewhat confused concept 'pure time preference'. It is assumed in most, though not all, economic literature that people prefer current to future consumption of the same quantity of goods. Henderson (1968) lists three reasons for believing that individuals normally have a positive time preference rate, so that future benefits should be discounted. These are that there may be some uncertainty that a future benefit will be paid out; that we are all going to die so may not be around to enjoy promised future consumption; and that if real income rises over time, later increments of consumption will yield less utility than will present consumption. None of the reasons for postulating a positive pure time preference rate is particularly convincing. Uncertainty about the repayment of loans is reflected in equity yields, but it seems to be improbable that the average investor is very much concerned about the risk that National Savings will not be repaid or that building societies will collapse. Although people may be aware of the possibility of an early death they will usually plan as if they expect to live to a normal age. Within the time horizon of a normal life expectancy the fact of human mortality is unlikely to affect most people's evaluation of future benefits. The fear of having an inadequate income in old age is likely completely to outweigh any concern about dying while a surplus of wealth is still unconsumed. As has been argued, most people probably plan for a family unit rather than for themselves alone, so that they may expect their spouse or children to be around even if they should die prematurely. The third argument may be relevant to an aggregated social time preference rate but it is not applicable to individual households. As has been shown, the common experience of households is that their income will fall for the last twenty years or so of their lifespan and the marginal utility of income may therefore be expected to rise. Even if a country is enjoying rapid economic growth, and if old people are given a share in increasing wealth through rising pensions or dividend income, it is very unlikely that they would enjoy a larger income in retirement than they did when at work.

As Feldstein has pointed out, 'for the community as a whole, it is impossible to redistribute consumption through time by merely monetary borrowing–lending transactions' (1964, p. 369). But different sections of the community can transfer purchasing power to each other. Young unmarried people and established households during peak earning periods can hand over some of their rights to immediate consumption to house buyers or to those in retirement. Retired couples will be able to reclaim loans that they made when they were themselves in the peak earning years. As has been argued, in a static society, with no population growth and with opportunities for private investment in productive enterprise, these interchanges of the 'right to consume' might be achieved without the emergence of positive or negative interest rates. However, even if capital could not be employed productively and only intergenerational lending and borrowing took place, it seems likely that interest rates would be positive. For many forms of consumption the choice is not (as it is usually shown in the models of consumer behaviour discussed below) between immediate or future consumption but between periods of consumption that may begin earlier or later. A chair is not consumed when it is bought but may last for a lifetime. Houses are only a special form of durable good of which there are many other species. While people may prefer to spread out their purchase of instantly consumable goods and services, such as food and entertainment, over their lifetimes they will usually want to buy and enjoy durable goods as soon as possible. This desire to obtain houses, furniture, TV sets and many other durable goods before sufficient purchasing power has been acquired could lead to positive interest rates even in a world without productive investment opportunities. The demand for interest-free loans would exceed the supply and those who are prepared to wait to buy their video recorders might expect to receive some compensation from those who borrow from them because they want to start their period of consumption straight away. As an advertisement for credit card facilities argues persuasively: 'today our households are amazingly complicated places, filled with elaborate equipment, frequently changed . . . Our budgets are correspondingly complex . . . Using your [credit card] account . . . you can smooth the peaks and troughs of your overall budget.'

In the real world, opportunities for productive investment are normally available: £100 today may be exchanged for £110 next year because it can be invested in some capitalist enterprise that will increase the actual quantity of goods available. This means, in effect, that those who want to consume more than they can buy with their immediate income are penalised, while those who wish to postpone consumption receive a bonus. Even if inter-generational demands for loans and creation of savings were balanced, the extra demand for investment capital would normally make interest rates positive.

The basic problem in trying to analyse the concept of time preference is to distinguish between the underlying preferences of individuals for future or present consumption and the ways in which they will behave when faced with positive interest rates. Henderson and Quandt (1980) define the rate of time preference as the minimum compensation required by an individual to postpone consumption from one period to a later period. If there are two periods, t_0 and t_1, where t_1 is later than t_0, then the rate of time preference

$$n_{t_0 t_1} = -\frac{\partial C_{t_1}}{\partial C_{t_0}} - 1$$

where C_{t_0} is the consumption in period t_0 and C_{t_1} that in period t_1. But they then argue that rates of time preference may be negative and state that the consumer's 'subjective rates of time preference are derived from his consumption-utility function and depend upon the levels of his consumption expenditure. They are independent of the market rates of interest . . .' (Henderson and Quandt, 1980, p. 327). Laidler (1974) calls the situation where the choice is between 'equal amounts of consumption' in each period the 'rate of time preference proper'. Feldstein (1964) has used the term a 'pure time preference discount rate'.

The terminology of subjective or proper rates of time preference is perhaps somewhat confusing and it may be useful to develop Feldstein's argument that there is a time preference function. An individual who has made no time adjustments to his expected income flow will have certain preferences, which may involve moving his consumption pattern over time. He may wish to substitute some future for present consumption or vice versa. If he wishes to postpone consumption, the utility of future purchasing power will presumably fall as he obtains an increasing supply. If interest rates were zero he would obtain all the future purchasing power he wanted up to the point where the marginal utility of future and present consumption were equal. This would be where the marginal rate of time preference was zero. In a two-period case, if C_0 is the utility received from current consumption and C_1 is that gained from future consumption, the consumer would lend money (or buy future purchasing power) until $\partial C_1/\partial C_0 = 0$.

The existence of a positive interest rate is likely to persuade households to buy more future purchasing power since this will not have a lower 'price' relative to current consumption. As has been made clear in the literature, however, (Laidler, 1974, Dasgupta and Pearce, 1972, Henderson and Quandt, 1980, for example) a rise in interest rates will not necessarily increase savings. The substitution effect of the lower price of future consumption may be offset by the income effect. Thus a household saving to buy a new car or in order to build up a fund for retirement might increase their current consumption if higher interest rates made their savings accumulate more rapidly. In the real world, of course, the situation is complicated by the existence of inflation, and a consumer who expects an increase in interest rates to be matched by a corresponding increase in inflation may allow his level of savings to remain unchanged.

Laidler's 'rate of time preference proper' relates to the marginal rate of substitution between present and future goods when 'equal quantities of them are available in each period'. This is just a special case of a consumer who is assumed to prefer present consumption (since future goods are discounted) and who expects to have a constant real income. As the conventional indifference curve analysis shows, marginal time preference rates would change constantly as consumers increased their holding of rights to future consumption. Even with this original equal holding of present and future goods and one-for-one exchange rate (or zero interest rates) there would be a continuous series of actual marginal preference rates as present income was exchanged for future purchasing power. The exchange rate between present and future consumption must also depend upon the size of the 'quantities of goods' or amounts of income available in the two periods. If the 'quantities of goods' available in each period are very small, so that consumers are near to the bare subsistence level, then they will be much less likely to choose to postpone consumption than when the purchasing power to buy large quantities of goods is available. The 'pure' or 'proper' rate of time preference therefore appears to be not a single rate but the series of rates that would be chosen by an individual consumer or household when interest rates are zero (£1 of consumption this year can be exchanged for £1 of consumption next year).

It is perhaps useful to attempt to summarise the rate of time preference concept in terms of the demand for present or future purchasing power and the distinction between 'pure', 'subjective' or 'proper' and what we may call 'unqualified' rates of time preference. Those who deal in present and future purchasing power may be consumers or suppliers of either 'commodity'. Some people, given their current and expected income flows, would like to forgo some present consumption and exchange this for future purchasing power. They will have a demand schedule for the 'commodity' future purchasing power. But instead of having to pay for this commodity they may find that (whenever interest rates are higher than the rate of inflation) they can gain a reward for postponing consumption. Some 'lenders' may be induced to buy more future purchasing power when the price falls (interest rates rise) though others may do the opposite. The net result of a fall in the price of future consumption for an individual depends upon whether the income or substitution effect is strongest. The marginal utility of increments of future purchasing power will fall as the stock increases so that a rational 'lender' will increase his stock until the marginal utility equals the price. But in the special case of transfers of purchasing power through time, 'lenders' will soon reach the point where one unit of future purchasing power would yield less utility than one unit of current purchasing power and their orginally negative 'rate of time preference proper' becomes positive. Beyond this point they need the reward of a positive rate of interest to persuade them to make any further loans. They will then continue to exchange current for future purchasing power until the reward they receive equals the loss of utility resulting from the transaction. As already argued, this is where the (positive) marginal rate of time preference equals the available interest rate.

Another group of people, the 'borrowers', wish to exchange some future consumption for extra present consumption. They will usually find that they must pay the 'price' of a positive real interest, and will need to surrender a larger number of units of future purchasing power for a smaller number of units of current purchasing power. This will mean that their demand for present purchasing power is likely to be lower than it would be if interest rates were zero and present and future consumption could be exchanged on a unit-for-unit basis. Both income and substitution effects will work in the same direction. Of course individuals may have a very strong need to increase their present consumption so that the demand for loans may be inelastic in relation to price. But, if interest rates become high enough, potential borrowers might eventually have their demand for loans reduced to zero and then be turned into lenders themselves. They could change from being consumers to suppliers of current capital. Their marginal rate of time preference would start and remain positive but would fall if they could obtain the first units of purchasing power at a lower price than they were prepared to pay (i.e. if the interest rate was below their initial 'rate of time preference proper'). If the market interest rate was higher than their marginal rate of time preference, or price they were prepared to pay for the first unit of current purchasing power, then they would lend instead of borrowing and their marginal rate of time preference would rise as more current purchasing power was surrendered until it equalled the rate of interest.

Much of the preceding analysis has been no more than an attempt to work out the meaning of established theory about individual time preference. But at least one new emphasis arises from the discussion. This is that the importance and prevalence of negative time preference rates may be underestimated. Laidler's definition of the 'rate of time preference proper' assumes that future benefits will be discounted. Henderson and Quandt mention the possibility that 'subjective' rates of time preference may be negative but do not develop this point. Much of the literature is concerned with social time preference (discussed later in this chapter) where the future is always assumed to be discounted, and if social time preference is based on individual preferences then it follows that these rates must be positive too. But if the demand for capital for productive investment did not exist then, as has been argued, the needs of borrowers and lenders might be approximately equal. The demand for capital to be used for productive purposes, however, normally ensures that marginal time preference rates are positive. Some people would be prepared to postpone consumption even if the current purchasing power they had to surrender was greater than the future purchasing power that they would gain in exchange. But faced by positive interest rates they can fulfil all their needs for future purchasing power and will be persuaded to lend more money until their marginal time preference rate becomes positive. At the time of writing, however, most real interest rates in Britain are negative.

The measurement of the return received on loans in the real world involves various complications. Uncertainty, changes in capital values and the effects of taxation and inflation must all be considered. The rate of return on government stock is known with virtual certainty but the yield on British government stock is also affected by the date that interest payments are due, the relationship between the market price and the redemption price (which may give a certain tax-free capital gain), the redemption date and expectations about the future movement of interest rates and the price of gilt-edged stock. To overcome some of these difficulties, the interest yield on twenty different government stocks all standing above 100 (and thus containing no guaranteed capital gain element) as shown in the *Financial Times* on 28 July 1980 was averaged. The average interest yield shown was 12.977 per cent (standard deviation = 0.36 per cent). Inflation at that time was over 20 per cent. Suppose that potential investors had the moderately optimistic belief that the average inflation rate over the next year would drop to 15 per cent and that they expected to pay tax on any interest received at the standard rate of 30 per cent. In these circumstances an investment in average 'above par' government stock of £1000 would be worth only £948.5 in real terms in one year's time. To obtain £948.5 worth of purchasing power one year into the future would involve surrendering £1000 worth of current purchasing power. (No allowance was made in the calculations for the possibility of deferring the tax payments on unearned income.)

Building society interest on ordinary paid up shares is currently 10.5 per cent (with income tax at the rate of 30 per cent already paid). With current inflation rates, building society investors are thus accepting negative interest rates. The figures in Table 7.2 show the estimated real rates of return on a one-year investment in an

TABLE 7.2

Real interest rates for one-year investment in average UK building society accounts and building society receipts of capital

Year	Real interest rate for one-year investment %	Rate of discount of present benefit	Receipts of capital 1970 prices £m
1970	−4.45	4.66	(1490)
1971	−2.53	2.60	(1859)
1972	−4.20	4.39	4519
1973	−8.59	9.39	4729
1974	−13.94	16.20	4292
1975	−8.46	9.24	4901
1976	−8.01	8.71	4770
1977	−2.00	2.04	5753
1978	−6.83	7.33	5882
1979	−10.12	11.27	6194

Source: Central Statistical Office (1980).

Note: The capital receipt figures for 1970 and 1971 relate to *net* inflows of capital. In calculating the average building society interest rate on ordinary accounts the rate shown in *Financial Statistics* for each year was deflated by the amount of the average rate of inflation from the year that the investment was made to the succeeding year, using index of retail prices data. The effects of interest rates and inflation were combined using the formula

$$[(1 + r) \left(\frac{1}{1 + i} \right) - 1] \, 100$$

where r is the interest rate earned and i the rate of inflation, both divided by 100. The 'rate of discount of present benefit' figures were calculated from the model

$$V = (1 + r) \left(\frac{1}{1 + i} \right)$$

$$R = \left(\frac{1}{V} - 1 \right) 100$$

$$= \left(\frac{1 + i}{1 + r} - 1 \right) 100$$

where V is the net value of £1 after investment for one year and R is the real rate at which *present* income received in the future is discounted.

average building society account during the period 1970–79 together with figures for cash inflows and the implied rate of discount of *present* consumption. These figures show that throughout the period 1970–79 investors making a one-year investment in an average building society account would have received a negative interest rate. Real rates for longer-term investments are difficult to calculate precisely, but these would also have been negative during this period except possibly for an occasional very lucky dating of investment, receipt of interest and withdrawal. The 'rate of discount' column shows the effective discounting of present benefits received in one year's time. Interest rates appear to have had little effect on the inflow of capital to building societies (though the comparison with alternative rates in National Savings and government securities would also affect the flow of funds). Despite negative real interest rates, savers continued to invest on a large scale and must either have been ignorant of real interest rates or have had negative rates of time preference.

A preference for future rather than present consumption is undoubtedly widespread in an affluent society and the assumption that discounting the future is the standard procedure for individuals needs to be examined. The existence of a demand for capital for productive purposes may mean that there is a reward for postponing consumption that has nothing to do with the balance of time preference and that marginal time preference rates will become positive. But with negative real interest rates the volume of lenders is apparently undiminished. If there were no means of employing capital productively and income was evenly distributed, inter-generational movements of purchasing power could lead to negative, zero or positive interest rates. The demand to buy expensive durable goods before sufficient income had been saved might lead to an excess demand for current purchasing power and to positive interest rates. But the volume of money saved for the future is likely to be greater than that used for 'surplus' consumption. The unequal distribution of income must also be important in the real world. Relatively affluent households may have a strong desire to postpone some possible consumption. Institutions managing pension funds create a large demand for future income. When, as at present, there are few investment opportunities that will yield a return as high as the expected rate of inflation, it is not surprising that 'lenders' are compelled to accept negative real interest rates. The large-scale storage of consumer goods is not usually practicable. The development of inflation has often been associated with an increase in saving as people seek to ensure that they have adequate purchasing power available for their non-earning old age. Until they can meet their minimum requirements for retirement, households may wish to postpone some present consumption and if the market will not provide positive real interest for loans they may have a negative marginal rate of time preference.

The effect of real interest rates on the saving required to produce £1000 of purchasing power in twenty years' time is shown in Figure 7.1. The figures illustrated in Figure 7.1 are given in Table 7.3. They show the well-known powerful influence of rates of compound interest on the growth of savings funds. Within the range of +5 per cent to −5 per cent real interest rates, the sum required to produce

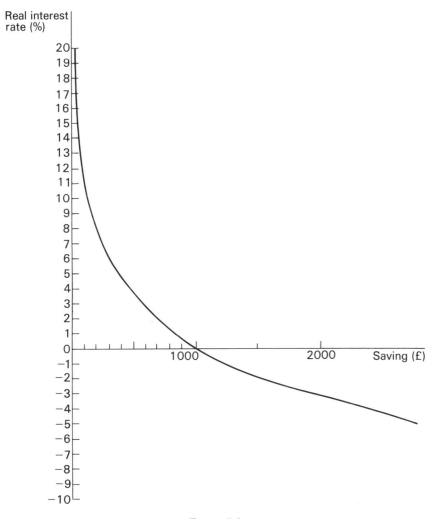

Figure 7.1
*Saving required to produce £1000 purchasing power in 20 years' time
with different real interest rates*

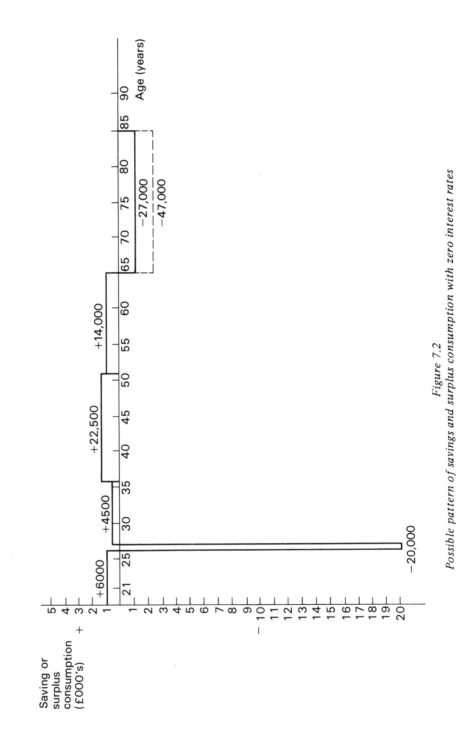

Figure 7.2
Possible pattern of savings and surplus consumption with zero interest rates

TABLE 7.3
*Sum required to produce £1000 in 20 years' time
with different real interest rates*

Rate of interest (with allowance for inflation) %	Sum required £
20	26.1
15	61.1
10	148.6
5	376.9
4	456.4
3	553.7
2	673.0
1	819.5
0	1000.0
−2	1497.9
−5	2789.5

£1000 of purchasing power in twenty years' time varies from £376.9 to £2789.5. The figures could also be regarded as the sums required to produce £1000 of purchasing power at constant prices given zero interest rates and different rates of inflation or deflation. Thus the sum required to be set aside today to provide £1000 at constant prices in twenty years' time, with a zero interest rate and a constant 2 per cent inflation rate, would be £1497.9.

The savings and 'surplus consumption' patterns of an imaginary household similar to that described in the earlier discussion of inter-generational transfers, with zero interest and zero inflation, is illustrated in Figure 7.2. It is assumed that the household consists originally of a man and woman of the same age who jointly save £1000 a year from the ages of 20 to 25 (Couples living apart but saving to get married can be regarded as a household for the purposes of this model.) At 26 the couple marry and buy a house that costs £20,000 more than their income for the year. (The couple may either borrow £20,000 or borrow £14,000 and use their accumulated savings of £6000.) It is assumed that their savings and consumption pattern is as shown in Table 7.4. The savings patterns shown are intended to reflect possible earnings from the wife and increased earnings from the husband from the ages of 36 to 50, and then some fall in average joint earning power between 51 and retirement at 65. On retirement the couple would have net cash savings of £27,000,

TABLE 7.4
Hypothetical savings and 'surplus consumption' pattern for a household

Age range	Annual saving £	Annual surplus consumption £
20–25	1000	–
26	–	20,000
27–35	500	–
36–50	1500	–
51–64	1000	–
65–84	–	1350(2350)

which would amount to £1350 a year if they both died on their eighty-fifth birthday. The global sum would be increased to £47,000, or £2350 a year, if they sold their house, for its original purchase price, on retirement. If the house was sold and the proceeds spent, the movements of purchasing power over time would cancel out, and the couple would leave neither assets (apart from durable household and other goods) nor debts.

The existence of positive real interest rates could have a very considerable effect on the financial position of this hypothetical household. It is assumed that the householders invested all savings at the going rate of interest on the last day of each year of their age (i.e. the savings for the year in which they were 20 were invested on the day before their twenty-first birthday); that they used the savings and interest for years 20–25 as part payment for the house; that the house was bought on their twenty-sixth birthday; that all other savings made were the same as in the zero-interest case; and that the debt on the house was allowed to stand, with interest charges until retirement. In these circumstances the couple would find that, with a constant 10 per cent interest rate, their savings on their sixty-fifth birthday would amount to the magnificent sum of £316,815. But the debt on their house would have increased to the even more formidable amount of £505,438. The solvency of the unfortunate couple would, in these circumstances, depend upon whether they were able to find somewhere to live if they sold their house, and the rate of inflation in house prices over the thirty-nine years between their twenty-sixth and sixty-fifth birthdays. If the householders wished to use their savings to pay the house debt on their fifty-first birthday, they would find that they had savings of £76,021 but a debt of £133,098. In order to pay the house debt on their fifty-first birthday an annual saving (starting in their twenty-seventh year) of £1353 would be necessary (i.e. repayment of £12,284 over twenty-five years at 10 per cent interest rate). If the 'zero-interest' pattern of saving and surplus consumption was followed, and if the constant interest rate was only 2.5 per cent then the hypothetical couple would find that they had savings of £64,714 on their sixty-fifth birthday while the debt on their house amounted to only £35,658, giving a net surplus for their retirement of £29,056, a very similar sum to that found in the zero interest rate case. The main figures for the 'settlement at 65' situation are repeated in Table 7.5.

TABLE 7.5

Surplus or deficit at age 65 for couple with savings and surplus consumption pattern shown in Table 7.4 for different real interest rates

Real interest rate %	Net surplus (+) or deficit (−) £
0	+27,000
2.5	+29,056
10	−188,623

The situation with positive real interest rates can be shown as a general model if two alterations are made that avoid unnecessary complication. It is assumed that there are two annual amounts saved, S_1 for each year before house purchase and S_2 for each year after the house purchase year, and that the house purchase (like investment) was made at the end rather than the beginning of the year. Then if the interest rate divided by 100 is r, the house is bought in year a at a cost C in excess of available income for that year, and the total years from starting work to retirement are n, then the net cash savings at the time of retirement, NB, would be given by

$$NB = S_2 \sum_{j=0}^{j=n-a-1} (1+r)^j - \left[C - S_2 \sum_{i=1}^{i=a-1} (1+r)^i \right] (1+r)^{n-a}.$$

The implications of changes in money interest rates and of the rate of inflation on inter-temporal movements of consumption in the real world are not easy to determine. Households following the pattern of early savings, borrowing for house purchase and then renewed savings (including repayment of the house loan) are likely to be made worse off when real interest rates rise unless they were already making relatively large savings. The imaginary household represented in Table 7.5 would have a net surplus at the age of 65 turned into a large deficit if interest rates rose from 2.5 per cent to 10 per cent and if they tried to maintain the same pattern of saving and borrowing. In reality, rises in interest rates are likely to force the typical house-buying family to increase its rate of saving so that the interest, and some capital, can be repaid from their mortgage. Their position on retirement will then depend on the general rate of inflation, the rate of inflation of house prices, whether they can arrange to turn the capital value of their house into income, and the yield obtained from their investments. A permanent rise in real interest rates could make households worse off during the 'middle years' when they are repaying the house loan, but better off on retirement when they have become net lenders. Changes in tax levels on earned and unearned income and the possibility of making capital gains or losses on investments add to the complications and uncertainties of the real world situation.

The effect of interest rates on the choice between present and future consumption has often been examined with the use of indifference curves and the equivalent of budget constraint lines. If a consumer knows what income he will receive in a current time period and (with reasonable certainty) in a future time period then he can adjust his consumption position by borrowing or lending. It is assumed in this simplified analysis that all income will be consumed in the two time periods taken together and, usually, that the time periods are year t and year $t + 1$. In the two extreme cases households could consume all their income in year t by borrowing the maximum amount possible on the promise of repayment from the expected future income or could lend the whole of their present income for repayment at the end of period $t + 1$.

In Figure 7.3 the indifference curve analysis has been used for two time periods, but the customary one-year gap has been extended to twenty years. The effect of this is to increase the influence of the interest rate level. It is assumed that there is no inflation and that any inter-temporal transactions other than those affecting years 1 and 21 can be ignored. The consumer is assumed to know that he will receive an income of £5000 at the end of both year 1 and year 21. The budget constraint *ab* shows the position with a constant 2.5 per cent interest rate. The maximum possible consumption in year 1 would be £8051, while that in year 21 would be £13,193.

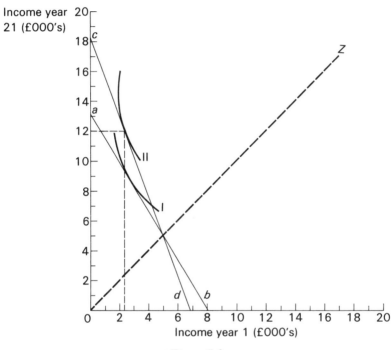

Figure 7.3
Choice between present and future consumption with different interest rates

With a 5 per cent interest rate the equivalent sums would be £6884 and £18,266, as shown by the budget constraint *cd*. If I was the consumer's indifference curve that was tangential to budget constraint *ab*, then the consumer would save £2441.1 from his year 1 income, consuming £2558.9 in year 1 and £9000 at the end of year 21. With a 5 per cent interest rate, and if curve II mapped the consumer's indifference between different amounts of present and future consumption, then £2361.8 would be spent in year 1 and £12,000 at the end of year 21. The line OZ marks the point at which the consumer would not transfer any purchasing power. If the income to be received in each of the two periods is the same, then the OZ line will be at an angle of 45° to the horizontal axis. An indifference curve tangential to a budget line where it is cut by the OZ line would measure zero time preference. The indifference curves drawn in Figure 7.3 show a situation where the substitution effect of a rise in interest rates is stronger than the income effect so that more year 1 income is saved at the higher interest rate. But a curve could have been drawn that would have shown a reduction in saving at the higher interest rate. Thus if a consumer had a fixed requirement for £7000 purchasing power in year 21 he would save £1220.5 and spend £3779.5 with a 2.5 per cent interest rate. With the higher interest rate of 5 per cent, this consumer would save £753.8 and spend £4246.2 in year 1. Indifference curves tangential to the budget constraint lines to the right of the OZ line would map the preferences of those choosing to increase their present consumption by borrowing, with the given interest rates.

3. THE PERMANENT INCOME HYPOTHESIS

It is not easy to integrate discussion of the permanent income hypothesis into a study dealing with economic problems and time. The main concern of the permanent income debate has been with the nature of the consumption function, with the relationship between changes in real income and consumption and savings, and with the macroeconomic implications of any conclusions. But some parts of the discussion are also relevant to our present concern with the choices open to consumers in allocating expenditure over time.

Friedman's seminal monograph (1957) was inspired by the apparent conflict between the nature of the consumption function postulated in Keynes' *General Theory* and empirical evidence. Keynes had argued that, 'as a rule', a greater proportion of income would be saved as real income increased. But empirical evidence, such as that collected by Kuznets (1946, 1952) and relating to the USA for the period 1869–1929, has shown that long-term rises in real income have been associated with a constant percentage of income saved. Where savings and consumption percentages remain constant despite large changes in average income levels, the average and marginal propensity to save (or to consume) will be equal. However, sets of individual budget studies have produced estimates of a marginal propensity to consume that were lower than the average propensity figures. The starting point of Friedman's study was, therefore, the problem created by 'the inadequacy of a consumption function relating consumption or savings solely to current income' (1957, p. 4).

Friedman argued that, if a consumer has complete certainty about his income, prices and interest rates in the future, then he would only have two possible motives for spending more or less than the total of his current income or consumption. Firstly he would seek to 'straighten out' his stream of expenditure by lending or borrowing. This is equivalent to the adjustments over time discussed in section 2 of this chapter, though Friedman did not distinguish between movements of purchasing power for current consumption and the desire to buy and enjoy durable goods before they can be paid for out of current income. Friedman's second motive is to earn interest from loans (or to be paid for looking after someone else's claim to purchasing power when interest rates are negative). This part of his analysis is based on Fisher's well-known treatment of the theory of interest. Friedman's basic argument is that the income that people actually receive for each arbitrarily determined time period may be either greater or less than their long-term expectations of income. It is these long-term expectations that determine consumers' saving and spending patterns. According to Friedman, the income of what he calls 'consumer units' consists of a 'permanent' and a 'transitory' component. The permanent component reflects '. . . the effect of those factors that the unit regards as determining its capital value or wealth; the non-human wealth it owns; the personal attributes of the earners in the unit, such as their training, ability, personality; the attributes of the economic activity of the earners, such as the occupation followed, the location of the economic activity, and so on' (1957, p. 21). Friedman deliberately avoids giving a precise definition of 'permanent income' since, he argues, this depends upon the actual behaviour of individuals, and cannot always be predicted. One possible meaning of 'permanent income' is the mean of the probability distribution of a consumer's expected future income, as judged by himself. Consumers' estimates will be affected by the length of their time horizon. If C_p is permanent consumption, i is the rate of interest, w is the relative importance of property and non-property income or the 'ratio of nonhuman wealth to income', u is a variable measuring the consumer's time preference (for consumption) and y_p is permanent income, then

$$C_p = K\,(i,\,w,\,u)\,y_p.$$

If y is total income, C is total consumption and y_t and C_t are transitory income and consumption, then

$$y = y_p + y_t$$

and

$$C = C_p + C_t.$$

An important assumption of the hypothesis is that the correlation between transitory income and transitory consumption is zero. The average marginal propensity to consume of transitory income is therefore zero. This appears to be a surprising conclusion since it is apparent that people do sometimes spend unexpected additions to their income on consumption. Friedman attempts to overcome this objection by arguing that the increased expenditure is likely to take the form of an extra purchase of durable goods and that this, when applied to the classification of empirical data, should be counted as saving. He also argues that extra spending from transitory income may be offset by reduced spending where, for example, the method of obtaining the transitory income (such as working on a North Sea oil rig) reduces opportunities for consumption.

A considerable part of Friedman's original development of the permanent income hypothesis was devoted to an examination of empirical evidence. He believed that the hypothesis was reasonably consistent both with budget studies and data from time-series studies. In the analysis of budget studies he found that the average propensity to consume was consistently higher than the marginal propensity for each cross-section study. Modigliani's 'life cycle hypothesis' (1966), developed at the same time as the permanent income hypothesis, puts forward very similar arguments to those of Friedman. According to Modigliani, consumption is related to permanent income, the consumption multiplier depending upon interest rates, the ratio of non-human to total wealth, the ages of members of the family, and time.

Much of the debate about the acceptability of Friedman's hypothesis has centred around the statistical problems involved in defining and measuring permanent income, and is not particularly relevant to this study of problems of time. The hypothesis has also been criticised by Houthakker (1958) for dealing largely with an imaginary world of certainty and because the argument that people will not spend part of an unexpected temporary increase in income on extra consumption seems to by psychologically unsound. But some of Friedman's observations are of interest for our discussion of movements of purchasing power through time. Friedman's assumption that consumers take a long-term view of their affairs and base their consumption and savings decisions on this plan rather than on short-term fluctuations in their income is broadly in agreement with the arguments of this chapter. According to Friedman's evidence, however, this long-term view may not stretch beyond a time horizon of about three years. One of Friedman's basic ideas is that measurements of income related to arbitrary time periods (usually the time taken for the earth to circle the sun) rather than to the events of people's lives is inadequate.

Friedman argues that increases in stocks of durable consumer goods should be regarded as savings, and only their 'use value' treated as consumption. This raises some interesting problems in relation to the discussion in section 2 of this chapter, where the emphasis was placed on the contrast between immediate or postponed consumption. Holdings of wealth can, of course, take numerous forms and it is not uncommon for stamps or works of art to be bought purely as a store of value. Even bottles of wine or tins of corned beef could be used as savings by those who believed that the cost of storage would be more than offset by inflation in their money value. But when goods are bought in order to be consumed, they can only be regarded as savings in a rather special way. The goods may retain some exchange value that will generally diminish with time though in a few cases, such as antique furniture or vintage cars, the exchange value at constant prices may remain constant or even increase. But there is an essential difference between the purchase of consumer durables and 'pure' saving. 'Pure' savings in building societies' accounts or shares represent claims on society that can be used for consumption. The consumption of a household can be increased at any time by turning its savings into consumer goods or services. Those owning durable goods used for consumption can reduce their level of consumption by selling the good and saving the proceeds or they can buy some other good with the sale price and thus exchange one form of consumption for another. But unlike the possessor of 'pure' savings, owners of durable goods cannot increase their level of consumption. They do not hold any reserves of unused purchasing power.

The concepts of 'wealth' or 'net assets' tend to confuse this distinction between what may be called 'goods in consumption' and unused reserves of purchasing power. All forms of assets are regarded as wealth by statisticians and tax-collectors and also, usually, by economists. The amount that a man is 'worth' when he dies will include the money value of his grand piano as well as that of his shareholdings. Wealth may be classified according to its liquidity (the ease with which it can be turned into cash), but no special treatment is given to durable goods that are 'being consumed' or yielding a stream of services. But, as already argued, when we are concerned with the distribution of consumption over time there is an important difference between 'pure' holdings of claims to purchasing power and the ownership of durable goods that retain some value even while they are being 'consumed'. A man who pays £5000 for a car is engaging in an act of consumption. It is possible for him to sell the car and forgo some of the future services that it would yield and he can use the proceeds either to buy a store of purchasing power or to engage in some alternative form of consumption. But the choice of increasing his level of consumption, which would have been open to him if he had put his £5000 into a building society account, is not available to the car owner. It is obviously true, as Friedman has argued, that a household that has spent a high proportion of its income on durable goods is in a different position from a 'consumer unit' that has spent most of its income on holidays and other goods and services that perish as they are consumed. (The second family is not necessarily worse off than the first as it may have spent income on increasing 'human capital' by acquiring some marketable skills. Defenders of the British so-called 'public' school system often extol the virtues of those who forgo the ownership of a car or some other consumer durable in order to give their children an education that will provide a superior earning power.) But if there is a difference between the purchase of consumer durables and the purchase of immediately perishable goods and services, so also is there a distinction between holding wealth in the form of goods that are being consumed and the ownership of unused claims to purchasing power. This distinction exists even when the complication of the probable existence of positive interest rates is ignored. A very important part of the demand to move consumption forward in time, and to consume more than current income would allow, arises not from the desire to even-out income fluctuations but, as was shown in section 2, because consumers wish to acquire durable goods as soon as possible.

The arguments for treating durable goods as wealth are generally held to apply *a fortiori* to owner-occupied houses. For very many households the value of their house (or net value after the deduction of any outstanding mortgage debt) is the major part of their wealth. In official studies of expenditure and the level of retail prices in

Britain, house purchase is regarded as a form of saving (although the interest payments on mortgages are treated as expenditure). Nevertheless, from the point of view of the distribution of saving and consumption through time, owner-occupied houses are just a very important form of durable good. Buying a house to live in represents an act of consumption, not an acquisition of a store of unused purchasing power. Houses are a special case only in that they are of relatively high value, and because their value (if properly maintained) will generally at least keep pace with inflation. Since a household's need for house room will expand with the growth of family size, and then usually contract when children leave home, couples can move 'downmarket' in later life and use some of the proceeds as capital. But a house owner-occupier, like the owner of any other durable good, cannot use the wealth represented by his house to increase his level of consumption. He can only exchange enjoyment of the services provided by the house for some other form of consumption or for a holding of purchasing power. A family living in a caravan with £50,000 savings may, at any time, decide to increase their consumption of goods or services up to the value of their savings; a family living in a £50,000 house with no savings can change the pattern of their consumption but cannot increase its level.

4. THE GHEZ AND BECKER LIFETIME ALLOCATION MODEL

The study of the allocation of goods and time over a lifetime made by Ghez and Becker 1975) is based on the idea of the household as a producing unit, which has already been discussed in chapter 2. This important work combines the development of a theoretical model of the behaviour of individuals or households over a 'life-cycle' with empirical evidence on such issues as the relationship between wage rates, hours at work and the consumption of goods. The household is pictured as a producing unit that combines time with market goods to produce 'commodities', which are an ultimate source of satisfaction or, in economic jargon, 'enter directly into people's utility functions' (see discussion in chapter 2). Thus, presumably, a man listening to music on his radio combines time with a market good to produce utility for himself. If X_t is the input of the services yielded by market goods, L_t the input of personal time, and C_t the output of 'commodities' (all in time period t), then

$$C_t = f(X_t, L_t).$$

The total utility of an individual is a function of the utilities obtained from producing a series of these time-plus-goods 'commodities' so that

$$U = U(C_1, C_2 \ldots C_t).$$

Time, in the Ghez and Becker model, can only be used in work (or gaining command over the supply of market goods) or in producing commodities in the household. If N_t is work time and the total time period to which decisions relate is θ, then the time constraint is given by

$$L_t + N_t = \theta.$$

Ghez and Becker draw some theoretical conclusions from their model. In the first place these were related to a world with zero interest rates and zero time preference rates. The optimum position for an individual at each age would be found where the 'increment in output from an additional dollar spent on time should equal the increment in output from an additional dollar spent on goods' (1975, pp. 5–6). 'Spending' a dollar on time must be interpreted as giving up the opportunity to earn a dollar's worth of market goods by transferring time from work to what Ghez and Becker call household production time or home time. For the choice between consumption at different time periods the model shows that to reach an optimum position the marginal rate of substitution between commodity consumption at different periods must equal the discounted value of the marginal costs of production.

An important deduction from the Ghez–Becker model is that while wage rates are rising households substitute 'goods for time' and present commodities for future ones. The first substitution implies that people would work longer hours as wage rates rise and that leisure time or home time is at its lowest point when earnings are at their peak. If a positive instead of a zero interest rate is assumed to exist then, according to the Ghez–Becker model, the peak in hours worked will be moved forward in time and will occur before the peak wage rate per hour. Becker and Ghez argue that the income effect of an increased hourly wage rate is eliminated from their model by the assumption that households have a perfect knowledge of the future and can foresee all changes in their earning capacity. Another rather complex deduction from the model is that (with a zero interest rate) the consumption of goods will be positively associated with wage rates over the life cycle if 'substitution between goods and time is easier than intertemporal substitution between non-market activities produced at different points in time' (p. 36). Substitution between goods and time appears to mean (Ghez and Becker provide very few explanatory examples) that people produce the commodities that they want to consume during their home time with more goods and less time. How this is supposed to work is not made clear. It is obvious that households can buy a dishwasher and then put a smaller input of time into the process of producing the 'commodity' of clean crockery. But it is not easy to see in what way the time input required for such activities as reading a novel, sleeping or watching television can be reduced by buying more market good inputs. In their study of actual US data, Ghez and Becker come to the not very surprising conclusion that consumption increases with earnings during a man's working life and the even less unexpected conclusion that the consumption of goods tends to increase with family size.

The empirical evidence analysed by Becker in a series of regressions does generally support the conclusion of the model that hours worked per year are positively related to hourly earnings. Becker found some difficulty in measuring consumption time, but the regression coefficients for male hourly wages (with consumption time as the dependent variable) were all negative, with high t-values, except for college graduates where the coefficients were positive but with low t-test values. If consumption time as defined by Becker was negatively associated with hourly wage rates this implies a positive association with hours worked. Becker's statistical analysis was based on US census data for 1959. A sub-sample of 34,000 male workers was used. This means that the data relate to different people at different ages and with different hourly earnings. The well-known problem of drawing conclusions about people's behaviour over time from cross-section data therefore applies to this study. We cannot be sure that the present generation of 20-year-old men will react to changes in their hourly wage rate when they are 60 in the same way as the current generation of 60-year-old workers. Unfortunately, time-series data on cohorts of workers at different stages in their working life are not generally available. (If such data did exist it might be difficult to make allowances for changes in the availability of work over long time periods and to distinguish between changes in money wages and in real earnings.) Some British cross-section data (Tables 7.6 and 7.7) are of interest for comparison with the American figures. An analysis of changes in hours worked over time was contained in chapter 6 (Table 6.1).

It is only with considerable caution that any conclusions can be

TABLE 7.6
Earnings and hours, full-time men, GB, April 1976

Age	Manual		Non-Manual	
	Earnings per hour	Average hours worked per week	Earnings per hour	Average hours worked per week
Under 18	67.9	41.9	66.1	38.7
18–20	103.8	43.2	101.1	38.6
21–24	131.7	44.4	143.0	38.4
25–29	141.3	45.7	184.1	38.5
30–39	146.4	46.2	224.3	38.5
40–49	144.9	45.8	237.9	38.4
50–59	140.4	44.7	225.7	38.5
60–64	131.7	44.1	195.2	38.4
65 and over	117.8	43.7	—	—

Source: Department of Employment (1978a).

TABLE 7.7
Earnings and hours, full-time women, GB, April 1976

Age	Manual		Non-Manual	
	Earnings per hour	Average hours worked per week	Earnings per hour	Average hours worked per week
Under 18	68.0	39.8	68.1	37.7
18–20	89.8	39.7	91.8	37.6
21–24	97.6	39.7	121.5	36.4
25–29	101.2	39.8	142.9	35.9
30–39	102.7	39.2	144.9	36.2
40–49	102.2	39.2	144.0	36.2
50–59	102.2	39.1	143.4	36.7
60–64	96.8	39.1	—	—

Source: Department of Employment (1978a).

drawn from these figures. It is apparent that there is relatively little variation in the average hours worked shown in these figures aggregated into age groups. The earnings figures do not include any allowance for extra overtime payments, but overtime working is included in the average hours worked. (If overtime hours were deducted, all the male manual workers would be shown to be working almost exactly for an average working week of forty hours.) Linear

TABLE 7.8
Earnings and hours data − statistical analysis

	Intercept	Slope	R^2
Male manual			
Linear	38.08	0.05	0.87
Log	20.09	5.06	0.82
Male non-manual			
Linear	38.71	−0.001	0.53
Log	39.44	−0.19	0.63
Female manual			
Linear	40.90	−0.01	0.31
Log	45.19	−1.26	0.29
Female non-manual			
Linear	39.24	−0.02	0.83
Log	47.08	−2.18	0.82

and (natural) log regression equations were fitted to the hours and earnings data, and coefficients of determination (R^2) were calculated. The results are shown in Table 7.8. Except for male manual workers, all the slope coefficients were negative (and very small). It was only for male manual workers that there was any evidence that the length of the working week increased with hourly earnings. The R^2 values were high for male manual and female non-manual workers. There was little difference between the results shown by the untransformed linear and log equations. It is of some interest that the *b* (slope) coefficients for both male and female non-manual workers were very small and negative.

This is similar to some results of Becker's study of US data where he found that there was a rather weak positive relationship between earnings and 'consumption time' for college graduates indicating that hours worked tended to fall with an increase in earnings. Non-manual workers in Britain usually have less opportunity than manual workers to undertake paid overtime. In *British Labour Statistics 1976* (Department of Employment, 1978a) the average hours of overtime for all male manual workers was 5.1 while for male non-manual workers the equivalent figure was only 1.2 hours. The relative strength of the income and substitution effects is very unlikely to be constant over all marginal additions to the wage rate. Non-manual workers in Britain and college graduates in the USA both had higher average hourly earnings than manual or non-college graduate workers. It may be that additions to a higher base wage are less likely to persuade workers to devote more time to paid work than are additions to a lower base. A man earning £2.00 an hour may surrender some more free time when his hourly wage rate increases to £2.05 whereas a worker having a pay increase of from £5.00 to £5.05 may not be persuaded to work any more hours a week and could even choose to keep his income constant and reduce the length of his working week. (This could apply even if the higher paid worker received the same percentage increase as his lower-paid fellow worker and his hourly wage rate increased from £5.00 to £5.125.) Non-manual employees will often be paid at an annual rather than an hourly rate and there may be little association between hours worked and current earnings. Workers at the 'executive' level may often work for much longer periods than the minimum weekly hours demanded by their employers. Their motivation may be partly the future extra income that could come with promotion but it could equally well be that they are seeking success and influence, or they might even obtain more satisfaction from devoting some of their 'free' time to their normal jobs than from any available alternative use.

The Ghez–Becker model is an important and useful attempt to analyse theoretically how people might behave, given certain simplifying assumptions, in allocating their time between paid work and other activities over their lifecycle. It provides the beginnings of some kind of theory that can be used and developed. Despite the statistical work in the study, however, its applicability to real-world situations is not clearly established. Some of the basic criticisms made in chapter 2 about Becker's pioneering work on the theory of time in economics also apply to the Ghez–Becker study. The rigid work/non-work division of time is much too simple. Workers do not exchange 'free' time for paid work solely in order to obtain command over a supply of market goods. The utility obtained from work may be an extremely important part of their lives and the hourly wage rate is only one factor, even if it is usually the most important, in determining how much time should be allocated to paid work. Ghez and Becker sometimes write as though time sold to an employer ceased to exist. They use the phrase 'the price of time', for example, as though it were synonymous with 'hourly wage rate'. This seems to imply that a worker having 'sold' some free time is completely indifferent about how he spends his working day. He sells his time to the highest bidder and then does not care whether he is put to work in the corridors of power or in the underground passages of a coal mine. In the real world the effect of a rise in wage rates or the willingness to exchange paid work for leisure will depend on the relative utilities obtained from work plus wages or the preferred leisure activity. Ghez and Becker seem to assume a constant hourly wage rate at any one period of time and do not discuss the problems that arise when marginal wage rates (overtime payments) are higher than the average wage rate. The existence of overtime payments for extra hours worked must affect the interpretation of data relating total hours worked to average hourly earnings. Suppose that statistics recorded a rise in average earnings from £3.00 to £3.50 and an increase in the average working week from forty to forty-five hours. This rise might come from an increase in the basic wage rate for each hour worked or from an offer, accepted by workers, of £7.50 for an extra one hour's work per day. The implication for the relationship between earnings and hours worked would be rather different in the two cases.

The basic Becker concept of the household as a producing unit, combining goods and time to produce commodities, can be applied to some human activities more readily than to others. Non-working time, as argued in chapter 6, is used for widely different activities and a simple classification of time into 'market' and 'non-market' or work and leisure categories is unrealistic. As argued in chapter 6, it is not easy to make a logical distinction between work and some leisure activities. If a consumer works overtime to earn money to pay a decorator to paint the outside of his house then, according to Ghez and Becker, he is selling his time in order to gain control of market goods. But if the consumer does not work overtime and paints the house himself then he is combining time and market goods to produce a commodity that enters directly into his utility function. The distinction is, perhaps, somewhat subtle, and the choice between the two alternatives will depend not only on the consumer's potential hourly earnings, but also on the decorator's charges and the consumer's ranking of the utility that he expects to receive from spending extra time at his daily job or from undertaking the home decorating.

5. THE TIME DISTRIBUTION OF THE BENEFITS FROM INVESTMENT

When investment is carried out, the benefits will normally be obtained over a period of time in the future, but the distribution of benefits over time is likely to be different for each investment project. It is therefore necessary to find a method of comparing different streams of benefits. Investment in a lorry might start to produce benefits in less than a month (including the period of manufacture) but end after three or four years, whereas an investment in a nuclear power station might not yield any benefits for several years but, once started, the benefit stream could continue for a very long time. It is apparent that a satisfactory investment appraisal cannot be based on a simple comparison of the total stream of benefits and costs for different investment projects when the distributions over time differ. It is generally assumed that as benefits move further into the future their current value falls, but there is considerable uncertainty about the appropriate rate of discount and still some discussion about which discounting technique should be adopted. Discussion about the appropriate rate at which future benefits should be discounted has usually been linked with the use of cost-benefit analysis and the appraisal of investment projects in the public sector. The problem of comparing investments with different distributions of benefits over time is not confined to the public sector, but it is usually, perhaps somewhat optimistically, assumed that market forces will decide the issue in the private sector. Investments that yield benefits mainly in the relatively distant future are more likely to be undertaken in the public sector. Companies that are concerned with their current share price and the immediate interests of the shareholders are unlikely to invest in projects that will not yield any benefit for ten or twenty years (although they may wish to safeguard the company's future by searching for some new source of their basic raw materials or carrying out research in order to develop a new product). Public sector decisions are more likely to relate to long-term investment and they also have to satisfy different objectives, such as increasing general welfare, where the timing of the receipt of benefits cannot be ignored.

The three 'standard' arguments for the existence of positive time preference rates (the uncertainty about the provision of future benefits; the certainty of death, which will prevent the enjoyment of future benefits; and the expectations of rising levels of wealth) have already been discussed in section 2 of this chapter where it was argued that they were all unconvincing in application to individuals. Curiously, economists who believe that positive time preference rates result from some built-in characteristics of human nature appear to have neglected one strong argument that might support their case. This is, as already argued in section 2, that people will prefer to start to enjoy consumer durables as soon as possible. But once their immediate needs are satisfied, consumers will often find that any further consumption of 'immediately consumable' goods is undesirable. They may very well prefer jam tomorrow rather than extra jam today. A rational consumer might be ready to exchange a second large ice-cream, which he must eat today, for a smaller ice-cream tomorrow, thus showing negative marginal time preference. But consumers will normally prefer to have an armchair or a TV set this year rather than next year, because these consumer durables start to yield a flow of benefits as soon as they are obtained, and the benefits can be expected to extend indefinitely into the future. Many households will therefore be willing to borrow from future income in order to obtain at least some durable goods as soon as possible. There are not many families who would be content to live in a tent until they had saved the full purchase price for a house. On the other hand, there is a strong demand to save for retirement and old age and, in a reasonably affluent society, time preference rates might well be neutral or negative. When there is a demand for capital for investment this may mean that even those with negative time preference rates may be able to earn interest on their savings. But, at the time of writing, British interest rates are lower than the rate of inflation so that real interest rates are negative. As lending at fixed interest rates still continues, people must either be very optimistic about future inflation levels or have negative time preference rates.

It is therefore assumed in the following discussion that time preference rates can be neutral, positive or negative and that the arguments suggesting that consumers normally prefer present to future consumption are not conclusive. The standard earnings pattern of households means that there is also a strong demand to postpone the consumption of some part of income. For the moment, however, it is assumed that when the yield from investment is taken into account, as well as personal time preference rates, then future benefits from investment are worth less than present benefits (though even this assumption is qualified later). This means that the analysis can be carried on in the usual form by discussing the discounting of future rather than of present benefits.

Before considering the basic problem of the choice of a discount rate, some attention must be given to the forms of discounting technique that may be used. This is a topic that has greatly exercised the minds of economists and no more is attempted here than a brief summary of the position. The general consensus of opinion is that the two most satisfactory techniques are the measurement of 'net present value' (NPV) or of the 'internal rate of return' (IRR), with the net present value method being most widely preferred. The net present value of a stream of benefits is the current value, discounted at some chosen rate, minus the cost of the investment. If B_i is the annual benefits resulting from the investment, C is the cost of the investment (all of which is assumed here to be incurred at the inception of the project), r is the chosen discount rate and the investment yields benefits for n years, then the net present value is given by

$$NPV = \sum_{i=1}^{n} \frac{B_i}{(1 + r)^i} - C.$$

Suppose that an investment project will cost £1 million and that the net annual benefits are known to be:

Year 1 = £100,000
Year 2 = £200,000
Year 3 = £300,000
Year 4 = £400,000
Year 5 = £500,000

At the end of five years the investment is worn out and yields no further benefits. If there was no discounting (because the rate of time preference was zero) then the project would yield a surplus of £500,000 more than the cost of investment. But with different discount rates the project could show a positive or negative net present value. The figures in Table 7.9 show the net present value for this stream of benefits for different interest rates. Discounting at 5 per cent reduces the money surplus of £500,000 to a net present value of +£256,610. With interest rates at 5 per cent this is the amount by which the value of a company undertaking the investment would be increased. It is also the maximum sum that a profit-maximising firm would be prepared to pay to be allowed to make the investment. The net present value falls with increases in the discount rate and is only just worth undertaking at a rate of 12 per cent. For discount rates of 13 per cent and above, the net present value would be negative and the investment project should not be carried out.

If the same total money benefits were distributed differently

TABLE 7.9

Net present value of hypothetical five-year flow of benefits
at different discount rates from £1 million investment

Discount rate %	Net present value £
5	+256,610
10	+65,220
11	+31,990
12	+179
13	--30,253
14	−59,379
15	−87,290
20	−210,350

over the five-year period then, of course, the net present values could be changed significantly. Suppose that (with the same investment cost) the distribution of benefits was reversed in time so that it became:

Year 1 = £500,000
Year 2 = £400,000
Year 3 = £300,000
Year 4 = £200,000
Year 5 = £100,000

In this case the investment would be worthwhile even at a discount rate of 20 per cent, when it would have a net present value of +£4650.

The alternative discounting technique is the internal rate of return method. This involves calculating the rate of discount that would make the present value of the stream of benefits exactly equal to the cost of the investment. If the same symbols are used as for the NPV formula, then the internal rate of return is the value of r that satisfies the equation

$$\sum_{i=1}^{n} \frac{B_i}{(1 + r)^i} - C = 0.$$

An investment would be undertaken if the internal rate of return was higher than the rate of interest that a firm must pay to borrow money or, for a public sector investment, higher than the social time preference rate. The value of r is not easy to calculate and involves solving a complex equation or using a suitable computer programme. An approximation can be obtained by trial and error, however, and for the first, increasing, stream of benefits example the internal rate of return would be just over 12 per cent.

When a decision is being made on the acceptance or rejection of an individual investment project, both the IRR and the NPV appraisal techniques will give the same answer (assuming that the rate of interest with which the internal rate is compared is the same as the rate of discount used in the net present value method). For rates of interest (or discount) below the internal rate of return the net present value would be positive so that the investment project would be accepted by both criteria. If the rate of interest was higher than the internal rate of return then the net present value would be negative and the investment project would be rejected. There may, however, be restrictions on the supply of capital available at the chosen discount or time preference rate and, in a capital-rationing situation, some projects with a positive net present value or an internal rate of return greater than the interest rate may be rejected. (The reasons why interest rates do not reflect the scarcity of capital cannot be explored within the confines of this study.) It may thus be necessary to rank potentially acceptable investment projects and in these circumstances the two techniques do not always give the same answer. Given its expected income streams, each project will have a fixed internal rate of return. But the net present value will vary with the rate of discount, and as the discount rate increases so projects that yield a bigger proportion of benefits at a more distant date will become less attractive relative to projects yielding most of their benefits at an earlier time period. The discount rate used in calculating net present values, if it represents the rate of interest required from investment or the appropriate time preference rate, must be lower than or equal to the internal rate of return for all acceptable projects. This means that the NPV method of discounting will be relatively more favourable to 'late yield' investment projects. In some cases, when the IRR measurement ranks an 'early yield' project above a 'late yield' project, the position may be reversed if the net present value criterion is used.

Suppose that two projects, *A* and *B*, both lasting for only two years, produced benefits as follows:

	A	B
Year 1	£100	£200
Year 2	£210	£100

If the cost of both projects was £256.8, the internal rate of return of *A* would be 12.0 per cent while *B* would have the superior internal rate of return of 12.5 per cent. But at a discount rate of 10 per cent both projects would have the same net present value of £7.7, while at 9 per cent the NPV criterion ranks project *A* more highly than *B*, with values of £11.7 and £10.8 respectively. In choosing between a project with a larger but 'later' total yield and one giving smaller but 'earlier' benefits there is no single right answer. As George and Shorey (1978) point out in their useful review of the problem, the objectives must be considered. If the investment decision is in the public sector and the objective is to maximise consumers' welfare, then discounting at a rate that reflects their time preference is demanded. This implies the use of the NPV criterion. But if the objective is to maximise the growth rate of the firm or public enterprise and the benefits can be re-invested at the internal rate of return level, then the IRR criterion is appropriate.

Both the IRR and the NPV criteria assume that the net benefits resulting from an investment can be re-invested. This assumption is considered again in the discussion of the choice of discount rate. In a general equilibrium condition with a perfect market the yield from investment in all activities would become the same and would also equal the rate of time preference, so that the IRR and the NPV techniques would give the same answer. In the real world, uncertainty, government activity, imperfect knowledge and other factors mean that no single rate of return exists. But the assumption of the IRR discounting technique that the stream of benefits can be invested and earn interest at the same level as the internal rate of return seems somewhat implausible. If the internal rate of return is higher than the rate of interest at which money can be borrowed then this means that there cannot be widespread opportunities of investment yielding the IRR level of interest. Nor does it necessarily follow that further increments of investment made in the firm's (or public enterprise's) own business will produce the existing internal rate of return. There may well be a problem of scale or of the existence of indivisibilities. If the initial investment has produced a plant of approximately optimum size then the small additions to that plant that could be made by investing the benefits from its original investment might yield at a very low rate of return. The cost of a complete new plant would be much greater than the amount of annual benefits and in any case demand is unlikely to be able to absorb the products of a second plant at the existing price level. This suggests that the situations in which the IRR technique is more appropriate than the NPV technique are probably somewhat rare and unusual.

Of more importance than the discounting model, and of greater interest for this study, is the problem of choosing a discount rate. But this statement of the problem assumes that future benefits should be discounted. Although much of the discussion will be based on this assumption, it is only an assumption and has not been shown to be incontrovertibly true in all circumstances. The basic problem is how streams of benefits with different time patterns can be compared. As has already been argued in earlier sections of this chapter, there are certainly cases where the marginal rate of time preference for individuals is negative. It may be more desirable to have some food supplied for tomorrow's needs rather than being compelled to over-eat today.

The obvious requirement for discounting the flow of benefits from public investment projects is to find a discount rate that reflects the preferences of society for present or future consumption. This is the principle behind the search for what is generally called the 'social' time preference rate. Since individual consumers' patterns of time preference will vary considerably, it is apparent that a single rate that is supposed to represent the preferences of a whole nation can be based only on some very approximate average figure. Real-world complications such as the existence of uncertainty and inflation, and the effects of a government's policy, make it very difficult to infer 'pure' rates of time preference from consumers' behaviour. Some variations between individuals cancel out, but there is a possible bias affecting the lending and borrowing activities of consumers. People with higher incomes (this means larger 'permanent' income in Friedman's terminology) and institutions will lend larger sums of money than poorer people and their marginal rates of time preference may be very low or negative. Thus consumers with large incomes and institutions may have a disproportionate influence on market rates of interest. Even if lending only increases in proportion to income, this effect might follow with uneven income distribution. In 1978, *UK Family Expenditure Survey* data showed that, as income per family rose, savings as a percentage of income also tended to increase, though not consistently (Department of Employment, 1979b). Thus families with a gross income of £65.20 per week saved 0.64 per cent of their income while those receiving £158.96 average income saved 1.497 per cent. These figures were not adjusted to allow for family size or tax deductions.

This argument suggests that empirical evidence on time preference might produce estimates of average rates that are too low. But some economists have followed Pigou in believing that people in general may underestimate the value of future benefits, so that a social time preference rate based on consumers' preferences might be too high. Society, represented by the government, may feel that it has a responsibility for future generations whose interests are not reflected in time preference rates based on an average of individual preferences. There are, therefore, considerable difficulties involved in deciding what should be the level of a social time preference rate. Some writers, however, have argued that the social time preference rate, even if it can be determined, does not represent a satisfactory rate for discounting the benefits from public sector investment projects.

The alternative method for discounting future benefits in evaluating investment projects is to use the social opportunity cost rate. This reflects the opportunity cost of capital and would be measured by the market rate of interest that must be paid by businessmen who wish to make an investment. The case for using a discount rate based on social opportunity cost was developed by Hirshleifer in a paper on the evaluation of water-investment projects (Hirschleifer *et al.*, 1963). He argued that classical economic theory regarded the rate of interest as a rate of discount on future goods that balanced considerations of time preference and productivity. According to Hirshleifer, even if time preference was neutral, 'the influence of productivity alone would dictate a positive rate of interest' (p. 117). If public sector investments are made only in projects whose benefit streams have a net positive value when discounted at the market rate, this will ensure that these projects are preferred by consumers to any alternative use of capital. Critics of the social opportunity cost approach have pointed out that there is no single 'market rate' for capital in the private sector and that the definition of benefits may differ between public and private sector projects (Henderson, 1968).

The social opportunity cost arguments bring together two quite separate considerations. These are the choice between projects with benefits distributed differently over time and the need to ensure comparability between public and private sector projects. Hirshleifer's approach assumes that solving the second problem automatically also deals with the time preference issue. The official guidelines for investment by nationalised industries in the UK have been strongly influenced by the social opportunity cost arguments.

The review of the objectives of nationalised industries published in 1967 said that a 'test rate of discount' should be used that reflected the 'minimum rate of return to be expected on a marginal low-risk project undertaken for commerical reasons' (*Nationalised Industries*, 1967, p. 5, para. 9). A rate of 8 per cent in real terms was prescribed, and in 1969 this was raised to 10 per cent. The issue was re-examined in a National Economic Development Office Report published in 1976 and in a new White Paper produced in 1978. The 1978 paper reiterated the view that the discount rate must reflect the opportunity cost of capital arguing that 'if the industries do not cover the full costs of supplying goods and services efficiently, resources may be diverted from more to less worthwhile uses' (*The Nationalised Industries*, 1978, p. 7). A new 'required rate of return' of 5 per cent in real terms before tax was laid down and this was said to take into account the cost of finance to the private sector as well as social time preference.

An interesting paper by Scott (1977), which was written before the publication of the 1978 White Paper, argued that the test discount rate of 10 per cent was too high. Scott developed a concept of 'base-level income'. People at this low income level are sufficiently poor for the government to regard the social value of a marginal increment of income to them as being of the same value as a marginal increment to the government's own income. The rate of discount for public sector projects, Scott argued, should have two components. These are the social weight given to marginal additions to base income at different levels and a pure time preference factor. (This concept of 'pure time preference' as 'impatience', with the effect of income changes abstracted, adds yet another possible meaning for this term to those already discussed in section 2 of this chapter.) Time preference would therefore reflect the expected growth in national income, but measured by its effect on 'base income' plus the 'pure' preference for present rather than future consumption. Scott considered that this 'pure time preference' rate might be as low as 0.5 per cent but finally chose a 'best guess' figure of 1.5 per cent to allow for the possibility of the destruction of civilisation by a nuclear war. His 'best guess' for the discount rate was 4.5–6.0 per cent compared with the 10 per cent level prevailing when his article was written. Scott's approach represents the development of a form of social time discount rate. He argues that if private rates of return on capital are much higher than the social time preference rate then investment should be increased until marginal returns and the time preference rate are made equal.

As the discussion has shown, it is quite difficult to disentangle the choice between differently timed streams of benefits from the problem of allocating investment funds efficiently between alternative projects. While it is important that capital is not mis-allocated and that the public sector does not employ funds that would be more productively invested in private business, the use of a discount rate based only on social opportunity cost is very unsatisfactory. It means that the question of how to choose be-tween present and future consumption is not being answered at all. The social opportunity cost approach is particularly un-satisfactory if this is interpreted as simply reflecting some estimate of the 'going rate' at which private industry can borrow capital, and if it is assumed that all the benefits from private investment are themselves re-invested. Public investment does not necessarily take place at the expense of private sector investment. It may well be that a government can raise or create funds for public investment at the cost of a reduction in personal consumption. This need not have any effect on private investment levels. The situation will, of course, vary with the state of the economy but it would not be easy to find cases where public investment in Britain in recent years has prevented private investment from taking place. (This argument does not relate to total public expenditure and so does not imply that 'crowding out' may not occur.) There is no evidence to suggest that new road building has replaced private sector construction or even that a growth in public sector house building is associated with a fall in private sector house construction.

The assumption that all private investment net benefits are re-invested is quite unrealistic. The government in the UK takes 50 per cent of net surpluses for its own purposes in the form of Corporation Tax. Out of the remainder, about one-third is distributed to share-holders or paid in further tax credits to the government. (The average 'times covered' for dividends for a random sample of thirty-eight miscellaneous British industrial companies in mid-1980 was 3.2, with a standard deviation of 2.2.) The rest of the net surplus may be re-invested in the company, used to reduce outstanding debt or held as some form of liquid asset. Even where private firms do re-invest a large part of a stream of benefits, it does not follow that this practice is relevant for a public enterprise. The benefits from road investment take the form of journey time savings that are consumed by travellers. There is no way in which they can be re-invested since, in Britain, there is no direct charge made for the consumption of road space. Nevertheless, the total estimated annual stream of benefits from road investment is discounted at the level of the required rate of return.

The assumption of the re-investment of the whole of a stream of benefits has important consequences. It means that benefits that are distant in time have very little value, so that investment in major projects that may take many years to complete but that then produce benefits for a very long period of time, are discouraged. The figures in Table 7.10 show the present value of a benefit as a

TABLE 7.10
Present value as a percentage of future income

Discount rate %	Present value of benefit occurring in:		
	Year 20 %	Year 50 %	Year 75 %
5	37.7	8.7	2.6
10	14.9	0.85	0.08
20	2.6	0.01	0.0001

percentage of its actual value, for different time periods and discount rates. At a 10 per cent discount rate, the present value of a benefit of £10 million occurring in fifty years' time would be only £85,185, while the same sum received in seventy-five years' time at a 20 per cent discount rate would have a present value of £11.52. If the assumption that all benefits from any investment are themselves re-invested is discarded, then the discounting of benefits at a compound interest rate equivalent to the current earnings on investment capital is no longer justified.

There is a case for arguing that the 'one-stage' present value or internal rate of return discounting technique should be replaced by a method that separates out the 'return on capital' and time preference factors and that also enables the capital repayment period to be considered specifically. The arguments can be worked out by the use of an example. In Table 7.11 the first column of 'gross benefits' represents the benefits stream from an assumed investment of £1 million. If the opportunity cost rate of interest for the original investment was known to be 10 per cent, then the annual interest charges of £100,000 could be deducted from the gross benefits. This sum might be paid as actual interest charges to the providers of capital (who are assumed to use the payments for consumption) or, if internal capital was used, it would be an

TABLE 7.11
Discounting future benefits when all surpluses are used for consumption

Year	Gross benefits £	Net benefits	
		10-year repayment £	8-year repayment £
1	190,000	27,255	2,556
2	200,000	37,255	12,556
3	210,000	47,255	22,556
4	220,000	57,255	32,556
5	230,000	67,255	42,556
6	250,000	87,255	62,556
7	220,000	57,255	32,556
8	210,000	47,255	22,556
9	200,000	37,255	200,000
10	200,000	37,255	200,000

accounting deduction to allow for the return that could have been earned if the capital had been loaned. Again it must be assumed that the notional interest payments are handed over to shareholders, or to the government, and are used for consumption. In the case of public investment in roads, or any other 'free' service, the benefits are all consumed directly and the question of distribution does not arise. (There may be an anomaly in comparing the results of public and private enterprise when the former depends only on fixed interest capital while the latter uses shareholders' funds. Interest payments are deducted from gross profits, but payments to shareholders for the capital that they have provided are made from 'net' profits. The same objection applies to comparisons between private companies with different gearing ratios.) The net present value discounting technique assumes that the capital will be repaid at the end of the life of the investment.

It has been assumed in the figures in Table 7.11 that some gross benefits are paid into a separate sinking fund, which earns interest at the opportunity cost rate of 10 per cent. The figures in the second column show net benefits after payment of £100,000 interest and of an annual sum into the sinking fund of £62,745. The figures in column three show the net benefit stream if the capital was written off in eight years (by annual payments of £87,444). If the 'pure' time preference discount rate is assumed to be 3 per cent (the highest figure suggested by Scott) and the net benefit streams are discounted at this rate, then three different estimates of net present value can be obtained from the figures in Table 7.11. These are the normal net present value of the original gross benefit stream and the discounted values of the ten-year and eight-year repayment net benefit streams. The net present value figures are:

Gross benefits discounted at 10% = £1,302,775 − £1,000,000
= £302,775
Net benefits discounted at 3%,
10-year repayment = £389,610
Net benefits discounted at 3%,
8-year repayment = £499,362

This technique would not necessarily favour all 'later' benefit streams compared with 'earlier' streams but it could mean that some schemes with very late benefits accruing, which would be rejected by standard NPV discounting at most discount rates, would be considered viable. Very large-scale and long-term investment projects, such as the construction of a new port, or of a tidal barrier for obtaining energy from the flow of the tides, tend to be rejected if it is assumed that all 'distant' benefits must be discounted at the rate of interest that could be earned by relatively short-term current investment. Some projects can be justified by special arguments that have nothing to do with time preference. There may be cases, for example, where benefits are interdependent. If long-term energy sources are not developed then the yields from any other form of investment might be greatly reduced, or even disappear. But it seems clear that a rigid application of full social opportunity cost discounting to the whole of a stream of benefits could distort the true time preference of the community. Suppose that effective choice in the real world lay between two alternative public sector projects, such as investment in either the gas or electricity industries. It will then be necessary to compare the value of the relative yields over the lifetime of each of the alternative investments and to take account of their time distributions. But if the product is sold at a price that covers renewals but allows no surplus for new investment, then the only discounting that is necessary is to allow for the time preferences of the community. The possible earnings if the annual product of gas or electricity sales was invested in some other industry is no longer of relevance. In the case of road investment, capital rationing makes it reasonably certain that the yield will be at least equal to that of any alternative investment. The de facto choice is then between alternative road schemes that may well have streams of benefits with very different time distribution patterns. There seems to be no reason why roads with more 'distant' benefit streams should be penalised by using discount rates that reflect possible investment earnings, in the transport or any other industry, rather than 'pure' time preference.

The argument could be carried one stage further. When there is no re-investment it is not entirely clear why social time preference should take the form of a compounded annual discount rate. Beyond certain time horizons there might be no regularly increasing dislike for further lengthening of the period of waiting for consumption. Little and Mirrlees (1974), in writing about 'pure' time preference (defined in the Scott sense with the effect of rising living standards removed), argue that governments may wish to 'give future consumption a smaller weight'. They seem to be thinking of rates of discount, but it is possible that a system of weights rather than a fixed discount rate could be used for measuring the relative importance of benefits received at different time periods. The weights applied by governments to benefits in major long-term capital projects might give relatively more importance to 'distant' benefits than would any discounting technique using compound interest.

CHAPTER 8

Conclusions

*Dost thou love life? Then do not squander time, for that's the
stuff life is made of.* [Benjamin Franklin]

The intention of this chapter of conclusions is not to summarise
the whole of this study on diverse aspects of economics and time
but to underline what are believed to be some of the more interesting
arguments that have emerged from it. Although time is commonly
described as a scarce resource in economic literature, it is still often
treated rather differently from the more familiar inputs of labour
and materials and outputs of goods and services. The problems
of its allocation have not yet been fully or consistently integrated
into economic analysis. One area in which this is apparent, which
has been discussed in chapters 2, 4 and 6, is that relating to work,
wages and leisure.

Discussions of the determination of wages and of the relationship
between earnings and hours worked often seem to be based on the
unstated assumption that all working time is homogeneous and that,
having sold some time to their employers, workers are no longer
interested in how it is spent. But the time given to paid work is a
very important part of people's lives and the utility they obtain from
it is a major factor in their welfare. Workers obtain both wages
and some utility or disutility from paid work. If an enterprise rejects
all other considerations except profit maximisation, then the job
satisfaction and general happiness of its workers will only be relevant
in so far as these affect productivity. But when the wider objective
of increasing or maximising welfare is relevant then the utility
obtained from work, though it may be difficult to measure, cannot
be ignored. The welfare of workers has not, of course, been totally
neglected in the real world. Legislation has dealt with many aspects
of safety and working conditions, but the process has been one of

gradually eliminating obvious causes of ill-health or discontent. The benefits from a positive work utility are not often taken into account in economic analysis. If the maximisation of the welfare of society was the objective in operating an enterprise, then both efficiency in producing the product and worker satisfaction are relevant. Some potential improvements in the level of output per manhour might be shown to yield a net reduction in welfare. A firm in a competitive industry would not be able to take notice of workers' preferences if its competitors could produce their output more cheaply by ignoring them, so that government action would probably be required. In a public enterprise it may be possible to take account of the welfare of workers, though the trade-off between their preferences and the interests of society as a whole may be very difficult to make. In practice, it would probably be only where there was a clearly apparent relationship between some proposed reorganisation inside an industry and the welfare of its workers that the desirability of obtaining an increase in productivity might be questioned. But it would constitute a step forward if public enterprises were able to think of the welfare of their workers not merely in a negative sense, by providing a satisfactory working temperature or adequate toilets, but more positively in terms of job satisfaction. Workers spend about one-fifth of their lives at work between leaving school and retirement. The wages they are paid represent part of the benefit they receive from this use of their time. But the level of utility that workers obtain from the employment of their time at work must also have an important influence on the welfare of society.

Consideration of the utility of paid work leads to another issue, also considered in chapters 2, 4 and 6, that of the availability of work. It is not possible to say whether the need to work is a built-in characteristic of human nature or a result of conditioning by the societies in which most men live. Keynes seemed to regard the desire to work as being a flaw in human nature but one that it would be difficult to eradicate. Writing in 1930 but looking forward to a future of plenty, with an abundance of leisure available, he argued that

> For many ages to come the old Adam will be so strong in us that everybody will need to do some work if he is to be contented. We shall do more things for ourselves than is usual with the rich today, only too glad to have small duties and tasks and routines. But beyond this, we shall endeavour to spread the bread thin on the butter to make what work there is still to be done as widely shared as possible. Three-hour shifts or a

fifteen-hour week may put off the problem for a great while. For three
hours a day is quite enough to satisfy the old Adam in most of us!
[Keynes, 1972, pp. 328-9]

Whether the desire to work needs to be eradicated or should be
preserved as representing one of the more admirable characteristics
of human nature can be debated, but Keynes' conclusion about
the sharing of work does make sense. If the marginal utility of work
falls over the length of a working day then the sharing of work may
increase welfare, even if it involves some loss in efficiency in the
output of goods and services. But if work means producing goods
or services for others to consume then there is no fundamental
reason why it should ever be in short supply. Despite the invention
of the microprocessor, it is not quite so easy to look forward from
1980 to a future of plenty as it was for Keynes fifty years ago.
The depletion of resources and the growth of population both
threaten to postpone or cancel the coming of Keynes' golden age.
But even if some fortunate parts of the world can live in great
prosperity with automated factories producing most of their inhabitants' requirements, this need not mean the disappearance of
work opportunities. Human wants are virtually unlimited and there
are still plenty of raw materials that can be turned into products
by human labour and skill. When they are in prison in Britain some
men use the long hours at their disposal to make attractive boxes,
gypsy caravans and other models out of such unpromising material
as used matchsticks. These products would be 'uneconomic' outside
prison because the alternative-use value of the working time used
up would make the goods too expensive for the market. But given
the disappearance of existing work opportunities, many new goods
and services involving labour-intensive production methods could
be put on the market. If there is a future long-term shortage of
work opportunities, this will not be the inevitable result of the
development of technology but rather the avoidable product of
a failure in the working of the economy.

Even if work-sharing is practical and new opportunities for working
for others are discovered, the use of non-working time will become
of increasing importance. Although economists have now started
to study the problems of non-work time, this is a relatively recent
development. But if we are concerned with the optimum use of
time then the employment of non-working time should be just as
much a central concern of economics as is the determination of
wage levels or the amount of time devoted to paid work. About

82 per cent of the time of the whole population is used for non-paid-work activities. It was argued in chapter 6 that the concepts of work and leisure are unsatisfactory. The Cairncross–Becker model of the household as a productive unit combining goods and time to produce commodities (or some ultimate form of satisfaction) is useful but does not explain all non-work activities.

One possible classification of the ways in which human beings spend their time would be to divide activities into those that are carried out primarily for their own sake and those that produce indirect utility in the form of some end-product or service but must also have some direct utility or disutility for the participant. The first category consists of true leisure activities. People read a novel or go for a walk for the direct pleasure that results. But even leisure pursuits may involve other associated activities that are undertaken mainly in order to make the leisure activity possible. In order to play rugger, a whole 'package' of activities may be necessary including travel, changing and bathing. The second category, yielding indirect benefits, includes housework, home repairs and improvement, child care, personal hygiene and the special sub-category of paid work (or work to produce a good or service that is sold). But some of these 'indirect benefit' activities, including paid work, may also yield a high positive direct utility. It is not possible to generalise about the motivation for some activities. Gardening may be undertaken in order to produce cabbages, for the pleasure of the gardening itself or for a combination of these purposes. The discussion in chapter 2 suggested that money income is complementary to non-paid-work activities, and that the income effect of an increase in basic wages is likely to offset the substitution effect. Rising real wages in Britain, the USA and other countries have been associated with a fall in the number of hours worked. High overtime payments, as might be expected, are associated with longer working hours.

Time only becomes relevant to human beings when they are alive, and the gains that result from prolonging life expectancy or preventing accidents were discussed in chapter 3. Transferring resources from consumption to medical research or accident prevention may involve reducing the quality of life for most people. This means that, at the margin, governments may have to choose between the 'quantity' of life and its quality, in so far as this is influenced by the supply of goods and services. The quantity of life or 'human time' is also determined by the size of the population of the world and of individual countries. There are no market forces to bring populations to an optimum level. An analogy with congestion theory showed how world population might be expected to grow above any optimum level that made allowance for a decline in the quality of life with increasing population. In present calculations about the value of saving life, no allowance is made for the quality of life involved. This seems to be mistaken in the case of people who are incurably ill.

The fixing by the state or by agreements of maximum hours for a working day can result in the accumulation of surplus capital equipment. It was shown in chapter 4 that where shift-system working is impracticable and when the length of the working day is rigidly determined extra capital equipment may be required to reach a given output per unit of time. A special case of this problem was discussed in chapter 5 where the value of time savings (resulting from road improvements) for goods vehicles was considered. State control over drivers' hours tends also to limit the period during which vehicles can be used. This means, it is argued, that time savings should have a value representing the extra productive capacity of the vehicle. Such values range from 218 per cent to 398 per cent of those currently used by the Department of Transport in road-investment appraisal.

Some aspects of time and technical change were also discussed in chapter 4. Most technical development has been regarded as 'labour saving' in economic analysis. It has been assumed that the time input is held constant and that labour will be replaced by machinery. The net effect on total employment has been analysed as a trade-off between the amount of labour displaced and the possible new demand arising from an expansion in the output of the product and from the need for workers to make the new capital equipment. But many innovations could also be described as being 'time saving' if the labour input remained constant. The 'labour-saving' alternative will be chosen by a profit-maximising firm and it is the more efficient in using all scarce resources except time. However, if the chosen objective is the allocation of time between different activities in a way that maximises welfare, then there could be situations in which the reduction of the time input is the best reaction to a 'labour- or time-saving' technical change. As already argued, 'work-sharing' may sometimes constitute a respectable policy.

The Pigou–Hicks classification of technological change requires some expansion when distribution theory is not the main matter of interest. Five categories of technical innovation are suggested in this study: raw-material saving; techniques creating new products;

those that produce a better-quality product than was previously available; capital-savings techniques; and labour- or time-saving innovations.

The meaning given to the term 'productivity increase' is not always very exact. It is apparent that the not uncommon practice of measuring output only in relation to units of time and labour inputs, such as manhours, may be an inaccurate guide to productivity changes. But it is also uncertain whether technical changes that allow depletable raw materials to be turned into consumer goods in a shorter time period should necessarily be regarded as improving productivity.

Given the assumption that individual workers are able to vary the average length of their daily earning period (either by working for a longer time at their normal job or by finding extra separate employment), it is possible to examine the process of choosing whether or not to buy domestic labour-saving capital equipment using a simple model based on time as the only currency. The average or marginal utilities per time unit purchased by undertaking different activities are equivalent to a system of weights. If normal wages were paid to those who undertake housework, the level of investment in domestic capital equipment would be determined by the market in the same way as investment in capital goods in manufacturing or service industries.

The substitution of unpaid do-it-yourself labour for paid professional labour in home improvement work can also be examined with a model using time as currency. The hourly cost of professional labour is likely to be above the level of average earnings, but do-it-yourself workers may take longer over their home improvement schemes than would professional workers so that the amounts of time consumed in earning extra income or in doing-it-yourself may be approximately equal. But for some people the utility obtained per time unit from working on their own home improvement may be considerably higher than that of doing additional paid work. It is obvious that, other things being the same, the likelihood of choosing the do-it-yourself method of completing home improvements will be inversely correlated with the level of earnings.

The main benefit of transport improvements is to reduce journey times. The value of these travel time savings will depend upon the relative utility of travel and that of the best alternative use of the time. For paid-work time savings, the value of any additional output and the utility change to the traveller should both be considered. The evidence of what travellers will be prepared to pay to reduce their journey time is not always easy to interpret. Rich people will normally value a time saving in the same transport mode more than would a poorer person. But the mode of transport is also relevant. A man travelling in a Rolls Royce on a wet day may not value a given time saving as highly as a poorer man who is making his journey on a bicycle or motorbike. In the past, the non-work time-savings values used in Britain have been based on the value judgement that both the rich and the poor man's minute should have the same value. The Leitch Committee has recommended abandoning this practice and also suggested that time savings on the journey to work should be valued at a higher rate than those gained on other non-work-time journeys. The adoption of these recommendations could mean building more roads in richer areas, raising the estimated rate of return from road building, and investing in roads with heavy flows of cars rather than in those carrying a high proportion of lorries.

The discussion of the choice between present and future consumption in chapter 7 led to the development of some doubts about the usual assumption that both individuals and society have a positive time preference valuing immediate more than postponed consumption. There are regular patterns of transfers of income between people in different generations but there is no reason why these should not balance out, producing a zero time preference rate. People wanting to save to form a household, or for retirement, lend to those needing to buy a house or purchase a stock of consumer durables. These inter-generational transfers can even-out the discrepancies between earnings and income over a lifetime. The position is complicated because capital can be productive, so that the payment of positive interest may induce people to lend more of their income than they would do with zero interest rates. Marginal time preference rates will then become positive. But during the last ten years in Britain, large-scale lending to building societies has taken place at rates of interest that become negative when they are adjusted for inflation. The purchase of government stock and of 'average' ordinary shares would also show negative yields during many recent years. Further complications result from the existence of uncertainty, but it is apparent that households in a reasonably affluent country like Britain do not want to consume all their income when they receive it, and that saving does take place even with negative real interest rates.

Wealth, for the economist and the tax collector, is usually defined to include owner-occupied houses and durable goods. But when considered in relation to the choice between present and future consumption it would seem to be more logical to classify the purchase of a house to live in, or of durable goods, as being a form of consumption rather than of saving. Durable goods can be exchanged for some alternative form of consumption, but the proceeds from their sale cannot be used to raise the seller's total level of consumption.

An examination of methods of discounting future benefits in investment appraisal accepted the conventional judgement on the superiority of the net present value technique. The social time preference rate of discount, if it can be determined, would be appropriate for use in the appraisal of public investment. The social opportunity cost rate may be relevant when it is necessary to ensure that the rates of return from public and private investment are comparable, but it does not itself help to measure the value of streams of benefits (from either public or private investment) that have different patterns of distribution over time.

The problem of appraising large-scale public investments yielding most of their benefits in the relatively distant future was also discussed in chapter 7. Even with low discount rates, 'distant' benefits will have little present value. The assumption that all benefits are re-invested and can earn the going rate of interest is crucial. It means that discounting at a compound rate of interest (as carried out in both the internal rate of return and present value discount techniques) is required. Where the assumption of re-invesment is not justified, then a system of weights representing the government's estimate of social time preference could be used for public investment appraisal.

Although it might not be apparent to anyone reading a random selection of articles from the professional journals, economics is concerned with human beings and their welfare, or happiness. The goods and services that the economy produces are not ends in themselves but are means that people can use in their search for well-being. Happiness is a product of the way in which people spend their time. There are many aspects of the search for welfare with which the economist, as such, is not concerned. Economic analysis cannot tell a man how to choose his wife, suggest what books he should read or prescribe a happiness-maximising philosophy of life for his adoption. But if the boundaries of economics should not be extended too far, neither should they be defined over-narrowly. The economic problems associated with the problem of allocating time so that it yields the most welfare for individuals and for society are formidably extensive. It is not sufficient to seek to secure that the 'right' amount of paid work is available and that a mixture of goods and services with the greatest potential for providing happiness is provided. The direct happiness or un-happiness generated by different methods of producing and distri-buting goods is also relevant. The utility or disutility that paid work yields for the worker may make as significant a contribution to the welfare of society as do the wages the worker receives or the value of the goods that he produces.

The process of retail distribution is not only a means of conveying goods from producers to consumers but may itself add to or subtract from human happiness. The activity of shopping is an important use of time and there is no reason why the utility that it yields should be ignored. The organisation of shops and shopping hours that is most efficient in distributing a given quantity of goods for the smallest consumption of scarce resources might be the least efficient in yielding satisfaction to the shoppers. A totally automated delivery to homes by pipeline that increased economic efficiency would reduce welfare for those who preferred the activity of shopping to any available alternative use for the time.

The market mechanism can deal with some of these problems. Workers may sometimes be able to choose between higher wages but less pleasant work and lower money receipts but more utility from the time spent undertaking paid work. Shoppers may have the option of personal service and higher prices or cheaper goods with a greatly reduced level of human contact. But this will not always be the case. Workers may have no influence on a reorgan-isation of their work tasks and the working of the market may not take account of the rival wishes of shop workers and shoppers about otpimum shopping hours. Economists need to consider the implica-tions of market failure in this area, as elsewhere. If economics takes notice of the social costs of production, such as noise and water pollution, it should also be concerned with the level of utility pro-duced by time devoted to 'economic' activity. It does not necessarily follow that the gain in welfare from minimising the resources con-sumed by an economic activity offsets any consequent loss in welfare that may affect those who participate in the activity.

If the economist is concerned with the production of goods and services and their sale in the market, there is no reason why he should not also have something to say about activities in the house-hold. It is true that final acts of consumption depend upon individual preferences that the economist will not normally seek to influence (so long as the right price 'signals' are conveyed). But decisions about the acquisition of household equipment that will contribute to the output of services by the household 'producing unit' and that will influence the allocation of time, may be suitable for economic analysis. Buying a washing machine is a different kind of decision from buying a hat. The product of clean clothes will not be sold on the market; otherwise the purchase of a washing machine is not dissimilar from a firm's investment in new plant. Similarly, the choice between professional or 'internal' do-it-yourself service in the household is analogous to decisions in a firm about whether such services as transport should be provided internally or hired from an outside organisation.

The decision to undertake 'pure' leisure activities, carried out for their own sake, is as already argued a matter for unguided personal preference. The only emphasis that results from considering leisure activities from the point of view of optimising the utility received from the consumption of time is that their importance is underlined. No one has tried to measure the contribution to total happiness made by 'pure' leisure pursuits but it must be very considerable. Although the importance of the utility gained from the time spent at work has been stressed in this study, this does not mean that work time makes a large positive contribution to human happiness. Indeed, the lack of attention given to this aspect of paid work means that job satisfaction in modern industry may often be low and the total welfare gained from being at work may be reduced by low or negative marginal utility obtained from the last units of time devoted to work. The 33.2 per cent of people's lives devoted to sleep may yield little, if any, direct happiness and the considerable amount of time used up by cooking and housework (an average of 7.8 per cent for the whole population) may also produce little direct pleasure. Even measured by the size of the time allocation, 'pure' leisure activities are important. The single activity of watching TV was the fourth most important, using 4.1 per cent of all time in the Multinational Project study.

There is a tendency, amongst politicians if not amongst economists, to regard some activities as not being part of the 'real' economy or to consider that the output of goods is in some way more worthwhile than the provision of services. If the criterion is the contribution made to human happiness, this judgement may be misguided. Writing a play may be as productive as manufacturing detergent and a course in musical appreciation could add as much to the sum of welfare as a series of lectures on engineering or economics.

Suggestions for the extension of the boundaries of economics may not be very welcome when it is apparent that there are still so many unresolved issues even in the more well-developed areas of the subject. Few, if any, of the points and suggestions made in the study are entirely new, but it is hoped that the attempt to apply the criterion of maximising the welfare obtained from the use of the scarce resource of human time to some of the problems of economic analysis is not without interest or value, and that further discussion of the many issues involved may have been encouraged.

Bibliography

Alonso, W. (1964) *Location and Land Use: Towards a General Theory of Land Rent* Cambridge, Mass., Harvard University Press

Becker, G. S. (1965) 'A theory of the allocation of time' *Economic Journal* September

Beesley, M. E. (1965) 'The value of time spent travelling: some new evidence' *Economica, 32*, pp. 174–85

Böhm-Bawerk, E. (1959) *Capital and Interest* South Holland, Ill., Libertarian Press

Bondi, H. (1970) *Relativity and Common Sense* London, Heinemann

Bromwich, M. (1978) *The Economics of Capital Budgeting* Harmondsworth, Penguin Books

Bruzelius, Nils (1979) *The Value of Travel Time* London, Croom Helm

Bullock, N., Dickens, P., Shapcott, M. and Steadman, P. (1974) 'Time budgets and models of urban activity patterns' *Social Trends* no. 5, pp. 45–63

Button, K. J. (1976) *Urban Economics* London, Macmillan

Cairncross, A. K. (1958) 'Economic schizophrenia' *Scottish Journal of Political Economy* February

Carlstein, T. and Thrift, N. (1978) 'Afterword: towards a time–space structural approach to society and environment' in *Timing Space and Spacing Time* Vol. 2, London, Edward Arnold

Central Statistical Office (1980) *Financial Statistics* London, HMSO

Commerical Motor (1979) *Tables of Operating Costs and Guide to Rates 1979* London, IPC Transport Press

Das, Mia (1978) *Travel to Work in Britain: A Selective Review* TRRL Lab. Report 849, Crowthorne, TRRL

Dasgupta, A. K. and Pearce, D. W. (1972) *Cost Benefit Analysis* London, Macmillan

221

Dawson, R. F. F. (1967) *Cost of Road Accidents in Great Britain* Reading, RRL Report, LR79

Dawson, R. F. F. (1971) *Current Costs of Road Accidents in Great Britain* Reading, RRL Report, LR396

Dawson, R. and Everall, P. (1972) *The Value of Motorists' Time; A Study in Italy* Reading, TRRL Report, LR426

Department of Employment (1978a) *British Labour Statistics Year Book 1976* London, HMSO

Department of Employment (1978b) *Gazette* London, HMSO, December

Department of Employment (1979a) *New Earnings Survey, 1978* London, HMSO

Department of Employment (1979b) *Family Expenditure Survey, 1978* London, HMSO.

Department of Employment (1980) *New Earnings Survey, April 1979* London, HMSO

Department of the Environment (1975) *1972/3 National Travel Survey* London, HMSO

Department of the Environment (1976) *Transport Policy* Vol. 2, London, HMSO

Department of Transport (1978) *Highway Economics Note* No. 2, London

Department of Transport (1979a) *National Travel Survey 1975/6* London

Department of Transport (1979b) *The Allocation of Road Track Costs* London

Department of Transport (1980) *Highway Economics Note* No. 2, 1980 revision, London

DeSerpa, A. C. (1971) 'A theory of the economics of time' *Economic Journal* December

Evans, A. W. (1972) 'On the theory of the valuation and allocation of time' *Scottish Journal of Political Economy* February

Feldstein, M. C. (1964) 'The social time preference discount rate in cost benefit analysis' *Economic Journal* June

Ferber, R. (1973) 'Consumer economics, a survey' *Journal of Economic Literature* December

Ferguson, C. E. (1969) *The Neoclassical Theory of Production and Distribution* London, Cambridge University Press

Friedman, M. (1957) *A Theory of the Consumption Function* National Bureau of Economic Research, No. 63, Princeton, NJ, Princeton University Press

George, K. and Shorey, J. (1978) *The Allocation of Resources* London, Allen and Unwin

Ghez, G. and Becker, G. S. (1975) *The Allocation of Time and Goods over the Life Cycle* New York, National Bureau of Economic Research, Columbia University Press

Gilbert, F. and Pfouts, R. (1958) 'A theory of the responsiveness of hours of work to changes in wage rates' *Review of Economics and Statistics* May

Goodwin, P. B. (1978) 'Travel choice and time budgets' in D. Hensher and Q. Dalvi (eds) *Determinants of Travel Choice* Farnborough, Saxon House

Harrison, A. J. and Quarmby, D. A. (1969) *The Value of Time in Transport Planning: A Review in Theoretical and Practical Research on an Estimation of Time-Saving* Paris, E.C.M.T.

Heertje, A. (1977) *Economics and Technical Change* London, Weidenfeld and Nicolson

Heggie, I. (1976) 'A diagnostic survey of urban journey-to-work behaviour' in *Modal Choice and the Value of Travel Time* Oxford, Oxford University Press

Henderson, P. D. (1968) 'Investment criteria for public enterprises' in R. Turvey (ed.) *Public Enterprise* Harmondsworth, Penguin Books

Henderson, J. and Quandt, R. E. (1980) *Microeconomic Theory* (3rd edition) New York, McGraw Hill

Hensher, D. A. (1976) 'The value of commuter travel time savings: using an alternative valuation model' *Journal of Transport Economics* September

Hicks, J. R. (1963) *The Theory of Wages* (2nd edition) London, Macmillan

Hirshleifer, J., De Haven, J. and Milliman, J. (1963) *Water Supply* Chicago, University of Chicago Press

Houthakker, H. S. (1958) 'The permanent income hypothesis' *American Economic Review* June

Jenkins, C. and Sherman, B. (1979) *The Collapse of Work* London, Eyre Methuen

Jennings, A. and Sharp, C. (1976) The value of travel time savings and transport investment appraisal' in I. Heggie (ed.) *Modal Choice and the Value of Travel Time* Oxford, Oxford University Press

Jones-Lee, M. W. (1976) *The Value of Life* London, Martin Robertson

Keynes, J. M. (1972) *Essays in Persuasion – Economic Possibilities for our Grandchildren* London, Macmillan (first published 1930)

Kreps, J. M. (1971) *Lifetime Allocation of Work and Income* Durham, North Carolina, Duke University Press

Kula, E. (1980) 'Derivation of time preference rates: a comparative study' Leicester, unpublished PhD thesis

Kuznets, S. (1946) *National Product since 1869* New York, National Bureau of Economic Research

Kuznets, S. (1952) 'Proportion of capital formation to national product' *American Economic Review* May

Laidler, D. (1974) *Introduction to Microeconomics* Oxford, Philip Allan

Lancaster, K. (1966) 'A new approach to consumer theory' *Journal of Political Economy* April

Layard, P. and Walters, A. (1978) *Microeconomic Theory* New York, McGraw Hill

Leitch Committee (1978) *Report of the Advisory Committee on Trunk Road Assessment* London, HMSO

Linder, S. B. (1970) *The Harried Leisure Class* New York and London, Columbia

Little, I. and Mirrlees, J. (1974) *Project Appraisal and Planning for Developing Countries* London, Heinemann

Mahler, H. (1980) 'People' *Scientific American* Setpember

Marx, K. (1946) *Selected Works* Vol. I, London, Lawrence and Wishart

Marx, K. (1961) *Capital* London, Lawrence and Wishart

Melbin, M. (1978) 'The colonization of time' in T. Carlstein *et al.* (eds) *Human Activity and Time Geography* London, Edward Arnold

Mishan, E. (1970) 'What's wrong with Roskill' *Journal of Transport Economics* September

Mishan, E. (1971) 'Evaluation of life and limb: a theoretical approach' *Journal of Political Economy* August

Modigliani, F. (1966) 'The life cycle hypothesis of savings, the demand for wealth, and the supply of capital' *Social Research* Summer

National Economic Development Office (1976) *A Study of UK Nationalised Industries: their role in the economy and control in the future* London, HMSO, November

Nationalised Industries, A Review of Economic and Financial Objectives (1967) Cmnd 3437, London, HMSO

Needleman, L. (1975) *Valuing Other People's Lives* University of Leicester, Economics Discussion Paper No. 5

Nelson, J. R. (1968) 'The value of travel time' in S. B. Chase (ed.) *Problems in Public Expenditure Analysis* Washington, DC, The Brookings Institution

Office of Population Censuses and Surveys (1973) *The General Household Survey, 1971* London, HMSO

Owen, J. D. (1970) *The Price of Leisure* Montreal, McGill-Queen's University Press

Pigou, A. C. (1960) *The Economics of Welfare* (4th edition) London, Macmillan

Quarmby, D. A. (1967) 'Choice of travel modes for the journey to work' *Journal of Transport Economics and Policy* September

Reynolds, D. J. (1956) 'The cost of road accidents' *Journal of the Royal Statistical Society* Series A, *4*

Richardson, H. (1973) *The Economics of Urban Size* Farnborough, Saxon House

Robbins, L. (1930) 'On the elasticity of demand of income in terms of effort' *Economica* June

Robbins, L. (1945) *An Essay on the Nature and Significance of Economic Science* London, Macmillan

Robinson, J. and Converse, P. (1972) 'The impact of television on mass media usages: a cross-national comparison' in A. Szalai (ed.) *The Use of Time* The Hague, Mouton, pp. 197–212

Samuelson, P. (1948) *Economics* New York, McGraw Hill

Schelling, T. C. (1968) 'The life you save may be your own' in S. B. Chase (ed.) *Problems in Public Expenditure Analysis* Washington, DC, The Brookings Institution

Scott, M. F. G. (1977) 'The test rate of discount and changes in base-level income in the United Kingdom' *Economic Journal* June

Shackle, G. L. S. (1958) *Time in Economics* Amsterdam, North-Holland

Shackle, G. L. S. (1969) *Decision Order and Time in Human Affairs* (2nd edition) Cambridge, Cambridge University Press

Sharp, C. H. (1951) 'Public and private financing of industrial enterprise' *Economic Journal* December

Sharp, C. H. (1970) *The Allocation of Freight Traffic – A Survey* London, Ministry of Transport

Sharp, C. H. (1973) *Transport Economics* London, Macmillan

Sharp, C. H. (1979) 'The environmental impact of transport and the public interest' *Journal of Transport Economics and Policy* January

Sharp, C. H. and Jennings, A. (1976) *Transport and the Environment* Leicester, Leicester University Press

Soule, G. (1955) *Time for Living* New York, Viking Press

Szalai, A. (ed.) (1972) *The Use of Time* The Hague, Mouton

Tanner, J. C. (1979) *Expenditure of Time and Money on Travel* TRRL Supplementary Report 466, Crowthorne, TRRL

The Financial and Economic Obligations of the Nationalised Industries (1961) Cmnd 1337, London, HMSO

The Nationalised Industries (1978) Cmnd 7131, London, HMSO

Thomas, T. C. and Thompson, G. I. (1970) *The Value of Time Saved by Trip Purpose* Stanford Research Institute, Menlo Park

Tipping, D. (1968) 'Time savings in transport studies' *Economic Journal* December

Vickerman, R. W. (1975) *The Economics of Leisure and Recreation* London and Basingstoke, Macmillan

Wabe, J. A. (1971) 'A study of house prices as a means of establishing the value of journey time, the rate of time preference and the valuation of some aspects of environment in the London Metroplitan region' *Applied Economics, 3*

Warnes, A. M. (1972) 'Estimates of journey-to-work distances from census statistics' *Regional Studies, 6*

Webb, M. G. (1973) *The Economics of Nationalized Industries* London, Nelson

Weisbrod, B. A. (1961) *Economics of Public Health: Measuring the Economic Impact of Diseases* University of Pennsylvania Press

Winston, G. C. (1966) 'An international comparison of income and hours of work' *Review of Economics and Statistics* February

Index